W9-AWH-911

Unreasonable Leadership

Transforming yourself, your team, and your
organization to achieve extraordinary results

By Gary Chartrand

Executive Chairman & Former CEO, Acosta, Inc.
with Chuck Day

Foreword by New York Giants Head Coach Tom Coughlin

Unreasonable Leadership Book LLC
www.unreasonableleaders.com

ISBN: 978-0-9830818-1-4

This book is printed on acid-free paper.

Printed in the United States of America

Table of Contents

Introduction

I truly believe that we live in the greatest country in the world and that America has done more for mankind than any other country in the civilized world. American capitalism is the chief reason why. Our free enterprise system offers virtually unlimited opportunities for everyone to exercise and enjoy personal freedom, to pursue their God-given potential and realize "the great American dream," especially when they demonstrate personal responsibility along the way. I am living proof of the American dream, and I am very proud of it. At the same time, I am also very humbled by it. My family and I have been blessed beyond our wildest imaginations, and we remain ever grateful for the opportunities we have been given.

I have written *Unreasonable Leadership* to express my belief in what is possible in America and to capture and share an entrepreneurial success story that exemplifies what our free enterprise system enables one to attain. The startling growth of Acosta, Inc., a sales & marketing agency servicing the $700 billion supermarket industry, demonstrates how an established company can undergo progressive transformation and flourish—provided that its leaders temper their risk-averse tendencies with selective yet bold out-of-the-box thinking. This is a story about refusing to accept the status quo and being willing—almost desiring—to march confidently into the *discomfort* zone and remain resolutely "unreasonable" to achieve the progress envisioned.

Trite as it may sound, the one constant in our lives is change. To be relevant, to grow and prosper, the leaders of an organization must not just acknowledge this reality but embrace it wholeheartedly and help direct this continuous change. The alternative is to accept the proverbial death of a thousand cuts and face the stark reality that, sooner or later, the organizations they lead will become irrelevant and die. You don't have to look very far to witness countless examples of companies, organizations, institutions, and the like that have fallen into this death trap.

That's no way to run a company! It certainly was not the way I was going to lead my company, which found itself in the midst of a radically changing world in 1996 when I became its chief executive. And make no mistake: that's exactly where Acosta found itself. It was my job as CEO to think through, define, and then drive a bold, progressive agenda to ensure Acosta's future as an independent enterprise. By not accepting our industry's status quo, by being relentlessly and pleasantly unreasonable, we were able to achieve our ultimate goal: to extend Acosta's reach into every significant market across the country.

Descriptive accounts of the critical meetings and decisions that guided Acosta's ambitious national expansion comprise the story line for this account of strategic moves. I also have made a point to include a description of the deceptively simple financial formula that made possible the 100 acquisitions that were necessary over a 35-year span. This formula made a vital contribution to Acosta's growth. What began as a local enterprise serving a single market in northeast Florida became first a pace-setting regional leader and then the industry leader serving every market throughout the U.S. and Canada.

In this same time span, our company would grow its annual revenues from $500,000 to nearly $1 billion and would transform itself into a full-service sales and marketing juggernaut. Moreover, Acosta's growth also transformed an industry. What had been a business realm of more than 2,500 independent food brokers would be consolidated into an industry with three national players representing nearly 90 percent of the business.

Unreasonable Leadership is an American success story rich in lessons learned. It illustrates how sheer resiliency and a relentless focus on creating and executing a vision transformed not only a company but also an entire industry. The book details Acosta's national expansion strategy and the company's evolution amid the equally dramatic changes reshaping the supermarket industry, the ways and reasons that merger partners were selected, and the monstrous task of molding Acosta's acquisitions into a single business entity with a common culture that now stands atop its industry.

Included, too, is a frank acknowledgment of the myriad challenges and troubles our leadership team confronted and the management lessons we had to recognize, understand, absorb, and put to work. I have been equally frank about acknowledging the growing pains, sleepless nights, and surprises that accompanied our bold expansion strategy. Some came literally out of the blue.

Unreasonable Leadership is, I submit, a noteworthy legacy of the leadership that built—from the ground up—the entire sales and marketing agency business as it exists today. The Acosta story is rich in riveting lessons about leadership and management for virtually anyone in business and anyone who aspires to lead in business, government, education, the nonprofit sector, or any sector that furthers the American opportunity for success. It is my hope that your read will be an entertaining and enjoyable experience and will cause you to think about being "unreasonable" yourself.

In his heart a man plans his course,
But the LORD determines his steps.
– Proverbs 16:9

Gary Chartrand
Ponte Vedra Beach, Florida
September 2009

Acknowledgments

You'll hear my colleagues quip that I know I need help to accomplish unreasonable goals. That was certainly true when it came time to plunge into this book project. I have had lots of help from a wealth of colleagues, former colleagues, business associates, and friends. The encouraging words they all have provided along the way were vastly more beneficial than these people may realize.

Retired Acosta executives Pete Jones, Mike Keohane, and H.C. Sims were generous with their time and dug deep into their memories and personal files to recreate important conversations and recount pivotal moments, including many critical decisions made in the years before I joined Acosta. Peggy Dallas, the widow of my mentor Del Dallas, graciously shared insights, letters, and memories of her husband's long and distinguished career. Helpful as well was information sent by Martha Albritton, the widow of the late Robert "Hy" Albritton; Hy was Acosta's president in the 1960s and early 1970s.

Absolutely invaluable were the perspectives, insights, and recollections provided by a number of valued business associates who also have been longtime friends of mine: at Clorox, retired Chairman Craig Sullivan and Senior Vice President–Chief Customer Officer Grant LaMontagne; at Minute Maid, General Manager and Vice President Mike Saint John; at Campbell Soup Co., President–International Larry McWilliams, former operations vice president at Minute Maid; at Ken's Salad Dressing, President John Pritchard, also a former Nestlé executive whom I first hired as a young manager at Carnation; at Nestlé, retired sales executive Nino Cristofoli; at H.J. Heinz Co., Dave Moran; and at MAI Alper, retired CEO Vic del Regno. Acosta wouldn't be the company it is today—and my career would not have prospered as it has—without the assistance of these gentlemen, whose specific contributions will be described in the pages ahead. I am eternally grateful for their help and friendship.

I am equally grateful for the assistance (and camaraderie) that my Acosta colleagues provided, not only for this book but also throughout our years together. Greg Delaney, our Chief Financial Officer, has provided a steady voice on financial matters and remains one of my best friends. Treasurer and Senior Vice President Sandy Ramsey always provided me with the facts and analysis needed to make good decisions. "Always there when I needed him" is a phrase I can use to praise the contributions of several men, including Senior Vice President Brian Baldwin; President of Operations Jamie Gronowski; Robert Hill, my successor as Acosta's CEO; Jack Laurendeau, Vice Chairman who was always alongside me and never wavered on our quest to make it all work; Executive Vice President Jack Parker; and Drew Prusiecki, General Counsel and Secretary. My thanks, too, to a trio of retired Acosta executives, Greg McDonald, Rick Nist, and Bob McCarthy, whose foresight and willingness to unite in early 1998 helped create the cornerstone for Acosta's growth.

For some 15 years, Pat Chafin served ably as my executive assistant, and I am incredibly grateful for all of her assistance. The detailed records, notes, letters, and memos Pat dutifully kept throughout those 15 years were vital to this project.

Vilma Consuegra, Jean Moyer, and Amber Anthony of the Acosta communications staff delivered important information about both our company's history and current activities, as did Tom Boyle of the Muscular Dystrophy Association. More thanks go to Dr. Jane Shannon, senior consultant with My Executive Solutions, who helped us develop a succession plan in 2008. Jane's perspectives about "unreasonable leadership" were, and remain, most helpful.

I don't dare forget my good friend Tom Coughlin, head coach of the New York Giants, Super Bowl XLII champions, who took the time to write the book's Foreword. Tom is a true champion and, I believe, an "unreasonable" leader himself, never accepting the status quo and always striving to bring out the best in his players. I also must thank my close Ponte Vedra Beach pal Ernie Bono. Ernie's continued encouragement helped this project get started, and his keen observations help keep it rolling.

Finally, I couldn't have completed this book without the help of collaborator Chuck Day, who has worked tirelessly on this project. Chuck first approached me in the summer of 2007, after hearing my advice "never be afraid to ask" during a speech I made to his Rotary Club. I told him to contact me in about a year, when I would have a little more time. One year later, he was there knocking on my door and saying, "OK, let's go." Thank you, Chuck!

Most important of all have been the contributions, support, encouragement, and love of my family. My wife Nancy and our children, Jeff and Meredith, make it all worthwhile and are indeed priceless. I love you all more than I can say, and I thank you. For this book, Nancy remembered scores of important details and insights, while Jeff and Meredith lent support and offered the right words precisely when they were needed. I am truly blessed. The four of us are working together now to grow our family foundation created to benefit public education reform. The Chartrand Foundation will receive all proceeds from this book, which obligates me to offer one more "Thank you!"

To everyone who is about to read Acosta's saga, I hope you are energized to find an unreasonable goal of your own and pursue it.

Foreword

By Tom Coughlin
Head Coach, New York Giants
Super Bowl XLII Champions

In the summer of 2003, my wife Judy and I took a trip to Italy with several other couples, including Gary and Nancy Chartrand. Our Italian guide, who took us to some of the country's most impressive landmarks, had a habit of declaring, "We go!" as our daily itinerary was about to unfold. Before long, Gary was also declaring, "We go!"

Seldom has a two-word phrase summed up a man better than "We go!" captures Gary Chartrand.

He is always looking forward to his next challenge, whether it is improving his business, enriching his family and friends, or helping the lives of people he's never met. Gary is an extremely successful executive and corporate leader with Acosta. He is also a dynamic leader, unfailingly optimistic and confident. For someone just launching a career, he is an ideal role model. Gary is as successful in life as he is in business, a well-rounded man with a huge heart and a wonderful sense of humor—and he is my close friend.

We first met in 2001, brought together by a mutual friend, Ernie Bono. Ernie and I were enlisting Gary's support for the Jay Fund Foundation, the charity I founded in 1996 to help children with leukemia and their families. We wanted Acosta to be a major sponsor of the Jay Fund Golf Classic, held annually on the first Monday in May in Ponte Vedra Beach. The event kicks off with a fundraising dinner the previous night.

At that first meeting, I was impressed with Gary's demeanor, confidence, and eagerness to learn about the Jay Fund. My initial impressions have since been confirmed many times, as I have come to know Gary as a devoted husband and father and dedicated community leader.

Gary was immediately enthusiastic about the Golf Classic. He loves golf and the camaraderie that is such an important part of the game. More importantly, Gary loves his community. From the moment we sat down in his office, he was genuinely eager to help us. He had read and absorbed the Jay Fund materials we had sent him, and he had a strong interest in supporting philanthropic ventures such as ours.

Gary also loves football, the sport I have coached for more than 40 years, and we hit it off immediately. Within a few days, he pledged his support, and Gary and Nancy have been committed champions of the Jay Fund ever since. As I worked with Gary our friendship grew stronger, as did my appreciation for his business and leadership skills.

Those skills prompted me to ask Gary to serve on the Jay Fund board, beginning in October 2004. He is the kind of individual I've always enjoyed working with; Gary has a relentless work ethic, and he is direct, creative, and persistent.

As you are about to read, he also has a knack for keeping his eyes focused on the future: I knew as long as I was a head coach in the National Football League, the Jay Fund's future was secure. But late in 2006, when I was uncertain how much longer I would coach, I asked Gary to chair a development committee to ensure that the Jay Fund thrives in perpetuity. Gary was aware of how critical a financial influence the Jay Fund had become at Wolfson Children's Hospital and Nemours Children's Clinic in Jacksonville. As Dr. Michael Joyce, another loyal board member and a Nemours physician, had once observed, the Jay Fund had been absolutely critical to their quality of care.

In June 2007, Gary acted on my request, proposing that we establish an endowment for the Jay Fund. That became "Now and Forever," our capital campaign with a $5 million goal. Gary agreed to chair the campaign, and as I write these words, I am proud to say that we have achieved our goal—in hard economic times, no less. That is a testament to Gary Chartrand's leadership, vision, focus, energy, imagination, determination, and "We go!" attitude. Many of the outstanding people associated with the Jay Fund wish to remain anonymous, but Gary is at the forefront of our efforts, never afraid to ask for money. He is the consummate salesman, with a unique ability to rally the troops.

Gary has one more special virtue. He is never without a smile. I can never recall seeing any animosity in him. He makes everyone around him feel comfortable and puts smiles on others' faces with casual ease, a critical trait for any leader. Gary has a great sense of humor, which is liable to surface anywhere, particularly on the golf course. For instance, I'm certainly not a great golfer, which he once pointed out as only he can. "Gee Tom," Gary said with his devilish grin, "we spend more time looking for your ball than we actually do playing golf." All I could do was laugh with him.

I can empathize with Gary, too, because our careers are linked by common threads. In 2007, our season began with two stinging losses. But in the face of adversity, "resiliency" became a common theme, as did "team" and "we are one." We believed in one another, faced every challenge, and refused to lose. The players and coaches were convinced that somehow, some way, we were going to make a play and win a game.

And we did. Almost every victory we earned down the stretch was won in the waning minutes or seconds. It was a tremendous risk/reward journey, one that didn't allow for breathing room. But we thrived on that, winning an NFL record of 11 consecutive games away from our home stadium. We won at Tampa Bay and Dallas in our first two play-off games then kicked an overtime field goal to defeat Green Bay in the NFC Championship Game in -23 degree wind chill. Two weeks later, we capped our journey with another last-minute victory, this one over the undefeated New England Patriots in Super Bowl XLII, the same team to which we had lost five weeks earlier. We were underdogs in all four postseason games but won them all by applying the lessons we learned on our journey. Perhaps the most important of those lessons was *always* give it your best shot.

Among the family members and close friends who celebrated with us that night in Phoenix were Gary and Nancy, plus our friend who had first united us, Ernie Bono and his wife, Rita. It was very appropriate that they should join us, because Acosta is a championship company with Gary at the helm.

The Giants and Gary both overcame many of the same obstacles: many doubters, a lot of adversity, defeats and close calls along the way, and some soul-searching moments. Gary succeeded through leadership and hard work, and by creating the enthusiasm and support among his colleagues that is essential to any successful organization. Gary and Acosta had to be as resilient as our football team. Both have enjoyed success but still constantly strive to keep growing and improving.

You are about to read about the leadership style that worked for Gary Chartrand, a role model leader for any business and for any profession.

"We go!"

This book is dedicated to my wife, Nancy, and our two children, Jeff and Meredith, who have never wavered in their support of my journey of unreasonable goal setting and to the thousands of people who work at Acosta, living the values and making a difference every day for our clients.

Step 1

Understanding What Unreasonable Leadership Is All About

Its path is marked by character traits, intangibles, and experiences.

IT'S OK TO BE UNREASONABLE.

Indeed, it's admirable. What sounds contentious really describes the kind of leadership that envisions the future, finds and articulates the proverbial "big, hairy, audacious goal," holds fast to convictions, inspires colleagues to move beyond their comfort zones, silences the naysayers, and achieves the impossible mission—whatever it takes.

The unreasonable leader is the ever-determined eternal optimist who eagerly faces challenges head-on, usually with a smile and always with an intense desire to win, and win big. Moderate success is never enough, and the status quo is never to be accepted. Unreasonable leadership, I contend, is a mind-set as much as anything. If you intentionally think thoughts about creating breakthrough results, it will become a habit. When it becomes a habit, change will begin to take place, and your actions will reflect your thoughts. You will start accomplishing breakthrough results, and the more you think about them, the more you will achieve.

The 12 years I spent leading Acosta, Inc. as its CEO stand as a 21st-century affirmation of George Bernard Shaw's famous observation: "All progress comes from unreasonable people." The Acosta growth story chronicled in this book demonstrates how to develop the traits to capture the passions, hearts, and talents of an organization to bring about transformational change.

Unreasonable leadership is what propelled Acosta from a single-market company with just 12 employees to a growth platform that encompassed more than 100 mergers uniting as many as 200 companies and developed what is now a payroll of more than 16,000 in offices throughout the U.S. and Canada.

To help you understand what unreasonable leadership is all about, I will express my own thoughts based on my journey and what I have

1

learned along the way. I believe one can learn to become an unreasonable leader.

I did.

Unlikely as it may sound today to those who know me, in my teenage years, I viewed myself as shy, quiet, and, in social settings, uncomfortable and very reserved. No one worried much about self-esteem back then, but mine would have been assessed as being pretty low. At the same time, however, I had a desire to be successful. *How* was I going to be successful? Well, that wasn't clear, not at all. I just knew that I wanted to be successful. From the beginning, it seemed I always wanted more; I was always pushing myself beyond what was "reasonable." At critical times throughout my formative years, thinking about and doing something "unreasonable" helped me achieve my goal at the time.

Without knowing it, I had started out on the road to becoming an unreasonable leader. I had lots to learn.

That road first took me onto athletic fields, where my desire to achieve soon became especially evident. As captain of both my baseball and football teams, I constantly yearned to make a difference, to lead and inspire. Because I was thoroughly safe in my comfort zone in sports, my yearning seemed natural, practically second nature. On the baseball diamond and football gridiron, it was easy to develop "team." I believed in my teammates and passionately believed we could win. That desire, the will to win—and win big—kept those competitive juices flowing.

Winning has always been in my DNA, a principal reason why I loved every minute of competitive sports. As a young athlete, I learned there was a big difference between expecting to win and refusing to lose. Here is the way I see it: Two opposing athletes make their way onto the playing field, both expecting to win, but one of them refuses to lose. Now this is not foolproof, but more often than not, it comes down to *who wants it more, who thinks about it more, who is obsessed with it.*

Participating in organized sports also gave me the opportunity to understand *the power of "one team."* I put that understanding to work when I started my business career. I knew that building the *right* team with the *right* people was critical to my success. Not too far into my first "real job" with the Carnation Company, I discovered I had been blessed with a unique ability to get people feeling comfortable by doing nothing more than talking with them, specifically by asking them to tell me how they felt. And they would. By listening to people and helping them get what *they* wanted, I ended up getting what the company needed. In building a team, listening and being open with people has been, for me, the single most important lever I pulled in creating the foundation of trust.

At the end of the day, it's all about trust. Without trust, there is no relationship. Do I believe in this leader? Do I trust this person enough to follow him or her? The ability to relate to others and, conversely, to have people relate to you is what is critical. People don't connect with phonies! They can spot the "BS-ers" a mile away. They see right through the BS-ers, and through the games, backstabbing, and manipulation on which BS-ers rely. It's an immediate turn-off.

My dad's words, which he used as his internal measuring stick and handed to me, were always uppermost in my mind whenever I worked with others. "Are you doing the right thing? Don't bullshit people! Always tell the truth. At the end of the day, can you look in the mirror and see your integrity still intact?" All of these early imprints led me to a pretty simple understanding: In order to win, I couldn't do it alone. I had to build personal relationships with every one of my teammates. Then, I had to work hard alongside my teammates, demonstrate a strong sense of determination, and instill innovation. This realization was one of several early Ah ha! moments that led me further along the road to becoming an unreasonable leader.

The importance of brutally and honestly assessing myself was another early discovery. My internal drive for success was clear. I knew what I wanted to create in my life, and to do it. I knew I had to overcome my shyness and lack of self-confidence. It was as if I finally realized the value of my own education and was able to clearly recognize what I was lacking. I knew that overcoming this weakness was going to be out of my comfort zone. That led me to a very uncomfortable place. To overcome the discomfort, I had to think of and visualize myself doing what scared me to death. The more I thought about it, the easier it became to put into action.

During these early career years, I could not read enough. I immersed myself in the tapes and books of classic leadership gurus, such as Napoleon Hill's *Think and Grow Rich* and *The Law of Success*. I really worked hard to change what I knew would hold me back. Moving out of my comfort zone, I forced myself to interact and to develop a more outgoing, self-confident style. I practiced and absorbed the concepts I studied, pushing myself to try new behaviors. I began to shift my internal thinking and condition myself to be the leader I was aspiring to become. And I watched and learned from the leaders I admired, observing how they handled themselves and worked with others.

By then, what had become clear to me was that there were distinct contrasts distinguishing those who successfully led organizations and surpassed industry expectations from those who did not. I was determined to emulate the leaders and achievers.

The term "unreasonable" describes a leader who can inspire his or her colleagues to stretch and grow to achieve a daunting and seemingly unobtainable mission. As often as not, though, the specific actions the leader takes are *very* reasonable: improving personal strengths, eliminating or overcoming weaknesses, continually motivating and encouraging others, clearly painting the picture of the goal, charting progress along the way and adjusting as need be, rallying the troops as often as necessary, and doing whatever else it takes to succeed.

Throughout my career I have had the good fortune of working with many leaders, and my early observations of successful leaders have remained consistent with my later experiences.

Unreasonable leadership can be defined as having the courage and conviction to change the status quo. It's a matter of crystallizing the vision clearly, capturing the passion and heart of the team to execute in pursuit of the vision, and then getting out of the way to make it happen—even when the goal seems unobtainable. When I am asked to define the characteristics of an unreasonable leader (i.e., "How does one become an unreasonable leader?"), my first response is that it begins with a brutal and honest assessment of you, the leader, and a willingness to stretch oneself into a very uncomfortable place to grow those areas that are holding you back. Most of what holds us back in life is not that we cannot achieve but that we will not do what is necessary to achieve. Why? Because it is hard!

Here are a few characteristics and traits that distinguish what I term reasonable leadership from unreasonable leadership. Reasonable leaders simply do their jobs, and that's all. They understand their mission and purpose; they set goals and then go about executing those goals. Working primarily within their comfort zones, reasonable leaders fulfill their obligations and achieve ordinary success. End of story.

Unreasonable leaders, however, view their roles quite differently. They are driven internally by the beat of a very different drummer. Achieving "moderate" success doesn't cut it. Neither does the limited change that they are capable of making within their organizations. Unreasonable leaders want it all! The sky's the limit! And unreasonable leaders strive to continuously make an impact on all they do. They will go to a very uncomfortable place outside of their comfort zones to make it happen.

The key segments of the journey to unreasonable leadership for me began with a deep and honest evaluation of myself against various leadership dimensions and then proceeded as I focused on filling the gaps I found.

Here's a detailed description of what I call the *Dimensions of the Unreasonable Leader:*

Self-Confidence: This is one of the most challenging and sometimes elusive dimensions. True confidence, I believe, is being very comfortable in your own skin; for me, it took a while to grow into. Self-confidence is the ability to believe in yourself and in what you *alone* bring to the table—what no one else can. Having self-confidence is to understand your own uniqueness in the universe, realizing that God made only one of you and from the beginning of mankind to the end of mankind there will only be one you. Think about that!

It is fairly easy to recognize leaders who are self-confident. You can sense their presence when they walk into a room. It's in the way they carry themselves and how they express their opinions. Are they direct with you? Are they credible? Do they look you straight in the eyes and speak their views?

It's these basic indicators that I observed in my early career years. I watched how leaders carried themselves. I studied how they handled difficult situations. In effect, I became a college student all over again, although this time I picked leaders to study and was much more aggressive about studying and asking questions.

The more I watched and studied, the easier and more important it became to recognize those leaders who didn't have self-confidence, because I wasn't experiencing or feeling it within them. Everything about an insecure leader seemed to shout out, "I don't measure up. I don't know what I am doing. Somebody's going to discover that I don't know what the hell I am doing!" The guru has labeled this phenomenon "the imposter syndrome," and I experienced it firsthand as a young professional. I can remember times when everything from my body language to my tone of voice seemed to scream that I "didn't have it." At the time, I wasn't clear about how to "get it," either. But I did know that I needed to gain control of the negative thinking pattern.

A number of things helped me develop my own self-confidence:

- *A realization that I had special gifts and talents that were given to me and to use these gifts to the best of my ability.* To become the person I was capable of becoming. To do otherwise was sinful.
- *A series of wins.* With each win, I became more and more convinced of what I could achieve.
- *Positive self-talk.* I realized early on that I needed to focus on the positive side of things. To look for solutions rather than dwelling on the problems. My mind is the most powerful tool I have.
- *Practice.* Doing something over and over helped me get the content down cold—the sales pitch, the presentation, the speech. Nothing beats practicing to near perfection. Bill Gates spent thousands of hours on the computer in junior high school. Look at the difference it made!
- *The company I kept.* By surrounding myself with "winners," people who were positive, optimistic, and determined by nature, and by carefully selecting and intentionally being aware of my relationships, my colleagues and I created a network that learned how to win together.

As I began to shift my own perceptions about myself and what I was capable of achieving, things really began to change. Once that shift began, the momentum came fast and I was ready. I became more and more comfortable with speaking up and began seeing myself as a creative, out-of-the-box kind of guy. In turn, I began experiencing business life in a very different way.

Unreasonable leadership almost inherently creates unprecedented changes at rates of speed that can produce havoc. Without a strong sense of self-confidence, of knowing myself, and an unshakable belief in our company's abilities, I doubt I could have overcome all the naysayers I was to confront. My self-confidence was what convinced my colleagues to say, in effect, "We want on the bus with this guy!"

Vision: What my mentor Del Dallas saw, other great leaders see as well. A creative and visionary mind sees things not as they are, but as they can be. Vision paints the picture of the future and with enough color and detail so others can see it in their minds as well. While crafting the future state, the *power* of the story is what enables others to aspire to that future, too. With this skill comes a challenge: to motivate and energize others to take action, to move past the planning, analyzing, and scoping out of the vision, and to work forcefully toward realizing the vision. That's when the real work begins, because it will include overcoming obstacles, which certainly include those grumblers who think that whatever it takes—maybe the very objective itself—is dangerously high-risk.

Know what you want to create, *and* draw the path to get there! It is not enough to do "your best." You have to have the vision, the energy, and the persistence to do whatever it takes to *make it happen.*

Bring about transformational change: You can bring about transformational change when you can look into the future of your industry and predict what is going to happen. You then begin to see how this change will affect you. If it is negative, then the process of transformational change becomes essential. Others in our industry may not have wanted to believe it, or had perhaps concluded it was too hard or too difficult to make happen. Why didn't others create a vision to consolidate our industry? Most, I have concluded, were too comfortable; they were well-off and content, perhaps complacent. I was hungry and actually endured a time when the value of my assets and resources flat out declined.

Drive and passion to win (aka *refusing to lose*!): For as long as I can remember, I've had an inherent loathing for failure. Whether I was crouched behind the plate catching and helping my team reach the American Legion World Series, trying to convince the respective pet food divisions of Nestlé and Heinz that Acosta really could represent both of their brands equitably, or trying to build Acosta into the number one sales and marketing organization from coast to coast, *wanting to win, expecting to win*, and *refusing to lose* have always seemed natural to me. When you are winning on a consistent basis, failure becomes unacceptable: Failure is *not* an option! Fear of failure drives me, propels me—and fear of the unknown *energizes* me.

Think about all the business success stories you've heard, read, or experienced. A common denominator is always the leader's will to win. The will to win is the driving force—invariably a powerful contributor to all progress and achievements—no matter what you are doing: building a business, playing a round of golf, strengthening your marriage, guiding your family, or building your relationships along all walks of life. Self-confidence and a drive to succeed are responsible for every great achievement in life. They transform what's unreasonable to what's attainable.

Character: I knew early on that my boss Del really cared about me, and I didn't want to fail him. Robert Hill, Acosta's current CEO, doesn't want to fail me, and he works harder than any man I know. I care about him, too. When you care and the team knows it, the drive is powerful and the impact is deeper. You simply do whatever it takes, for each other and the team. You are able to teach your team how to refuse to lose. When selecting your team, always put the character of an individual ahead of competence. The right character will have far more impact on the success of the organization. Don't misunderstand me, though. You shouldn't lower your standards on competence. Just think character first.

Teamwork is essential: It's naïve to believe that hard work is something you do alone. How you *treat and work with* your colleagues, regardless of rank, will determine the outcome of your endeavors. No one can ever accomplish the ultimate goal by himself or herself. I have always believed that people working with you—I never say "for you" but "with you"—will rise to the level of expectations you set for them. Setting high expectations and clearly articulating *the results* you desire will provide the fuel for people to perform. I firmly believe in the concept of team. Trite as it can sound, we can all recognize that there is no "I" in team.

It's been my experience that when your work reflects your life purpose and when you surround yourself with the best, work no longer feels like work. There's an excitement and energy about it that's tangible. Enjoying the moments along the way with a good sense of playfulness and humor provides the balance. The team's intensity increases, and as the wins start to accumulate, team members identify themselves as winners. Expectations rise; although the work is tough, challenging, and long, the stories of *the win* are being created and shared. There's power in sharing those stories!

Integrity: I expect the highest of ethics of myself and others. A good reputation takes a long time to build, but it can be destroyed in an instant. Trust, passion, drive to succeed, being results-oriented—these are critical qualities of a leader of integrity. "Always do the right thing" keeps ringing in my ears from my father. Be honest with people, and they will trust you! Integrity is simply "doing the right thing." There have been numerous instances throughout my 25 years with Acosta when we could have taken some shortcuts and saved a lot of time and aggravation, as well as bundles of cash. We didn't take those shortcuts, though, because it wouldn't have been right. It's critical when you are building a team to surround yourself with individuals who are convinced—at their very core—to do the right thing on a consistently firm basis, to lead by doing what's right.

Expect only the best from people: Go ahead and set expectations high! Your people will get there. Set low expectations, and they'll be met, as well. It is critical to a leader's success to require the development of relationships. Rules without Relationships create Rebellion. If you don't have believability within your team, what I call a connection, you'll never gain credibility, only cynical talk at the water cooler. To inspire others, to motivate others, you must push others beyond their comfort zones and challenge them to reach beyond what they believe they are ready and able to reach. People don't care how much you know about them as long as they know how much you care about them.

Relationship building: The power of the relationship creates the desire to do virtually anything to support the team, its mission, and its goals. That requires your best intuitive skills.

Selfless leadership has always been about giving. It is also called servant leadership. Giving of myself to others and using my God-given talents to create and win big in the marketplace has worked for me. I've spent the better part of my life developing those talents to inspire others to become successful, devoting myself to others so that together we can make an impact and create something that has not been made before. As I began to view leadership as my life's mission and purpose, it became more about others and less about me. Giving of myself was about becoming more and more selfless and, in very practical ways, all about living it in my day-to-day work.

I believe selfless leadership is often demonstrated in the little ways that we serve others, yet it also can be demonstrated when we take a stand for those without a voice in the decision. I have always made it my business to ensure that others own a part of our business and share in the profits. Ownership creates a level of investment, of loyalty, and of heart that brings a whole new dynamic to the workplace. Ownership brings out the best in our associates. The company is not only *their* company but *our* company; the feeling is intangible, but real.

There was a time in 2003 when it would have been easy for me to have just gone along with a plan suggested to me after we brought in our new equity firm. Conventional wisdom dictated that the most efficient way to implement this plan would be to mandate a buyout of some 150-plus Acosta associates. Yes, they would have made a significant profit, yet they would no longer be owners. Something about that notion rubbed me the wrong way, and I wouldn't let that happen. We had made a commitment to each of these associates. Fortunately, our new equity partners endorsed my stand: I believed that our people were owners—in the real sense of the word—and should be treated as such. The good news is that because I felt so passionately about it, everyone agreed it was the right thing to do. A few years down the road, these same associates all prospered beyond their wildest dreams, and, for me, that's the best part of this story.

Courage to challenge the status quo: There's really no such thing as the status quo, and nothing bores an unreasonable leader more than accepting what passes for the status quo. In the final analysis, companies do one of two things: grow or decline. Staying the same is just not an option. If you choose dramatic growth, as an unreasonable leader always will, by definition, you must reject the status quo. Growing any business means reaching beyond what is comprehensible. Real change occurs when the improbable becomes thinkable. That's important to remember. *Real change occurs when the improbable becomes thinkable.* When my mentor and predecessor Del Dallas retired in late 1996, I praised him for his innate desire to break with the long-standing tradition that ours was strictly a local business. That's the only way breakthroughs come about. As proud as I am of what Acosta became on my watch, it was Del who first saw what a small local food broker could become. It was his foresight that ignited the revolution of an entire industry.

Work ethic: Work hard. Nothing is attainable without hard work, plain and simple. Nothing worthwhile is ever accomplished easily. To believe otherwise is naïve.

Decisiveness: Nothing gets accomplished if the leader struggles to make a call or begins to waffle once a decision has been made. Focus your energy and time toward the successful outcome, and look for new ways to solve problems as they surface. Instinctively, proactive unreasonable leaders are prone to look for opportunities and are reluctant to postpone the decision. Waiting to make the call rarely works.

Empowerment: Leading a team of people so that everyone's God-given talent is put to the best possible use is a rewarding experience. My successor, Robert Hill, transformed the Acosta business platform while he was the COO of the company. Robert said, "Give me the ball, coach," and I did. Because of Robert's leadership, our business exploded. He accomplished things others could not, and Robert continues to do so today. Jamie Gronowski, whose Denver firm became part of our Acosta family, also brought with him a conviction that the then-nascent natural foods sector merited special emphasis. "Run with it," I said. Jamie did, and he created a potent new profit center.

These examples reflect my style to challenge people and to be intolerant of those who are not fully immersed in the game. "All hands on deck!" is the way we work as a team. I'm no elitist, either. I never want to be known as the guy with all the answers, far from it. My favorite people are those who provide solutions and give me options, not just their opinions.

Openness: I assume good intentions and potential; this is how I let people in from the first moment I meet them. I pay attention to what they have to say and give them the benefit of the doubt early on. With a lot of leaders, you have to prove yourself first. I believe this is what distinguishes the leaders who perform spectacularly from those who perform well: The spectacular performers are spectacular because they were *open* to leveraging the potential of those on their teams and let them do better and greater things. Unreasonable leaders let go of control. This allows them to empower others.

Urgency: An unreasonable leader has an *active* mind that is always searching, always plotting, always planning, instinctively looking ahead and not behind. This kind of leader has difficulty with patience. These leaders are always reaching energetically with a level of intensity and focus toward the next win, the next achievement.

Emotional intelligence: What I have really come to appreciate is taking the time to focus on what made the difference in my own leadership journey. What did I bring to my role as leader to maximize the core strengths that were always within me? What are the things that limit me? What learning from past patterns have I faced and overcome? What am I still working on? Research indicates that the most effective people are those who understand themselves, both their strengths and their weaknesses. There's nothing unreasonable about that!

Knowing exactly what makes you tick, and why, allows you to develop strategies to deal with the multitude of demands and situations that any leader will confront, whether you lead a small business, lead a global corporation, or coach a kid's soccer team on a Saturday morning. Having a keen understanding of yourself helps you know when to seek the opinions and wisdom of your colleagues and when to consult outside experts. From the day I became CEO, I never forgot to remind myself of what I don't know.

Understanding yourself and how you instinctively behave begets still more understanding:

- It helps you recognize how you influence others to comprehend your point of view and, ideally, to embrace and support it should your point of view be adopted.
- It defines the kind of individual you really are and how you will likely respond in your own special way to the myriad problems, challenges, and opportunities shaped by the combination of a given business environment and its rules, as set by the prevailing establishment.

Here are more thoughts of which to be aware, generated by what is part and parcel to every self-respecting study of any business organization. Knowing your weaknesses may be as important as knowing your strengths. How so? Being aware of your weaknesses is the first step toward addressing and correcting those weaknesses and the unreasonable leader continually needs to improve himself or herself. Knowing your weaknesses can help you build a team whose other members have strengths that can offset your weaknesses so the team itself won't suffer from a potentially dangerous flaw.

Know what you don't know and do whatever it takes to develop these areas. When most people realize their weaknesses, they create a sense of hopelessness, and that can be very limiting. I turned my weaknesses into opportunities to develop and then challenged myself to act on these opportunities. I wound up turning my weaknesses into my biggest strengths, and I firmly believe that anyone can do this!

So where can this unreasonable leader come up short? Lots of places! Below are a few descriptions that can apply to an unreasonable leader's weaknesses:

Skeptical: It's the flip side to being ever so optimistic and maybe not necessarily the proverbial healthy skepticism, either. As I have come to understand, skepticism is a trait that can suggest to others that I am set in my ways and unable—or stubbornly unwilling—to appreciate viewpoints that are different from mine. This can be perilous. Left unchecked, being too skeptical can provoke colleagues and/or clients into becoming defensive and can lead to difficulty in developing consensus, something an effective leader must be able to build.

Overly cautious: A decisive leader sounds ideal. But there's a flip side here, too. Being decisive can breed unwarranted caution and can force the decision maker into endless and needless delays in the name of thoroughness and fact-gathering when, in fact, swift action may be critical. In the first three years of the Civil War, for instance, Union general George McClelland became infamous for waiting endlessly for more information and more favorable conditions. Lincoln finally got fed up and relieved him of command.

Overly bold: Bold leaders tend to have thick skins, so they can handle the critics who inevitably arise amid conflicts. Being bold communicates confidence in one's convictions. That's fine to a point. But being too bold can indicate cockiness and may make the leader appear indifferent to others' fears or concerns. In turn, teammates may feel their leader is insensitive about their feelings and couldn't care less about their opinions or ideas. A good leader needs to understand this and have almost a sixth sense about knowing when to be heroic and when to be humble.

Too creative: A creative mind full of imagination is a wonderful trait. But imagination, too, needs to be kept in check. If it is not, others may consider your ideas unrealistic, impractical, unusual, and—yes—shockingly unreasonable. An unreasonable leader can never afford to leave the team wondering about the validity of the goal.

Perceived aloofness: Not consulting others before making major decisions is a recipe for disaster. A colorful and charismatic leader can make people feel insignificant if he or she doesn't ask others for their opinions. It's important to keep in mind that everyone needs a share of the recognition for a job well done and to be shown that their individual and team efforts are being appreciated and noticed.

Too jovial: Over the years, my penchant for ribbing, teasing, and keeping everyone at ease earned me a reputation as a prankster. For instance, just before we made a key presentation, I had a habit of taking my teammates aside for a quick overview and concluding by saying, with a grin, "Now, don't screw it up." Most of the time, it served me well. As my longtime friend and former colleague John Pritchard will quip, "Gary has a unique ability to get away with a lot of things others can't." I guess so, although I can also remember occasions when a colleague would snarl, "If this is another of your jokes, it's no longer funny!" Then I knew I'd gone too far. Another indicator was the icy and penetrating "What in the world have you done *now?*" look from my wife, usually delivered amid a cold stony silence and obvious tension from my best intentions getting me in a pickle.

I really have tried to be mindful of being too jovial. Once you gain a greater understanding of yourself, you're bound to provide better leadership and enjoy a more satisfying career.

Reasonable

- Is acceptably satisfied with his or her job and responsibilities
- Has a team that does its job
- Develops a relationship only as a result of the work
- Values safety; is comfortable only with incremental change
- Is comfortable with moderate success; is risk-averse, accepts the status quo, and fears dreaming too big; plays the "what if this happens?" game to a fault
- Makes incremental improvements
- Tends to be masked and guarded
- Is appeasing and unduly eager to please others
- Is internally focused
- Is hesitant to make decisions and is slow to act

Unreasonable

- Creates a winning team and a winning culture
- Builds strong relationships based on trust
- Values risk taking; becomes energized by change, by pushing the limits; constantly questions the status quo and seizes innovative ideas to build upon; dreams big and plays the "why not?" game

- Creates significant change when the initial opportunity or challenge emerges; embraces the idea that whatever the mind can conceive and believe *can* be achieved
- Knows that a significant leap has to be a BHAG (big, hairy audacious goal) and insists that real change occurs when the improbable becomes thinkable
- Is willing to stand up for oneself, one's ideas, and one's beliefs
- Is decisive and self-confident

Acosta's growth story is an illustration of unreasonable leadership, one example that transformed not only a company but also an entire industry. It is a story that shows what is possible when a leadership team is determined to stretch beyond what most people consider reasonable. And it affirms that all progress is truly made by unreasonable people, rebelling against the status quo and growing outside of their comfort zones to achieve what others deem impossible. For me, it all started in an unlikely place, on a family farm outside of a small town in New Hampshire.

Food for Thought

All progress is made by unreasonable people because reasonable people adjust to their surroundings, whereas unreasonable people rebel against their surroundings and produce progress.

Long-term happiness requires short-term discomfort. That's because in the long run, people are happy only if they are learning, growing, and expanding; yet, in the short-term, a person or business can't learn, grow, or expand unless exposed to the discomforts of new ideas and new situations.

Step 2

Reflect on Your Own Journey to Becoming an Unreasonable Leader

My early years and how I began to develop unreasonable leadership skills.

If you had asked me at a young age, "Gary, what do want to be when you grow up?" I couldn't have told you. I just knew what I *didn't* want to be.

I did not want to be a chicken farmer in New Hampshire.

Chickens do three things: eat, lay eggs, and create waste. As a steward of the farm, therefore, one must keep the chickens fed, gather the eggs daily, and shovel and dispose of their waste periodically. Tell me, why is that something to aspire to?

My defiance was born of experience. My dad was a chicken farmer on the northeastern edge of Bedford, New Hampshire. When I lived there, Bedford was a little community of about 6,000 nestled along state Highway 101 just a stone's throw west of the Merrimack River. On the other side of the river was Manchester, then, as now, the state's largest city.

Please don't misunderstand; I loved my dad dearly and was mighty proud of what he did to earn an honorable and honest living. I still miss him. Pancreatic cancer cut dad's life short at age 62, far too soon. I am grateful for the scores of warm family memories from those years when we worked alongside one another.

As I saw it, my dad was the hardest working and most honest person on earth. He inspired me to work just as hard and to feel good about my accomplishments; I loved him for that, as I still do. But all the daily chores I had to complete to make our family enterprise move forward? Those I didn't love at all. So was I going to spend 40 or 45 years tackling them from dawn 'til dusk? I don't think so. I wanted something very different.

If he had had the choice, Dad probably wouldn't have been a chicken farmer, either. It was a business he started from scratch after returning home from World War II. While my dad was off serving his country, my grandfather had launched a chicken farm, almost by accident when he realized there was decent money to be made selling eggs. When Dad returned from the war, he took stock of what my grandfather had started and decided to buy 50 acres of land in Bedford to start his own farm—but with some resignation, I later concluded.

Down deep, Dad had really wanted to expand his education and go to college. But my grandfather, who was of French-Canadian roots and had originally immigrated to New Hampshire to work in the textile mills, didn't think a college education was all that important in the late 1940s. He believed a good job was enough. So my dad would pursue a life on a farm as a young adult. The work was hard and the days were long, so pursuing an extended education just never happened.

Dad did find time to follow business, though. He did so with great enthusiasm and loved it, monitoring the stock market's daily performance with the intensity of a Wall Street trader. The rest of us didn't need radio or television to learn what the Dow had done during the day. Dad's mood at the supper table was our leading indicator. If the market had climbed, he was happy. If it had tumbled, he was downcast or grumpy.

My dad's keen interest in business was a reflection of his great work ethic, which he passed to my brothers, Steve and Alan, and me. He was also well-read and became a student of the market and business itself. In fact, one of my few regrets to date is that my father didn't live to see the growth and success that Acosta was to enjoy and the rewards that success has brought to so many of my colleagues and me. Dad died in 1989, long before I ever seriously envisioned the national expansion of Acosta; too bad, he would have relished every episode of the adventure that was to come. Still, I believe Dad watches from up above with a big smile on his face.

As tedious and demanding as farm life could be, my dad and mom made the Chartrand family farm a truly wonderful place to grow up. My mom was the real deal: a woman who loved her husband and the kids they had together. I always have felt secure that my mom loved me with all her heart. I learned a great deal about nature on the farm, which instilled in me a deep and enduring respect for what farmers do that enables them to feed the masses. I learned many more enduring lessons about hard work and the rewards it can bring if you apply yourself. One of my favorite memories was honed by an unexpected wood-chopping adventure that interrupted my freshman year in college.

Thanks to the double-whammy of the 1973 Arab oil embargo and the usually frigid New England winter, the powers that be at the University of New Hampshire sent all of its students home for almost six weeks, starting with the traditional break for Christmas and the end of the fall semester. Heating oil was in short supply during 1973 to 1974, so much so that classes were abruptly suspended.

When I got home, Dad either asked me what I was going to do with myself for six weeks or—more likely—told me to *find* something worthwhile to do with myself because he wasn't about to watch me sit around and do nothing for all that time. There was plenty to choose from, including clearing a few acres of land.

"I'll make a deal with you," my dad said. "You clear the land of the trees, and you can keep the money you make selling the wood you're left with."

So I decided to chop and split firewood to sell to residents looking for an alternative to heating oil, which had been expensive to begin with and was getting ever more expensive. There was plenty of wood on those acres, so off I trudged into the frosty air.

After quickly taking stock of the timber that I needed to cut down, I came up with a plan. First, I would cut the wood into manageable four-foot lengths and then drag them to the edge of the woods, where I'd truck the wood back to the barn. From the barn, I'd cut the logs into shorter lengths ideal for burning in a fireplace or wood stove. Then I'd split the wood by hand, stack it into cords, and, finally, try to sell it all.

Making my project a great deal more desirable was the help I got from Nancy Piecuch. This cute-as-a-button high school cheerleader, who had at first concocted excuses to avoid going out with me, had become my high school sweetheart and was destined to become my bride four years later. Nancy helped me a great deal. Every night after I had cut wood all day, she came over to help me by stacking the wood as I split it. It was cold and windy, but she was right there with me. She also made a sign: *Cut Firewood – Fill up your trunk for $8*, which we stuck at the edge of our farm's driveway to attract everyone driving to and from Bedford along Rundlett Hill Road.

Anyone who has ever cut and split wood for just a few hours knows how tough a task this is, far tougher than what I've just described—and I cut it not for just a few hours, either, but for almost six weeks. A New Hampshire winter can be one cold, dreary stretch: short days, too little sunshine, too many clouds, and plenty of wind, snow, and ice. Still, Nancy and I made what I thought was good money for the time. "A whole lot," Nancy will say if asked. As I recall, the total came to about $1,600. For a college freshman in 1973, it was a hefty sum, and I still get a satisfying feeling of accomplishment when I recall it. I was never in better physical shape than I was after this six-week adventure.

I've come to feel even better about the memorable lesson I gained from that experience. My days cutting timber affirmed how tackling a task could reap nice rewards, especially if one added dashes of ingenuity and salesmanship. Without realizing it, I had identified a "target audience." Further up Rundlett Hill Road was a small college, St. Anslem's, which generated pretty good traffic. I had figured many of those drivers would be tempted by the chance to buy quality firewood. "Let me load up your trunk," I'd say, and many of them did.

Notwithstanding the lessons and rewards the farm brought me, there still was no way in the world I was ever going to be a chicken farmer. At some point during my high school years in nearby Manchester, I began to feel the desire to be a teacher and coach, not quite in that order. For two years I studied at Bishop Bradley, an all-boys Catholic high school run by the Christian Brothers, which then merged with two other Catholic schools to form Trinity High, where I spent my junior and senior years—and first got acquainted with Nancy.

At both schools I loved sports and played everything the typical jock of the early 1970s played. In the fall it was football, right guard on offense and middle linebacker on defense. In my senior year, my teammates paid me a huge compliment by electing me team captain. Basketball came next, although my hoops talents were really pretty meager. Baseball was perhaps my best sport, so in the spring, I'd be found behind the plate as Trinity's catcher—just where you'd expect to find a middle linebacker, right? Like many catchers, I was far better crouched behind the plate than I was standing at the plate with a bat in my hand. I couldn't hit worth a damn.

You could say that baseball, in a way, gave me my first opportunity to achieve something unreasonable. In the summer of my junior year, I landed a spot on one of Manchester's American Legion baseball teams, Sweeney Post. I hadn't planned to try out for the team, because I figured my chores on the farm came first. But the team's pitching coach urged me to try out anyway, and Dad had given the idea his blessing.

The pitching coach was delighted. Then again, he had a specific interest in my talent. Though I was no all-star, I could handle our team's number one hurler, the coach's son, better than anyone else on the team. He was a likable kid who would go on to make quite a name for himself in baseball: Mike Flanagan—yep, the same Mike Flanagan who helped the Baltimore Orioles win the World Series in 1983, who won the Cy Young Award in 1979, and was a mainstay of the pitching staffs of those great Orioles in the 1970s and 1980s.

Largely because I could catch Mike almost flawlessly, along with a dash of luck that a quirk of fate provided, I became our team's number one catcher. Mike's pitching talent left my hand throbbing in pain after a game, but it was worth it. We won a lot of games that summer—so many, in fact, that by season's end, we had earned a spot in the state championship game. Winning that game was a feat that a Manchester sports writer predicted was well beyond our reach; that's the unreasonable part of this little sandlot drama. This was my first real experience with a naysayer.

In a column preceding our big game, this sportswriter described how our opponents would steal us blind—all because of me. Specifically, he declared my throwing arm woefully weak. "They'll run all over this Chartrand kid," he wrote.

You can imagine how this Chartrand kid reacted.

Sure enough, in the first inning, a guy got on base and, on the very next pitch, promptly took off toward second. I gunned him down! The next guy who reached base also tried to steal second. I gunned him down, too, just like I threw out a brief parade of others who tried swiping second base. Better to be lucky than good, right?

Did we win the game? Of course we did. And with our state American Legion Championship in hand, it was on to the New England tournament in Connecticut. We won four straight games there, and off we went to the American Legion World Series. That was quite a prize; it gave me my first-ever airplane ride all the way to Portland, Oregon.

Unfortunately, the plane ride back home came all too quickly. I'd love to tell you that we won the double-elimination American Legion World Series too, but we didn't. Had Mike Flanagan been healthy, who knows? But Mike got hurt warming up for our opening game and never threw a single pitch. Our first loss was a heartbreaker, 1–0 in 14 innings. I can recount it as if it were yesterday.

In the bottom of the 14th, a guy reached third base with nobody out and scored on a well-executed suicide squeeze play; the runner broke for home seconds before the pitch hit the dirt, bounced off my chest, and scored the winning run. There wasn't a thing we could do. Baseball fundamentals dictate that when a runner on third breaks for home to start a squeeze, the pitcher is to forget about throwing the pitch that's been called and throw a high inside fastball. It prevents the batter from getting any wood on the ball and pushes him back, so the catcher can catch the pitch cleanly and tag out the approaching runner as he slides into home plate.

That's what we'd been taught. But although I saw the base runner break for home, our pitcher didn't. Instead of throwing the high hard one, he threw the curve ball I had originally called; the ball hit the dirt and bounced off my chest and we lost.

We lost again the next day, getting blown out, 19–0. I never wanted to remember much about that one. Still, there was one treat waiting for us back in New Hampshire: A week or so later, we were special guests of the Boston Red Sox at a game in Fenway Park. We got to go onto the field beforehand and were greeted by and shook hands with another special guest at that game: Ted Williams. That was a thrill.

Such memories and experiences nurtured my desire to teach and coach, so I majored in physical education at UNH and prepared accordingly. That included playing football for two years, a pursuit that afforded me an early lesson in cash flow management. You also might call it my second adventure in unreasonable leadership.

After discovering that the president of the fraternity received free room and board, I quickly adjusted my goal and, as a junior, was elected president of the fraternity.

Most of the UNH football players wound up joining the same fraternity, "Acacia." I was no different and, as a sophomore, was elected fraternity treasurer. I considered it an honor until I discovered how a handful of brothers, all football players, were habitually late paying their room and board bills. Money wasn't the problem, because they were on full scholarships. They just deliberately dragged their feet, which made it tough for our fraternity to pay its bills. I set out to end the problem.

I declared that if room bills for the upcoming year weren't paid by August 1, before the fall semester began, the fraternity would have the right to rent the rooming space to other students. My Acacia brothers approved the proposal, as did the UNH administration. I even had my dad show the agreement to a federal judge, his best friend, to verify that we were on solid legal ground. As August waned, about half a dozen football-playing brothers still hadn't paid and had also ignored the notification letters we'd sent them in July. So, after contacting the administration's college housing office, I rented the available rooms to others. "That's what we said we'd do, so we're going to do it!" I insisted, digging in my heels.

I was still digging in as the brouhaha erupted upon the delinquent brothers' arrival on campus a few weeks later. One of them, a real brute of a defensive lineman, was ready to tear me apart. He might have, too, had another hulk of a fraternity brother, Nick Ragusa, not come to my rescue. Nick was a six-foot, three-inch massive hunk of muscle, was my best friend in college, would be my best man at my wedding, and was ready to clench his own fists on my behalf. Fortunately, we made the new rule stick without having to resort to anything like that – but the lesson learned still packed a wallop. I learned a lot about myself that day. Having the courage to stand up for what is right and face conflict head on has served me well ever since.

So did another lesson, except at first I couldn't appreciate it. By the time I had completed the requisite student-teaching assignment in the spring of my senior year in college, I began to realize that the classroom and a coaching career weren't for me. By then, I also had grasped the reality that far fatter paychecks were more likely if I chose some other career.

But what career? I really didn't know. I did give some thought to sales, but then I decided "No way." I was too shy—way too shy. The very thought of standing before anyone and making a sales presentation terrified me back then.

Anyone who knows anything at all about me today no doubt is dumfounded by this statement. But it's the absolute truth. Selling wood for a couple of weeks one winter to neighbors and acquaintances was one thing. Selling just about anything else to complete strangers was a frightening prospect. I was so shy, in fact, that as a high school sophomore I had to ask a friend to first tell Nancy I wanted to ask her out. I had been too timid to call her myself. And because my friend began relaying my request with the words "I want to warn you ..." Nancy initially blew me off, figuring I wasn't to be trusted.

I was trustworthy! I was just too inhibited to demonstrate it.

That same shyness kept me from acting on the many misgivings I had about my career choice. I still graduated from UNH in December 1975 intent on teaching and coaching and suddenly learned how tough launching any career could be.

With the economy still in the grip of a brutal recession, even teaching jobs were hard to get. So I took whatever I could find, working as a substitute teacher during the day and waiting tables at night at the Mill Yard, a restaurant not far from my home. It was aptly named. The Mill Yard had been remodeled smack dab in the middle of what once was a world-renowned complex of textile mills, the ones that made Manchester the largest textile-producing city on the planet. There was a touch of irony in my working there, too: My mother's great-grandfather, Alfonzo Sanborn, was the architect of those mills.

For the time being, both jobs were OK. I just wanted to make some money so Nancy and I could get married the following May, as we had planned to do following her graduation from UNH.

What we hadn't planned was Nancy having to wait tables in a restaurant too, after our honeymoon. Initially, my bride was having no better luck finding a high school teaching job than I was. Our combined income was so modest that we qualified for a government-subsidized apartment in Manchester. But most of the time, we didn't care too much. We were newlyweds and in love; money wasn't all that important.

Ironically, at about the same time Nancy landed a full-time teaching job for the fall of 1976, I stumbled upon the job opportunity that would whisk us from Manchester to Maine.

Actually, the opportunity stumbled onto me. As Nancy and I sat watching a softball game one evening, an old high school pal, Billy Cullity, whose wife played for one of the teams, matter-of-factly told me about a job opening at Carnation, where he was working as a sales rep. He said Carnation was a fine company. What he described sounded enviable enough, and given the fact that I was on the verge of having to scour the want ads for whatever I might find, it didn't take me long to act on what my friend was suggesting.

"I'm going after that job!" I said to myself and then to Nancy.

In part, at least, my days on the gridiron and the baseball diamond paid off. Carnation's managers liked to hire athletes: They had concluded that a competitive zeal and a will to win were attributes possessed by a good sales representative. I also impressed Steve

Pearsall, the first of three managers who interviewed me. The other two, Rick Maily and Tom Caston, were also impressed with my wood-chopping story. By September 1976 I had a real job, representing Carnation products to about 80 grocers and supermarket managers in stores scattered through much of Maine.

So up the coast to Portland we went.

I feel indebted to Carnation to this day. The company took a big chance by hiring an inexperienced college kid who wasn't sure what he wanted to do, trained him well, and molded him first into a polished, confident sales rep and then into the manager of a six-member sales team. The seven years I spent with Carnation were terrific. To be sure, I brought a solid work ethic with me, and it thrived in Carnation's culture—which gave me an appreciation for organizational culture I will always remember.

Carnation was a great organization to work for, which made the work itself no work at all. And the harder I worked, the greater I felt. From day one, I was motivated to spend my entire eight hours with the store managers and grocers I called on. Whatever time I spent driving to get to them never counted. In turn, 10- and 12-hour days became routine. But it was time incredibly well spent, because tucked within those hours were innumerable impromptu learning experiences, about the grocery business in general and about relationships—with customers, competitors, and colleagues.

While calling on one of my stores, for instance, I was startled to find that Friskies cat food, one of my Carnation products, wasn't arranged on the shelf as it was expected it to be. Friskies, it had been drilled into our heads, should *always* be next to Purina Cat Chow—and at eye level (just as Friskies Buffet *always* belonged between 9Lives and the competing Purina brand). On that morning, my product was stacked in the corner of a distant and lower shelf. After bringing the store manager to the aisle, I won his permission to move the Friskies to where I knew it belonged. I did it myself, can by can.

On my next visit to that store three weeks later, though, I found the Friskies had been shoved back to where I had first discovered it. A guy standing next to me could see I was perplexed, if not miffed. He introduced himself as Dick, the sales rep of the independent food broker who represented 9Lives.

"I moved your Friskies back to where you first saw it," Dick readily acknowledged. He then explained how he knew all about

Carnation's insistence on positioning its products. "But let me tell you how things are," this sales veteran said candidly, making it clear that he had plenty of clout throughout his territory and wasn't about to be upstaged by some green 22-year-old company sales rep in his very first territory.

But rather than conspire and feud, this rep and I struck up a good professional relationship, worked out a mutually beneficial arrangement for the shelf space, and soon became friends. Dick had goals too, I reasoned, just like I did. This episode was an important early lesson about mutually beneficial negotiations and win–win relationships.

Another important early lesson was my campaign to sell a million pounds of Carnation hot cocoa mix. I had been promoted to my first sales management job by then, responsible not only for Maine but also New Hampshire and the eastern portion of Massachusetts, and I was ever eager. Even early on, I relished hitting unreasonable goals.

Hot cocoa isn't a tough sell in upper New England, given the fishermen, campers, hikers, and hunters who traipse up and down the region. Still, my million-pound goal was imposing at best; it was more than twice the number ever sold in any territory in a given period. Carnation hot cocoa is packaged in 30-ounce canisters, and a million pounds of it stirs into an ocean's worth of hot cocoa. That didn't matter to me. A million pounds was the mark I wanted our team to hit.

"But we won't come close, not with all the other tasks we have to tackle," my six-member team replied.

"OK," I reasoned quickly, "forget about all those other tasks for the next two weeks; let's blitz the territory and fire all our bullets exclusively for hot cocoa mix." Our aim was true, and we hit our goal: a million pounds—not so unreasonable after all.

What was most satisfying of all was the team-building that our campaign nurtured and the excitement that resulted. The memories of that campaign have both endured and come in handy over the years. Stretching beyond our comfort zones, taking some calculated risks, and reaching for a goal never before accomplished gave the team and me a real thrill. It also gave me great confidence that I could, in fact, motivate and direct a team to achieve great results.

Perhaps most important were the bonds of friendship I established during this time. Notably, one of my team members—and one of the first guys I ever hired—was John Pritchard. A one-time state highway patrolman, John too was embarking on a successful career. After a number of outstanding years with Carnation and Nestlé, he became president of Ken's Foods. Ken's is an Acosta client, and John remains one of my best friends in the business. Nancy and I make it a point to invite John and his wife, Connie, to our Colorado home just outside Beaver Creek each year for some skiing.

I also learned to cope with the frustration that comes with any managerial assignment. Another person assigned to my team was a preppy and attractive young lady from Cornell, whose first morning on the job began with her asking where her office was. As best I could, I explained that she didn't have an office and needed to make do with her car, the road, and whatever working space she chose to carve out within her residence. That task was easy. But the male chauvinism that endured in our business at the time proved overwhelming for her. And I didn't begin to have either the experience or expertise the situation needed. The young lady became frustrated and soon left the company.

The situation remains vivid for several reasons. First, I learned as a young manager that I didn't really know how to handle this situation. That frustrated me. Had I been more experienced and equipped with the right tools, the situation may have turned out differently for her. More important were two key lessons: Know what you don't know, and don't be afraid to ask for help when presented with a difficult set of circumstances.

My own circumstances were about to change—with Carnation's blessing. Pat Dills, my supervisor, had become an early mentor and helped advance my career. In early 1982, a second promotion beckoned, and I was weighing going to Houston or Jacksonville as an assistant district manager: "cowboy or redneck?" as I put it privately.

I chose "redneck" because Jacksonville wound up being more appealing. For one thing, moving there would keep us on the East Coast, an important consideration to Nancy. Her family's heritage had never really included anyone living far from our hometown, and Jacksonville was much closer to New Hampshire than Houston was. With other factors being pretty much a wash, it was "Jacksonville, here we come."

In no time at all, though, northern Florida seemed about as far away from New England as it could be. At some point in my life, I imagine I might have joined in singing "Dixie," but certainly not in the rousing fashion expected of all participants at an industry-related dinner we attended not too long after our arrival. Shouting "Dixie" might be more descriptive—standing and singing at the top of our lungs with everyone.

"What was *that* all about?" Nancy asked almost in disbelief on our way home. Just life in the Deep South, we figured. We both shrugged. Conversation during another dinner function not long afterward left my wife momentarily wondering if the South might have won the Civil War.

Still, neither of us spent any time wondering if I had made the right career decision. Carnation's corporate culture in Jacksonville and throughout Florida was as stimulating as it had been in our Boston office, renditions of "Dixie" notwithstanding. I also had the good fortune of working for another great boss, Mark Gupton. He was supportive from the moment I arrived. Nancy probably put it best; Carnation, she'd often say, was like family and was an organization that I never seriously considered leaving.

So it was purely by chance that I was introduced to Acosta's Mike Keohane sometime late in the summer of 1983 at a business gathering at Hidden Hills Country Club in Jacksonville. It was an industry gathering of some kind that had attracted both me and Mike, who by then had become one of Acosta's four owners. Neither of us can remember exactly what we first said to each other. What Mike does recall, though, is what he was thinking. "As soon as I saw Gary," Mike later recounted, "I knew we had been recruiting the wrong guy."

Acosta was a growing company in the early 1980s and was almost always looking for promising new talent. Evidently, the company had had its eye on someone else at Hidden Hills Country Club that afternoon. Without my knowing it, Mike suddenly had turned his attention to me. In no time at all, our initial conversation prompted others. In fact, Mike soon was calling me often enough that Nancy began getting curious.

I kept telling her it was nothing more than a casual exchange of ideas that wouldn't lead to anything. At first, maybe that's what I really thought. "It's just some good interviewing experience," I would say.

"Well, then, why don't you tell him to stop calling?" Nancy suggested at one point.

I didn't, though, and so Mike didn't stop.

Before long, he and Acosta CEO Del Dallas were in full recruiting mode. I knew next to nothing about the company itself, and what little I knew about the food brokerage business I had observed from my vantage point with Carnation. Yet the more Del Dallas talked, the more intriguing Acosta Sales & Marketing Company sounded. Once I proved myself, there would likely be an ownership opportunity, Del explained. I concluded he wasn't just blowing smoke once he and Mike had outlined the company's tradition of having what you could call "ownership spans" of about 10 years and could demonstrate it by reviewing Acosta's ownership history.

What had initially sounded intriguing began to sound increasingly appealing, so much so that in October of 1983, I asked to meet with Acosta's president, Pete Jones, whose office was in Tampa. From what I was later told, Pete was impressed by the fact that this prospective hire had specifically asked to see him. He also liked my background and the questions I asked during what I remember as a very good meeting.

Even so, the thought of leaving Carnation had me squirming. They had hired me when I had badly needed a job, and they had trained me, supported me, and promoted me and were continuing to make an investment in my future. To walk away after barely a year in Jacksonville was no easy step.

"Put down the pros and cons on a sheet of paper," advised my dad, who happened to be visiting us that fall. "Then do what you think is best. It's your call."

Privately, though, I sensed Dad was urging me to accept Acosta's offer, one that would have me handling its all-important Clorox account. More than once, my father told me that having an ownership position in your own business was almost always better than working for somebody else.

As much as anything, the ownership opportunity that Acosta kept citing was what led me to walk into Mark Gupton's office in late October and resign my position with Carnation. It wasn't an easy message to deliver.

But it was a piece of cake compared with the task of consoling Nancy. I'll never forget coming home that evening, walking into our kitchen, and making it official. Even though Nancy had assured me time and again that she would support whatever decision I made, my wife was devastated by the news. A few minutes later, I found her sobbing on our living room couch, so I pleaded, "You said you'd support whatever decision I made."

"I didn't think you'd make *that one!*" Nancy stammered. It was like bolting from the family, she said tearfully. And it was. Hell, we'd even gotten used to singing "Dixie."

Yet, I'd also considered carefully the implications of staying with Carnation. Although Nancy looked forward to returning to New England, specifically Boston, the reality was something else: We could anticipate a steady string of moves all over the country and ultimately all the way to the company's southern California headquarters – assuming my career progressed as I was envisioning. The idea of being uprooted time and again wasn't appealing at all. Nor did I think it would appeal to Nancy or be in the best interests of our two children.

The reality of such a future with Carnation helped Nancy's tears subside—after maybe a week, that is. The first few days following my decision, she kept thinking about something else: how unreasonable I was being.

The fact is that I had made up my mind to pursue what I had concluded was a once-in-a-lifetime opportunity. There was no looking back. I had made a commitment, and there is great power in that.

So it was in October 1983 that I began my journey to learn all about the food brokerage business. It would prove to be a good journey, indeed. Ten years later, Acosta's board of directors appointed me to lead the organization into the future as president of the company.

Food for Thought

Until one is committed, there is hesitancy, the chance to draw back—always in self-selectiveness. Concerning all acts of initiatives and creation there is one elementary truth, the ignorance of which kills countless ideas and splendid plans. That the moment one commits oneself, and then province moves, too. All sorts of things occur to help one that would never otherwise have occurred. A whole stream of events and issues from the decision, raising in one's favor all manner of unforeseen incidents and meetings and material assistance which no man could have dreamed would have come his way. Are you in earnest? Seek this very minute whatever you can do or dream you can, begin it. Boldness has genius, power and magic in it. Only engage and the mind grows heated. Begin and then the task will be completed.

— Goethe

Step 3

Learn from Your Company's History

What worked and what didn't work at Acosta before I arrived.

I suppose it would be unreasonable to expect to find any connection other than the name itself linking the steadily expanding $4 million company I was joining in October 1983 with the original enterprise founded by Louis T. and Daniel Acosta in 1927. And yet you can find a connection—several of them, in fact. These ties don't show up all at once; you do need to dig a little to find them, because official company records and financial statements don't reveal much beyond routine facts and figures. But delve into decades-old letters, memos, sales presentations, and newspaper clippings, and you'll discover that some of the key practices and attitudes guiding twenty-first century Acosta, Inc., do in fact date to the early years, if not the very roots of L.T. Acosta & Company.

Hearing the perspectives and recollections of predecessors and former partners makes these links more visible. At times it's almost uncanny—enough to make me wonder if there was something in the water we've all sipped throughout the years. If nothing else, I have gained an even greater appreciation of our company's heritage. Here's a thumbnail description of the practices I found:

Always hire the best people. Not just good, but the best you can find. This has been the expressed maxim almost from day one. In fact, by the mid 1950s, Lou Acosta could see that the future of his family business depended on his finding capable people outside of the family. By the mid 1970s, "People make the difference!" was the rallying cry of Del Dallas, my predecessor and mentor.

Prepare and plan for the future. Acosta established a deferred profit-sharing plan in 1961, when the company's payroll totaled only 10 or 11 names—as it would well into the 1960s. That plan helped build a deep loyalty to the organization, which in turn helped attract succeeding generations of company leaders. Sharing in the success of the company with critical leaders throughout the organization has been a long-standing philosophy of Acosta Sales & Marketing.

Perpetuate the business. You couldn't find even a hint of an exit strategy within Acosta. From the 1950s on, Acosta's original owners became consistently focused on continuing the business and expanding it, albeit in Jacksonville. Out of that focus grew the ongoing practice of actively recruiting promising new talent and, in turn, the wise notion of preparing a new generation of company leaders every 10 years or so.

Operate conservatively. In a business sector that had a reputation for the ostentatious and extravagant, Acosta always stood apart. It built relationships on performance and made a point of avoiding debt whenever possible. Robert "Hy" Albritton, who became company president in 1959, was an old-school businessman with mighty tight fists. His philosophy was right for the times, and it left Acosta poised to expand with catlike quickness when the opportunity arrived.

Stay ahead of the curve. Even when it was just a local company, Acosta acquired a sixth sense about where its business was headed. "Better to be first than to have to fight your way in later," was the advice former partner and secretary/treasurer H.C. Sims heard time and again once he joined Acosta in 1961. Whether it was adding product lines, broadening its reach, anticipating changes its clients were to make, or studying Florida's population growth trends, Acosta was typically a year or two ahead of its competitors.

Build ties with other companies in your industry. Arguably, this trait *predates* that 1927 morning when Acosta's doors first opened. While working as a grocery buyer in and around Sanford, Florida, in the 1920s, Lou Acosta struck up a friendship with a prosperous food broker in Jacksonville who sold him on starting his own business. Once he did, Lou soon developed informal ties with a food broker in Miami and another in Tampa. Because their businesses were each strictly local, they recommended each other to food manufacturers seeking new representatives across the state.

Although he couldn't have begun to realize it then, Lou Acosta's conversations were setting the first of several critical precedents for his little company. Not quite a half century later, these same precedents would help trigger the transformation of an entire industry.

There was a more immediate payoff to those conversations, too. T.W. Holt, the Jacksonville food broker who first encouraged Lou Acosta to strike out on his own, remained an ally and confidante to Lou Acosta for years. No doubt his counsel was valuable; compared with buying groceries in Sanford, launching a business in a big city like Jacksonville would have been an especially ambitious move at the time.

Lou got additional encouragement and assistance from two other brokers, Bonacker Brothers in Tampa and Bonacker & Leigh in Miami. Before long, the informal ties Acosta had formed with these two firms were strong enough to leave onlookers with the impression that the businesses were all part of a single organization. They never were, however; they were just good business pals who each gained important insights into food broker activities throughout the state. I guess we could presume the Acosta brothers' new enterprise had one more important ally: L.T. and Dan were third cousins of St. Elmo "Chic" Acosta, a prominent Jacksonville councilman during the early decades of the 20th century, and namesake of the downtown bridge that today spans the St. Johns River.

Notwithstanding these associations, the L.T. Acosta Company of the late 1920s was still a small business in every sense of the word. So was the food brokerage business itself, as it was then defined. No matter the town, part of the country, or product line, food brokers everywhere looked pretty much the same: collections of tiny, family-run companies, each one representing no more than a few products in one or two sectors of the grocery business. It was the ultimate in niche marketing long before anyone had coined the term.

At one point, there were as many as 2,500 food brokers scattered across the U.S. Look hard enough among them and you even could find enterprises that bore a passing resemblance to the Corleone family in *The Godfather*, without the guns and the goons, that is.

If "strictly business" was a pet phrase of Michael Corleone, it was also the Acosta brothers' singular focus, and a necessary one. After all, it wasn't long before the family business had to endure the Depression and then the war years, though in one respect, the era could be labeled the best of times—thanks to none other than the Clorox Company. That's as it should be, I guess.

The company that would later play such a pivotal role in Acosta's initial expansions first became an Acosta client in Jacksonville in 1933. So did another renowned brand, LaChoy Chinese food products. Our records indicate that, for a time, the Acosta brothers did purchase and stock Clorox cases outright, back when the bleach was packed in glass bottles, then resold them to grocers. How long that practice existed and why it was discontinued isn't clear. Company records don't offer any clues either.

Neither do the records shed much light on a disappointing episode of the company's first 30 years. For a number of those years, Lou Acosta handed the reins of the business to his younger brother. Dan's time at the helm turned out to be less than successful. From all indications, he had been quite the successful salesman and personally handled the Clorox account. But running the entire company was beyond Dan's capabilities due, in large part, to one or more personal weaknesses. By the early 1950s, Lou Acosta was back in charge and, before long, looking for help.

In hindsight, his salvation was prophetic: Acosta's first merger. After almost 30 years in business—a number of which had to be awfully challenging—it certainly was understandable for Lou Acosta to want to pass the torch. The man Lou convinced to accept it was a logical choice. Robert "Hy" Albritton was president of his own food broker-age, Common & Co., and knew an opportunity when he saw one. Here was a family business without a family member to run it now running toward him at a time when the grocery business was bustling, thanks to the continuing baby boom.

Moreover, Lou was especially eager to step aside. A provision of the 1956 merger agreement that united the two companies under the Acosta name called for Lou to retire within a year after the deal was completed unless circumstances required a longer transition period. Evidently, circumstances did, for it wasn't until February 1, 1959, that Hy Albritton officially became Acosta's president. Until then, he served as the company's executive vice president.

For me, it's particularly interesting to note that in assuming command, Albritton was one nervous and uncertain executive vice president. Some of it, of course, was simply human nature. A dash of mystery surrounds any new job, no matter the level of responsibilities, and merging one company into another is especially challenging. Yet much of Hy Albritton's trepidation was prompted by a specific provision of the merger that Lou Acosta proposed. Albritton was to gain controlling interest in the combined company in exchange for his $8,000 investment.

"We really had to scrape together that $8,000," remembers Albritton's widow, Martha. Now in her mid 90s, Martha Albritton still lives in Jacksonville. "It was our entire nest egg," she said, and putting it all on Acosta's future struck them as one mighty fateful bet.

That very feeling has proven to be a precedent setter of sorts. Just about everyone else who made an initial investment in L.T. Acosta Company, Inc., through the years did so with at least some trepidation—including me. We all had our futures on the line. As it turned out, none of us needed to have spent as much as a minute worrying.

Hy and Martha Albritton's $8,000 investment was to soar in value during the next 20 years. The investments by other partners that followed would soar, too, and stand as classic examples of the American free enterprise system at its best: invest, continually work hard, be patient, be fair, and earn a substantial reward.

Albritton's caution and unease reflected how he would run the company: in a word, *conservatively*. Like countless other veteran businessmen whose early working years were influenced by absorbing the pains of the Depression, Albritton ran a tight ship. He spent cautiously, zealously avoided debt, and was happy to avoid the limelight —other than when promoting products that Acosta represented required a little special attention. Albritton made it a point to operate out of a modest office and purchase modest, practical company cars; aging photos of vintage 1950s white Ford station wagons attest to it.

The boss's trust in the people who worked for him didn't extend especially far, and the small firm with which Albritton was entrusted remained small. Acosta's payroll barely totaled more than a dozen when Albritton became president, and that number didn't change appreciably for at least the next half dozen years. When H.C. Sims came aboard in September 1961, he remembers being "either employee number 10 or 11, I forget which one," H.C. laughs. At age 22, Sims was also one of Acosta's youngest hires, because Albritton was wary of hiring anyone under the age of 30. And H.C. learned early on not to expect dramatic boosts in his paycheck.

Soon after the Simses' first child was born, Albritton "mentioned something about having another mouth to feed, and indicated there would be a little more in my paycheck," Sims also recounts. Sure enough, he had earned a pay raise … of $5 a week. "Hy never had any children, so he never really understood what having a family could do to your household expenses," H.C. said.

But don't conclude that Acosta was a cold, uncaring place to work. It wasn't, not at all. Hy Albritton could be as compassionate as he was cautious and frugal. During the early 1960s, one of the company's younger sales representatives was involved in a horrific auto accident that killed his wife and left their young son seriously injured and permanently handicapped. The sales rep had been with Acosta for less than six months, and his own injuries kept him from working for several months afterward. Acosta continued paying his salary for a full year. The employee subsequently left the area to rejoin his family in West Virginia. Albritton understood fully, and the young man departed with Acosta's best wishes.

The sad tale offers a glimpse of what lay under the boss's often tough exterior. Albritton certainly knew his business well enough to also know that Acosta needed to hire and hold onto the very best people he could find and treat them well. He found some excellent people. Among those dozen or so employees hired during the 1960s was, of course, H.C. Sims, who spent his entire 35-year career with Acosta, including 21 years as secretary/treasurer from 1974 to 1995. Another was Charlie Hill. He, too, built a long and most successful career with Acosta and, in time, became a company vice president and minority owner.

It was under Hy Albritton's direction that profit-sharing and deferred-compensation plans began. The profit-sharing plan that began in 1961 automatically earmarked 15 percent of an employee's salary for an individual retirement fund. It was long-term thinking at its best. The fund was managed with care, and in some years its value alone grew by 15 percent—over and above any contributions from participants. Not even the periodic losses of lucrative accounts could slow the fund's steady growth. Albritton personally oversaw the program as the plan's trustee and continued in that capacity for a good nine years after he retired.

When Albritton did retire, he decided not to take a lump-sum payment from the sale of his controlling interest in the business. Instead, Hy established the practice of taking annual payments spread out over a 10-year period. This practice grew into the deferred-compensation plan that became an all-important template that helped initially finance Acosta's expansions in the 1970s and 1980s. And, yes, it was essentially the same plan that I begged my fellow owners to recast in 1999. You will learn why in Step 5 of this book.

What emerged from these various influences, mind-sets, and attitudes was a food brokerage that was consistently well run and self-disciplined. Acosta built solid relationships with its clients, attracted its share of new clients, generated yearly revenues of about $500,000 by

1974, and was consistently profitable. That's what veterans like H.C. Sims remember most of all—and with pride.

L.T. Acosta Company, Inc. was, all in all, a fine little sales company. It was a hard-working little sales company, too.

Close and long-standing relationships notwithstanding, a food broker's clients could still be very demanding, and a client could cancel its ties with a broker at any time simply by giving 30 days' notice. Practically speaking, that didn't occur very often, but it kept brokers on their toes.

Acosta's Clorox account was a case in point. To begin with, the renowned maker of bleach had consistently high expectations and challenging quotas. It was Acosta's job to convince the supermarkets and grocery stores it called on to advertise Clorox products in local newspapers and actively market Clorox products—not with ad dollars from Clorox, however, but with dollars from the supermarkets' and grocers' own coffers.

In turn, part of an Acosta sales rep's repertoire was clipping and saving copies of any and all ads that appeared, then periodically shipping them off to Clorox headquarters in Oakland, California, to demonstrate his success. Even within a modestly sized market like northeastern Florida, there were plenty of these episodes, because there were fewer large chains and many more independent stores.

Every now and then, Acosta had to ship off something else: photos of its entire staff. Clorox wanted graphic evidence that the numbers of representatives and staffers its various food broker organizations claimed to have toiling on the bleach maker's behalf were valid and not phantom figures pulled out of thin air to impress the folks back in Oakland. Clorox wasn't the only account with high expectations, either. Hellmann's, the mayonnaise maker, was another Acosta client that could be just as demanding.

Acosta's business was so demanding that Albritton's business horizons never extended beyond Jacksonville. As he saw it, there was absolutely no need to think any further. The Jacksonville "territory" that Acosta covered throughout the 1960s and early 1970s offered ample opportunities. It extended north into the southeastern corner of Georgia, west to Tallahassee, and southwest to about Ocala, Florida.

In Hy Albritton's mind, every last square mile of that expanse could be covered from his Jacksonville office. The very notion of establishing a branch office someplace other than Jacksonville was virtual heresy. Hy refused to even consider it. "He always felt that people operating out of another office wouldn't be giving him a good day's work," Sims recalls. Albritton finally relented a bit in the late 1960s, allowing Charlie Hill to establish a satellite office of sorts in Tallahassee; however, this one concession was motivated in part by the fact that Charlie's wife could serve as bookkeeper and office assistant. And because Charlie by then had purchased a portion of Dan Acosta's company stock and become a minority owner, Albritton could rely on Hill to deliver "a good day's work."

Still, Tallahassee was the lone exception to Hy's policy. Even by late 1973, when gasoline prices first skyrocketed and shortages erupted in the wake of the first OPEC oil embargo, Hy wouldn't consider anyone moving out, despite the increasing opportunities to reduce rising transportation expenses or the growing restlessness among Acosta's sales force.

Within a year or so, that restlessness would be harnessed, and dramatically so. In addition to H.C. Sims and Charlie Hill in 1961, Hy Albritton hired, in the summer of 1966, an eager young man from Mississippi whose business horizons were broader, much broader. His name was Delmar "Del" Dallas. I suppose it's not unreasonable to infer that, at some point, Hy Albritton and Del Dallas would have discussed in some detail Acosta's long-term future. After all, it was Albritton who had first approached Del about joining Acosta and immediately appointed him vice president once he arrived in Jacksonville as the company's 13th associate. As the 1970s progressed, Albritton was confirming what had become obvious—that Dallas would succeed him as president and the majority partner in the business.

If Del and Hy did share ideas about the future, no one was remotely aware of what they might have discussed. Then again, maybe the two didn't confer, given what unfolded so quickly after Albritton put Del in charge as president and CEO in 1974 and retired at the end of that year.

Like me, Del Dallas grew up on a farm, but in Mississippi, not New England. He enrolled at Mississippi State University, had his college years interrupted by the Korean War, then returned and got his marketing degree in 1953. Soon thereafter, he joined Procter & Gamble as a sales representative.

Initially, P&G recruited Del for a position based in New Orleans. But because Del's young wife, Peggy, yearned to return to her native

North Carolina, Del had turned down the offer.

"If they offered you a job in New Orleans, they'll offer you a job someplace else," Peggy had reasoned. She was right. Soon thereafter, P&G hired Dallas as a sales rep for a territory based in Columbia, South Carolina. By 1964, Dallas had earned a string of promotions that resulted in his being appointed southeast division manager for the Clorox Company, at the time a Procter & Gamble subsidiary. Given Clorox's ties to Acosta, it wasn't long before Del and Hy Albritton became friends and prospective allies.

His 13 years with P&G and Clorox had afforded Del ample opportunity to appraise the food brokerage business. He concluded that he could grow the business beyond its local presence. Then based in Atlanta, he also began to tire of the regional sales executive's routine: leave home on Monday, spend the work week on the road making calls and conferring with customers, and return sometime late Friday afternoon—if then.

Ready for a change and a new challenge, Dallas at first thought he had found it with a brokerage firm in Nashville in the early days of 1966. But there was snow on the ground in Nashville when Del and Peggy arrived for a visit. A blustery winter wasn't in their plans, so, as he had once before, Del declined the offer.

"It just wasn't right for other reasons too," Peggy Dallas later recalled. "Still, we were pretty disappointed because we thought it was the best offer Del would ever receive."

Hy Albritton proved otherwise. The chance to join Acosta in Jacksonville, which had its strong ties to Clorox, was appealing, especially because it came with an opportunity to buy an interest in the business, as well as the possibility of becoming the majority owner at some point in the future.

It was a very strong possibility, too. As it had been in 1956, Acosta was again a family-run business with no more family in the wings. By the time he took the reins from Hy Albritton, Del undoubtedly knew there was an opportunity to take this fine little sales company and expand it. Del was a man with a great attitude, and he always believed that people with the right attitude would make the difference whenever opportunities presented themselves. He wouldn't waste time seeking opportunities, either.

Food for Thought

Promise yourself to be strong, that nothing can disturb your peace of mind. To talk health, happiness and prosperity to every person you meet. To make all your friends feel that there is something special in them. Look at the sunny side of everything and make your optimism come true. To think only of the best, to work only for the best and expect only the best. To be just as enthusiastic about the success of others as you are about your own. To forget the mistakes of the past and press on to the greater achievements of the future. To wear a cheerful countenance at all times and give every living creature you meet a smile. To give so much time to the improvement of yourself that you have no time to criticize others. To be too large for worry, too noble for anger, too strong for fear, and too happy to permit the presence of trouble.

— Christian D. Larson

Step 4

Study Other Unreasonable Leaders

Their wisdom and perspectives are priceless.

L.T. Acosta & Co. still looked and operated much like every other Jacksonville food broker in the autumn of 1974. Just 26 employees worked alongside Del Dallas, now the company's president and majority owner, the CEO as we would say today. But the modest payroll was deceiving. Del had bold, ambitious plans for this 47-year-old company—plans that would grow Acosta's payroll from 26 to 2,000 over the next 22 years and send revenues soaring. In that same 22-year span, revenues would double every three years. All Del needed was the opportunity to put his plan into action.

The opportunity arrived in a phone call. When he hung up the receiver, Mike Keohane abruptly put aside what he had been doing and marched quickly to Dallas's office with some very exciting news. Mike knew instinctively that the man who had recruited him to Acosta the preceding July would want to know right away what he had just learned. Clorox, Acosta's long-standing, number one client, was looking for new representation in the Tampa market.

It was all Del needed to hear. The opportunity he had been awaiting was suddenly staring him in the face, perhaps sooner than he had imagined. After briefly savoring what Mike Keohane was sharing with him, Del started making mental notes. "What to do first?" he kept asking himself as his strategy began taking shape.

Before Keohane left, Dallas gave him an important assignment. Then Del picked up his phone to make the call that would transform his company and stun an industry.

Clorox division sales manager Craig Sullivan had started reviewing a strategy of his own before he left his Boston office, even though he practically knew it cold. He also started anticipating the flurry of telephone calls he and fellow sales manager Jerry Todd would soon field. That the Clorox broker in Tampa had not been performing well had become almost common knowledge. It was that kind of business;

the string of disappointing results was apparent if one knew where to look, plus sales people talked constantly.

Initially, Sullivan informed Clorox's Tampa broker of his company's concerns. Step two was putting the broker on probation. But those actions only stalled the inevitable. It was time to make a change. It was a standard ritual: fly down to Florida, pull out the current National Food Brokers Association directory, flip to the pages listing all the brokers who served the Tampa Bay area, start compiling a list of candidates, and then cull from that list any brokers who were already representing the products of competitors. The phone calls would follow, both to the candidates who had made the first cut and from broker organizations eager to be of service.

Clorox was an attractive client, with an attractive family of familiar products, so the question was not "Who is interested?" but "Who *wouldn't* be interested?" Clorox also had demanding standards, however, so Sullivan and Todd needed to appraise broker organizations with care and respond to inquiries in the same manner. Devoting time to anyone other than serious, viable candidates would be a waste of time. That's what the Clorox Company expected of Craig Sullivan, a young but accomplished sales manager with a bright future. Of course, he knew the drill as well as anyone. After he set up shop in Tampa, he'd begun tackling his task with a sense of anticipation.

What Sullivan didn't expect was the voice at the other end of the phone that afternoon. "I understand you're interviewing brokers in Tampa," Del Dallas confirmed after the requisite friendly hello. "We want to throw our hat in the ring."

For an instant Sullivan was speechless, genuinely puzzled. Why in the world was Del Dallas asking that his Jacksonville company be allowed to make a pitch to be Clorox's sales representative in Tampa, some 240 miles across the state? It was more than unusual; it was unheard of and patently unreasonable. Clorox was represented across the country by close to 60 independent sales organizations, and every last one of them was a local business, nothing more – Acosta included. In fact, to the best of Sullivan's knowledge, every last firm listed in the National Food Brokers Association directory was a *local* business.

"Del, I appreciate your interest, but we're not interviewing Jacksonville brokers," Sullivan said. "We're interviewing *Tampa* brokers, and you're not in Tampa."

"Yes, we know that," Del answered quickly with confidence, "but we're still extremely interested and look forward to an opportunity to talk further and show you what we can do for Clorox in Tampa. Just give us the chance to explain what we have in mind."

Sullivan's first instinct was to snap, "Del, there's no way in hell we could even consider it." And there wasn't. Acosta had no business whatsoever in Tampa—no clients, no products to represent, no customer base, no office, no telephone listing, no nothing! What Acosta did have, however, was a determined, unreasonable leader named Del Dallas who wanted to grow his company. Yet, although Acosta meant something in Jacksonville, in Tampa, it meant *nothing*. In the brokerage world at that time, Tampa was as far away from Jacksonville as Timbuktu.

Just the same, Sullivan knew that he couldn't snap. Acosta had been Clorox's broker in Jacksonville for 41 years and counting—and its national broker of the year in each of the past two years, an unprecedented feat.

Besides, it *was* a tempting notion, Sullivan had to silently admit. Having Acosta and Del Dallas working for Clorox just about anywhere was an idea worth pursuing. That Del had worked for Clorox for a couple of years before joining Acosta made the notion almost heavenly. Del knew the business cold and was a very persuasive salesman—as he was demonstrating at that moment. Before he snapped back to attention, Sullivan was becoming half-sold himself. At the very least, Dallas and Acosta merited a little courtesy.

That's it! Sullivan reasoned. *Out of respect for its loyalty, decades of service, and laudable track record, we'll include Acosta in the first round of interviews solely to satisfy ourselves. Then we'll tell Del that his intentions are honorable and deeply appreciated but that we still firmly believe that Clorox's needs and long-term interests will be best served by one of the 47 food brokers based in Tampa.* Yes, that response would be fair to all and put the matter to rest.

With a "we'll get back to you" farewell, Sullivan ended the conversation, hung up the phone, and shared his plan with Jerry Todd. Yes, that would work, Todd nodded.

Let's hope so, Sullivan thought. It was still going to take some explaining to the guys at headquarters in Oakland. As he boarded his return flight to Boston, Sullivan wondered how much heat he might face for even suggesting Acosta be interviewed.

Back in Jacksonville, Mike Keohane was also looking up a phone number. It was the first critical step of that important assignment Del Dallas had given him. While Del made his pitch to Craig Sullivan, Keohane quickly prepared to make a pitch of his own.

There had been several reasons why Del had lured Keohane away from his solid and satisfying career with Procter & Gamble that summer of 1974. One of them was Mike's ties to the scores of people he had gotten to know in his 20 years with P&G. Better still, Keohane was both an astute judge of talent and a savvy, effective recruiter—as I would discover myself nine years later. In late 1974, it was exactly the kind of expertise Del Dallas needed. To realize his vision of Acosta, Del first would need what Acosta had always depended on: getting the best people he could find. Mike Keohane knew where to look. That's why he had been one of Dallas's first hires after Del had assumed command.

Now Keohane was actively on the hunt. Having found the number he needed, he dialed the man he had in mind to be Acosta's general manager in Tampa.

Turner "Pete" Jones had no desire to leave Procter & Gamble, nor any reason to consider it. For the moment, he was looking forward to a nice bonus check in late November. More importantly, after five years with P&G, he could look forward to more bonus checks and a glowing future.

As a P&G unit sales manager selling health and beauty care products in Tampa, he was on a fairly fast track within a blue-chip company and blessed with an enviable background. Jones had both his marketing degree and his MBA from the University of Tennessee and was an alumnus of P&G's acclaimed sales training program, revered as one of the finest in corporate America.

Already twice promoted, Jones could expect to leave Tampa for a "special assignment" at P&G's Cincinnati headquarters at some point not too far down the road. After that, he'd get his own district and then keep working his way up the corporate ladder, probably in other locales. Ultimately, if all went well, he'd wind up back in Cincinnati, the Queen City as it was known, a very nice place to live. Still, he had one misgiving. Pete Jones had no desire to leave Tampa. He and his family loved the Florida lifestyle, especially his young daughters. But they would adjust, he and his wife always told each other.

Not long after taking Mike Keohane's unexpected call late Friday afternoon, Pete began pondering whether to adjust his career plans. Mike's call had been perfectly timed and executed. There's always a bond among those with P&G ties, and the comfort level, as Pete calls it, was high from the get-go. With P&G having its own direct sales force, Pete barely knew what a food broker was. Even so, the great opportunity Keohane described sounded very intriguing, intriguing enough for Jones to want to learn more.

"Del and I want to come see you this weekend and talk further," Mike continued, alluding to the need to move fairly quickly. That was barely 24 hours away, but Jones readily agreed.

On Saturday, Jones heard Dallas and Keohane thoroughly outline Acosta's expansion plan for Tampa and the role they wanted him to play. As they spoke, Dallas had no doubt that Jones was ideally suited for the task. Jones knew the area and had built good professional relationships with all of the key retailers. Moreover, Jones had that P&G pedigree that would impress Clorox.

By the time additional discussions were wrapped up late Sunday, Jones was all but convinced. Tampa was where Pete and his family would remain, Dallas assured him, because his knowledge of the Tampa market was critical. "And you can still grow within the company," Del added. As much as anything, that assurance had both Jones and wife, Kay, ready to board Acosta's train.

There was just one nagging problem, a classic catch-22: Acosta had to land the Clorox account in Tampa before it could formally hire Pete Jones. But Acosta needed Pete Jones on board to land the Clorox account in Tampa. Pete wasn't about to risk his P&G career without the "bell cow account" being safe in the barn, nor could there be the slightest hint of what he was considering. "Let's ask Clorox to schedule the interview at night," someone finally suggested. It would give Jones the freedom to participate as needed without him shirking any of his daytime responsibilities.

"Okay by me," agreed Jerry Todd, who conducted the first round of interviews. *Why not?* he thought. *It's only going to be a courtesy interview anyway.*

No one within Acosta needed to say what was obvious. There was a ton of work to do and not much time to do it: gather the latest available market research—and make sure it *was* the latest; learn all there was to learn about Tampa and its grocers and supermarkets so Del, Mike, and company could demonstrate that *they* knew the area Acosta would be serving not only as well as any local broker did, but *better*;

prepare all the appropriate statistics showing how Acosta had continually expanded its clients' shipments and retail shelf space; prepare explanations about "concept selling," the company's training program, and Acosta's long-standing ties with Clorox; and dig up some maps and charts—maps and charts were always useful.

The result was to be a world-class presentation, finely tuned, carefully scripted, and, above all, *convincing*. Del, Mike, H.C., and Pete were embarking on what all unreasonable leaders do when the stakes are high and the odds are stacked against them. They prepared, not only expecting to win but, more importantly, refusing to lose. There is a mountain of difference! It's that attitude that motivates the real winners in this world.

At the same time, there was also the matter of creating a brand-new office out of thin air and lining up equipment, furnishings, and services to put in it, including *top quality* people, not just bodies. Pete Jones, as capable and proven as he was, certainly couldn't operate alone. Nor could he help set up a new office; for the time being, Pete was still a P&G employee.

Acosta's white Fords rolled up a ton of miles motoring to and from Tampa in the weeks leading up to the first November interview. Meanwhile, Del, Mike, and H.C. rolled up 12- and 15-hour days, and a few even longer because first and foremost, Acosta had to continue serving its Jacksonville clients.

H.C. Sims's description of those weeks is brief but vivid: "We flat-out busted our asses." But their asses were sturdy enough, Del would assure his colleagues, and it was going to be worth it. He really believed that, too.

Del Dallas had always yearned to run his own business. That's what had brought him to Acosta in the first place. That, plus his conviction that the food brokerage business he observed from different vantage points for a couple of decades was his opportunity of a lifetime. Here was a business that in many locales was profitable almost in spite of itself and ready to be turned on its head. Take all these little good-old-boy food brokers and strengthen them with professional salesmanship, Del's reasoning began. Hire some really quality professionals who had sales experience with national companies, plus the discipline and expertise that went with it. Fashion the salesmanship into ongoing training, add some analytical expertise and a dash of old-fashioned promotion, and food manufacturers and clients would flock to your door, his reasoning continued. That would give you a modern, state-of-the-art food brokerage business you could then expand all over.

How far? Del wasn't quite sure, but he knew it stretched well beyond Jacksonville, Florida, and here was the chance to start the march. All that was left to do now was make the most important sales pitch of his life, unreasonable as it was: *Why the Clorox Company should appoint a food broker in one territory to represent its products in another territory that the broker had never stepped foot in and was at least a half day's drive away.*

Jerry Todd still didn't want to believe it. So much so that he had trouble getting the words out of his mouth as he spoke to Craig Sullivan. Of the brokers he had interviewed in Tampa, three were worth further consideration. One of them, Todd said with noticeable hesitation in his voice, was L.T. Acosta & Co.

Predictably, Sullivan was skeptical and said so. "Jerry, we agreed we were not going to appoint anyone without business in Tampa, remember?" Sullivan said.

"But Craig, you've just got to see Del's presentation!" Todd replied. There was no hesitation in that statement at all. After what Jerry had seen, there was no way in hell Clorox could *not* consider Acosta.

In truth, Sullivan was not totally blindsided by Todd's report. Thumbing through an early November edition of *Supermarket News*, Craig had noticed a blind classified ad soliciting applicants for a sales opportunity in the Tampa Bay area. Sullivan figured out soon enough that Acosta had placed the ad, and even he had to smile a bit at Del Dallas's enterprise and diligence. A week or so later, he saw firsthand how effective classified advertising could be and why Jerry Todd couldn't cross Acosta off the candidates' list.

For Sullivan's convenience—and because he had no place else to meet anyway—Dallas arranged for the same suite in the same Admiral Benbow Inn near the Tampa–St. Pete airport where he had first so impressed Todd. His encore presentation was even better.

Among the people in the room with Del were a few Sullivan didn't recognize. But Dallas quickly had the Clorox sales manager riveted. "Simply magnificent, right down to the store count, coverage patterns, just about everything," Sullivan later recounted. Before the meeting ended, Sullivan and Todd were introduced to the two strange faces. Pete Jones was one of them.

"He'll be our general manager," Del pointed out, taking care to mention Jones's P&G background.

Mightily impressed though he was, Sullivan was still bothered by one factor. "You're still not *here*, Del," he said.

It may as well have been a cue. Dallas immediately pulled out not only a contingency lease for a Tampa office but also a bill for the office furniture he just purchased. "We *will* be here!" he promised with a flourish. "Just give us the business."

Now it was Sullivan's turn to hesitate as he called Clorox's home office to review the status of the Tampa appointment. He knew his boss's initial reaction to hearing that Acosta was one of the two candidates still standing would be exactly what his own had been when Todd reported to him about 10 days before. And it was. But at least it would bring a ranking Clorox headquarters executive to Tampa for the final round.

After the headquarters executive arrived, he and Sullivan were given essentially the same Acosta presentation that Dallas had been delivering, just as impressive, but still uncomfortably vague about one key factor.

"You haven't said anything about retail coverage," Del was told once again. "That's something we'll need right away."

This was another cue precisely delivered. It was all Del Dallas could do to keep a straight face, given what he had orchestrated so carefully. First, he circulated resumes. Then, he waited for the inevitable question: How can we be sure these people will ever be Acosta employees? After the inevitable question, he beckoned to one of his colleagues to open the door to an adjoining room.

One by one, all of the prospective Tampa office employees walked through the door and into the meeting—not just designated general manager Pete Jones, but supervisors, the staff members who would call on retail stores throughout the area, even the office secretary, some 12 or 13 people in all. It was reminiscent of a championship football game: Each person was given an introduction that included his or her background and specific responsibilities.

Clorox was blown away by the presentation and demonstration. The choice was obvious. Still, the decision didn't come without a good deal of serious soul-searching by Clorox. Del Dallas, Mike Keohane, and H.C. Sims knew that all too well and remained as nervous as they were confident. En route home the next day, they stopped several times to call the Jacksonville office, wondering if there had been any word from Sullivan. The call they were waiting for came after they arrived, in late November and just in time to add to the Thanksgiving holiday celebration.

A call Craig Sullivan had made earlier was pivotal as well. The furniture bill that Dallas had shown him after his second presentation had included the just-ordered phone number of the Tampa office. Sullivan had saved it, on a whim as much as anything. Just before his final flight back to Boston, Sullivan still had the number and dialed it, just for the heck of it, he mused.

Early that same morning, Mike Keohane arose well before dawn and headed toward Tampa. With the deal virtually done, there was plenty to do, and Mike wanted to give his new staff a helping hand in the new Tampa office space. When the phone rang, Mike was there to pick it up and said cheerfully to Craig Sullivan, "L.T. Acosta & Co. Good morning!"

Sullivan couldn't have known it at the time, but he was setting the precedent for Clorox to provide ongoing support to its long-time Jacksonville broker. That very precedent—and Sullivan himself—would assist me a little more than 24 years later during the early stages of Acosta's national expansion. Perhaps it helped Craig back then, too. By the time he helped me in late 1998, he was in the middle of his nearly 11-year run as Clorox Chairman and CEO. It was a great run, too, directed by a great CEO who always remained a sales guy at heart.

In December 1974, however, the decision Sullivan so strongly influenced as a division sales manager looked like one huge roll of the dice and a monstrous leap of faith. Clorox, after all, had had plenty of Tampa brokers from which to choose but rejected them all in favor of Acosta. "We were taking a pretty big risk because Tampa was an important market," Sullivan says now. "Our decision certainly wasn't going to sink the company, but we'd still have egg all over our faces if we had bet wrong."

Of course, Sullivan and Jerry Todd had bet right. None of them have ever forgotten their bet, either. Todd, ironically, would later join Acosta and enjoy a fine career with us. And in a January 1997 personal tribute to Del Dallas upon Del's retirement, Sullivan imparted much of the episode in an article he wrote for the company's monthly magazine. He also praised Del for his conviction, vision, and resolute intent to grow Acosta "at a time," even, Sullivan wrote, "when some people thought he was a little nuts."

Craig's commentary didn't include the word *unreasonable*, but it could have. Whatever Del's alleged frame of mind, his expansion bid was a huge roll of the dice in itself, much bigger than Clorox's roll had been. The rolling began while a brutal recession battered the U.S. economy. And had Acosta's number one client rejected his bid, how could Del have turned to any other clients? It would have been extremely difficult, Pete Jones remembers. "If Clorox had said no, why would numbers two or three say yes? I don't see how we could have begun expanding as we did had Clorox turned us down," Pete says. "We just had to succeed in Tampa, and we knew it."

But succeed with what? Even with Clorox's support, Del faced a "beware what you wish for" scenario. Capabilities and talent aside, Acosta was opening a brand-new office with one product in unfamiliar surroundings amid nothing but hostility from local food brokers. The local brokers' overriding reaction was, "Why don't you just go back to Jacksonville!" The locals were so irate that they refused to let Acosta join the local trade association for several years.

Once Pete was on board, Del ran into an imposing hurdle: What else can we sell in Tampa? What they found, with some help from Mike Keohane, was as unlikely a product as you could imagine: fireplace logs.

Fireplace logs in Florida? Yes, indeed. Duraflame was a 1968 creation of the California Cedar Products Co. A concoction of sawdust and petroleum wax molded into logs and packaged and ready for sale at fine stores everywhere. By the mid 1970s, its makers had moved east looking for markets and distributors.

Voila! Mike and Del thought. Their epiphany was due to Hy Albritton's old habit of paying attention to population trends and residential building because of the impact they had on supermarkets and grocery shopping. In turn, Acosta was well aware that new homes in rapidly growing communities all over Florida included fireplaces.

"We'll take it on. Let us have it!" Mike declared on his colleagues' behalf. Duraflame agreed and promptly gave Acosta *statewide* distribution rights, which Del Dallas then wielded as a tool for his earliest expansion efforts.

See what being unreasonable can do for your growth?

Taking full advantage of a product like Duraflame reflected Del Dallas's real genius, Pete Jones likes to observe. As he became one of Del's key confidantes and later Acosta's president, Pete likened Del to hockey legend Wayne Gretzky: Gretzky attributed his success to skating where the puck was *going* to be, not where it was. "In the same way," Pete says, "Del positioned Acosta to be where the business was going to be—before the market got there. Del was consistently ahead of the market."

Consider this: At the time, there were more than 40 food brokers in Jacksonville. Why didn't any of them expand beyond their home base? The answer I think Del would give is the same answer I will offer: They all had reasonable leaders.

Del Dallas was an unreasonable leader. The success that Del envisioned his expansion plan would reap didn't come overnight. Indeed, for several years, some of the profits the Jacksonville office generated subsidized the red ink being incurred in Tampa. It's a major reason why Del's next push didn't come until 1977, when Acosta opened an office in Birmingham, Alabama, the company's first serious move outside of Florida. A year later, with the nation's economy again humming along, Acosta made its first-ever acquisition, a Tampa brokerage firm, which merged into Pete Jones's operation. In 1979 came two more moves: first, a new office in Orlando, then the company's second acquisition, a brokerage firm in Mobile, Alabama. Acosta was well on its way to implementing a serious business plan to become the South's leading food brokerage firm.

Other than that distinction, these four moves now may seem almost trivial, compared with what was to come. Maybe so, but they were also leading indicators that stunned the conventional wisdom ruling the brokerage realm at the time. Moreover, what looked like reckless heresy to conventional thinkers looked very interesting to thinkers at Clorox and other manufacturers. *What next?* they started wondering.

An ever-quickening pace of expansion was to follow, as they soon saw. With the Duraflame logs tucked under its arm, Acosta opened its office in Miami in 1981—Act One of a decade-long play that would include seven more acquisitions, another brand-new office, and Acosta's entry into two more states: Georgia in 1983 and South Carolina in 1989. By the time the 1980s ended, Del Dallas had acquired numerous firms in various locations:

- Two firms to expand Acosta's presence in Miami
- Two more firms to further bolster Acosta's presence in Tampa
- A Jacksonville broker
- A Birmingham, Alabama, broker
- Raley Brothers, a brokerage of significance in Atlanta

"Once Del had gone into both Miami and Atlanta [the 1983 expansion], it became obvious what was happening," Craig Sullivan says. "Acosta was becoming pretty strong and we started following Del closely. We almost had to." Clorox did more than watch. By our staff's informal counts, its family of products was involved in some way in just about all of these expansions. All told, Clorox brands were represented in 26 of the first 27 markets Acosta entered through the mid 1990s. "I know the brokerage community often suspected something back then," Sullivan adds, "but these were not sweetheart deals, not ever." Rather, it was just smart business.

All that Acosta learned upon opening its Tampa office in 1974 was put to work as it expanded. In 1989, for example, Acosta established a South Carolina office to serve both Charleston and Greenville by relying on essentially the very same strategy that Del Dallas, Mike Keohane, and H.C. Sims used in Tampa 15 years earlier: Recruit seasoned Procter & Gamble sales representatives and pitch the account at night.

In the 15-year span that began in 1974, Acosta expanded 13 times via acquisitions (9) or new offices (4). From Acosta's vantage point, there was nothing unlucky about it, quite the contrary. By the end of 1989, Acosta had grown to 30 times its 1974 size and stood as a role-model regional powerhouse. Its influence was powerful, too. Acosta had the food brokerage world marching in a new direction, with Del Dallas unquestionably leading the parade.

Along the way, Acosta also acquired more products to represent, just as Del had planned. The majority, of course, came with the acquisitions, but representing all this new business still wasn't quite as easy as you might think. First, any acquisition could wind up with Acosta representing competing brands, such as Minute Maid and Tropicana orange juice—as was to happen in 1998. That's what the business considers a conflict and almost automatically requires the immediate resignation of one of the brands. Fairly uncommon at first, conflicts became an increasingly nettlesome problem as Del's expansion strategy continued. The more brokers he acquired, the greater the odds of a conflict. Nobody liked it, largely because Acosta did a laudable job in the field, as old letters lamenting these unavoidable parting of the ways document.

Second, tradition strictly prohibited a food broker from soliciting a manufacturer's business. Acosta needed to abide by that and wait until a manufacturer decided to "interview the market," as the process was called—much like when a company put its advertising activities up for review if it became disenchanted with its current agency. As successful as Del Dallas was, scores of capable local brokers flourished, and some of them were busy trying to expand themselves.

Despite these challenges, Acosta's roster of clients climbed steadily, as did revenues. Indeed, beginning in 1974, the company started its streak of doubling its dollar volume every three years. That streak would continue under Del's watch until he retired in 1996.

It was a good thing, too, because Del's bold expansion strategy needed dollars to pay for the acquisitions! Fortunately, he didn't need to pay for them all at once, thanks to a financial formula he developed. In a manner of speaking, Del turned back the clock.

When Hy Albritton retired in 1974, he decided he would be far better off being paid over 10 years. It also was far better for Del, the company's new majority owner, as well as for minority partners H.C. Sims and Charlie Hill and, later on, Pete Jones and Mike Keohane. Del applied that same thinking to his acquisition strategy.

If a broker being acquired had a market value of, say, $10 million, Acosta would pay 10 percent immediately—$1 million—then pay the remaining $9 million due over the next 10 years. The time frame could be adjusted depending on how the business performed: sooner if business exceeded expectations and later if business soured. Del's formula not only strengthened Acosta's cash flow but also kept the former owners engaged and interested—and that was of supreme importance.

You see, although Del Dallas wanted to build a much, much bigger Acosta, he had no desire at all to send the owners and key staffers of his acquisitions packing. In most cases, Del wanted them to stick around and help Acosta keep growing! People really did make the difference, he insisted. Moreover, those familiar faces helped maintain the relationships that the companies brought with them when they joined the Acosta family.

Besides, Acosta's existing staff already had more than enough to do as it was. Mike Keohane called those days the "culture of 1,000 hats." No matter the various titles, everyone did whatever was necessary. Before long, Mike became executive vice president, but he didn't hesitate to help unload samples off a truck docked at our Beach Boulevard headquarters. Mike's typical Tuesday began with a call on, say, Publix. Then it was back to the office to turn in purchase orders before heading off to Orlando to visit a string of Winn-Dixie or Super Foods stores. Once he completed those rounds, Mike would turn around and head for home.

By the late 1980s, Pete Jones was Acosta's president, but he still had direct sales responsibilities and continued to run the Tampa office. Indeed, about the only executive who did not have sales relationships to maintain was Del Dallas himself, yet even Del found time to call on the company's corporate principals while building the business.

One other consequential concept emerged from this culture of 1,000 hats: a much stronger and deeper management structure designed, in part, to perpetuate the business by carefully expanding ownership opportunities. Whether it was the raw pace of business or deep conviction, or perhaps both, Acosta's third generation of owners had recognized by the early 1990s the need to groom succeeding generations of company leaders, a roughly "10-year span of ownership," as Pete Jones once described Del Dallas's broad thinking. Indeed, Del more than once expressed his belief that the ideal age to retire was no later than 60. Essentially, Del believed that the business he was transforming steadily was becoming a young person's business, so why not establish a management structure to support his contention? In addition, he and his four minority partners had the luxury of such thinking. Their modest five-figure investments had mushroomed, and they could retire in comfort whenever they wished.

As you can imagine, such thinking was a powerful recruiting tool for attracting eager young professionals willing to roll up their sleeves. At least it was for one of them—me. The Tampa story, told so well by Del, H.C., Pete, and Mike, convinced me that these people knew how to win. Their unreasonable thinking resonated with me, and I wanted in.

Del had first introduced the possibility of my having a stake in

Acosta at the time I was being recruited. It was a possibility I had no trouble remembering, especially given the company's dizzying growth rate. The possibility of being promoted to vice president a year after I had joined the company only heightened my interest in an ownership position.

One year later, in 1984, Del delivered. He invited me to become Acosta's sixth owner. For a $35,000 investment, I could own an approximate 2 percent share of the company and be at the head of the class of Acosta's next generation of owners. It was a great feeling—even if my wife, Nancy, and I thought long and hard beforehand. The $35,000 represented our life savings to that point, $35,000 that we had worked hard and sacrificed to earn during the first eight years of our marriage. To roll the dice, I first had to be convinced that failure was not an option. I was indeed convinced of that. I can honestly say that I have awakened each morning over the past 26 years with one thought in mind: I refuse to lose! Today, words cannot describe how wise an investment that's turned out to be.

Del subsequently delivered on something else as well. In 1993, I became Acosta's president and heir apparent. Three years later, I succeeded Del Dallas as CEO. Overall, it was another great feeling, because our future looked incredibly bright, provided that we could stay ahead of the fast-paced and constantly changing marketplace.

Acosta's expansion across the South was continuing at a pace even greater than that of the 1980s. A 1990 acquisition of Carolina Brokers, Inc. put us in business in three North Carolina cities: Charlotte, Raleigh, and Asheville. The following year, we brought a second Charlotte broker into the family. In 1994, Acosta was doing business in Tennessee and Virginia; in 1995, we entered Arkansas and Mississippi, then Louisiana. Why, you could almost liken it to Sherman's march to the sea—in reverse. "Dixie," which Nancy and I had sung years ago, suddenly seemed like an appropriate tune.

But "Dixie" would become inappropriate soon enough. Acosta's bright future notwithstanding, I soon thought far beyond Dixie. And why wouldn't I? I saw what was possible by watching and studying my mentor, Del Dallas. Del wasn't afraid to ask for the order, nor was he afraid to ask people for their help when he needed it. I learned a great deal from him. Now, it was my turn to think big, be bold, and ask for the help I needed to execute what I saw was not only possible but also essential for our future.

What wasn't clear was just how I was going to finance this bold vision for our future. The one thing I knew for sure was that I wouldn't stand by and let all the naysayers tell me that my vision for the company was impossible to achieve. For 13 years I watched Del soar like an eagle. I wanted to soar just like he did.

Food for Thought

A man once found an eagle's egg and put it in the nest of a barnyard hen. The eagle hatched and grew up with the rest of a brood of chicks and thought he didn't look at all the same. He scratched the earth for worms and bugs and played the chickens' games.

The eagle clucked and cackled, he made a chicken's sound; he thrashed his wings but only flew some two feet off the ground. That's as high as chickens fly, the eagle had been told. The years passed, and one day when the eagle was quite old, he saw something magnificent flying very high and making great majestic circles up there in the sky. He'd never seen the likes of it. "What's that?" he asked in awe while he watched in wonder at the grace and power he saw.

"Why, that's an eagle," someone said. "He belongs up there, it's clear. Just as we, since we are chickens, belong earth-bound down here." The old eagle just accepted that; most everybody does. And he lived and died a chicken, for that's what he thought he was.

– Unknown

Step 5

An Unreasonable Imperative: "Never Be Afraid to Ask"

Asking is apt to win support from unexpected allies.

You never know what you might miss if you don't ask. More importantly, when you do ask, as often as not, you find opportunities that are within your reach. People who are in a position to help you will help you, especially if your plan will benefit them in the long run.

"I will never be afraid to ask!" I pledged to myself one evening just after my flight lifted off and headed home following yet another round of challenging meetings, this time in Houston. I had good reason to make that pledge. A few hours earlier, my willingness to ask had garnered assistance so critical to our expansion plan that it now seems almost heaven-sent. And within the next 12 months, my not being afraid to ask brought our company three more transformational opportunities.

What I had heard in Houston was one of those pivotal, life-alerting things that I should have marked down the instant Bob McCarthy and I heard it. But we couldn't lift a finger—that's how startling it was. So thank goodness Bob remembered and to this day can readily recall exactly when Ralph Cooper uttered his unbelievable endorsement.

It was mid afternoon on the Friday before Labor Day in 1998; September 4 to be exact, late enough on a sweltering summer day in Houston that my business partner and I probably started wondering if we would make our scheduled flights home for the approaching holiday weekend. Except the longer Ralph spoke, the less concerned Bob and I were about flying anywhere. Suddenly, the weekend could wait, and whenever it did start, we knew, we could celebrate wildly.

"I like your plan. If you can do what you're telling me you'll do, we'll be your first national client," Minute Maid's president Ralph Cooper was declaring. "We'll back you wherever you go. Northeast, southwest, west—wherever you're going, we're going with you, because what we need here is a national solution. I'll give you a handshake deal right now," Cooper continued, "and you need to give me the assurance that you won't dump us along the way."

I don't know if I was more ecstatic or stunned. Bob reacted in the same way.

In hindsight, I guess we shouldn't have been all that stunned. After all, we went to Houston seeking the continued business of Minute Maid, the orange juice-making subsidiary of the Coca-Cola Company. Asking for the order was what we sales guys were trained to do. Along with hearing me ask for the order, Cooper and his top lieutenants who arranged our meeting—Mike Saint John, vice president of sales, and Larry McWilliams, senior vice president and general manager of Minute Maid's North American operations—heard me explain our ambitious plan to build a national company and the rationale for expansion.

For the moment, however, we cautioned that we needed a month or two to digest phase one of our plan, which we completed that July. Acosta Sales & Marketing Company, the Jacksonville, Florida, company I served as CEO, had wrapped up the straightforward merger we proposed in the spring of 1998 to PMI/Eisenhart, Inc. PMI was the company where Bob McCarthy had been president and was, in several respects, Acosta's mirror image. PMI was a strong, Chicago-based sales and marketing agency that had been expanding in the Midwest much the way Acosta had expanded throughout the Southeast.

With our merger complete, Bob and I had been making the rounds to key clients, outlining our vision and strategy and expressing the hope that they would remain key clients of our newly combined organization. Minute Maid was one of Bob's most prized and most important clients and was critical to everything we hoped to achieve. Cooper's pledge was more than we could have hoped for.

Minute Maid, Cooper said, not only was intent on maintaining its relationship with Acosta/PMI but also was eager to grow our relationship, and dramatically so! At long last, here was a high-profile company willing to help us create what I long insisted we had to create: a truly *national* sales and marketing company in every respect, and one able to represent the makers of packaged food products in every supermarket and grocery store in every market across the country.

The trouble was that my conviction kept running headlong into our clients' conventional wisdom: "We'll never appoint anybody to represent us nationally, because our business is and will always be a regional business." I heard this ad nauseam.

Not any more it isn't, I said to myself. I believed that as strongly as I believed anything. As Bob and I now were discovering, Ralph Cooper wholeheartedly believed it, too. And the best was still to come. "So, how else can we help you?" Cooper asked.

"Frankly, I could use some money," I said without hesitation. *What's to lose?* I thought.

"How much?" Cooper wanted to know. He hadn't hesitated, either.

"Well, to tell you the truth, at least $25 million," I said, watching for his reaction.

Ralph never batted an eye. "Let me make some phone calls and get back to you," he said. To Bob and me, at least, Ralph's tone seemed optimistic, as did the strength of his handshake as we departed.

Ralph was good with his word, and within a week, he got back to me. In no time at all, I had in hand a $25 million loan from Coca-Cola, and at a very attractive rate of 4 percent. Working out all of the details and payment schedule with Coke's chief financial officer in Atlanta was "routine"—to the extent that being handed $25 million is ever *routine*. It surely wasn't routine for me. It was paramount to achieving our dream. As indispensable as that loan proved to be, we gained something even more valuable from that Friday afternoon meeting in Houston. It was a lesson I will always remember and a maxim certainly worthy of being the springboard for this saga about unreasonable leadership:

Never be afraid to ask. Even if at first it seems too bold or unreasonable!

The second lesson I learned at that time was just as dramatic. This time it was with my own leaders.

My colleagues might well have been thinking that what I was asking of them was both unreasonable and reason enough to have me declared certifiably insane. Acosta's managers had long been accustomed to my bold insistence that embracing the status quo was not going to ensure our viability for the future. The managers at PMI, however, were just getting to know me as a leader, so what I was about to ask them surely put them into shock.

Imagine the scene: There I stood before the assembled ownership group of our management team made up of approximately 60 people who owned the newly created Acosta/PMI Sales and Marketing Company. In my left hand was a copy of my deferred-compensation agreement. As concisely as I could, I explained the progress of our expansion effort and how it related to our gathering. At the same time, I spelled out the critical details. Given what I was about to ask, this was no time to be vague.

"I'll be the first person here to do what I am asking all of you to do," I said next. "Here's tangible proof of my conviction that each one of us will be far better off financially in the long term if we agree to do what I am about to do. I've been holding this for a reason," I continued, holding up my deferred-compensation agreement. Then I tore up the agreement. For a few awkward seconds, I stood silently to let the message sink in.

Where or when I came up with the idea is unimportant. You need only understand that it was the best illustration I could conceive to demonstrate my commitment to Acosta's future—before asking my fellow owners to scrap their individual deferred-compensation agreements. Here's why this was such an unreasonable yet necessary step. These agreements were in place to provide for everyone's retirement for all the years of hard work building the company. In closely held private-service businesses, this was a common way for owners to get their value out of the business. When owners purchased stock in our company, they bought the stock at book value. When they sold the stock, they sold at book value. Deferred-compensation agreements were put in place along with noncompete agreements to extend compensation for 10 years beyond retirement.

My request was to eliminate this liability on the company so the banks could get their arms around what our future liabilities would be. The banks insisted that these agreements had to be eliminated before they would lend us any more money. My selling point to the group was to change the stock buy-back agreements to redeem everyone's stock at *market* value, not *book* value. I had to convince all 60 people that the future market value and their individual stock value would be greater than their 10-year deferred payments after retirement – with no real evidence. Yet I believed with great conviction that it would be, just as I staunchly believed that not expanding nationally would put our business, as well as their individual agreements, at risk. Our entire expansion plan, and our future as a company, depended on it, I stressed.

That was true—assuming our expansion plan succeeded. But on this day in early 1999, the longer term was a long way off. We were still living and working in the short term. Here's what I did know: Our expansion plan was sound. Moreover, it unfolded almost exactly as Bob McCarthy and I envisioned. And Minute Maid was right alongside us too, just as Ralph Cooper had promised the preceding September.

It's just that what we were doing was breaking the mold and replacing it with a new mold, one the food brokerage business really hadn't seen; so much so, in fact, that the very term "food broker" would soon become passé and disappear altogether. Essentially, my colleagues and I were writing new rules of engagement for our business as we grew it. With deliberate and focused efforts, we were recreating an entire industry.

At the same time, there still were some old rules to obey, primarily the ones imposed by the banks. For the moment, at least, I won't subject you to any of the "financial-ese" and will just cut to the quick. Bank financing was extremely difficult, because the new business model we were creating hadn't matured to the point that we could assure lenders of sufficiently predictable cash flows to satisfy loan requirements. In addition, we could not quantify our future debt liabilities entangled in the deferred compensation agreements, so there was no way any financial institution was going to loan us the $30 million we needed to fund our ongoing expansion. The elimination of the deferred-compensation agreements was an absolute must—and an immediate necessity.

Minute Maid's understanding of this dilemma was one reason why it loaned us money. Ralph Cooper, Larry McWilliams and Mike Saint John saw that we needed a corporate angel with deep pockets. Along with an angel, I needed my colleagues' cooperation. The new deal I proposed was to change the stock buy-back agreement to *market* value from *book* value, although "pleading" better described my tone than "proposing." The change was, I declared, the only alternative available to satisfy the bankers and obtain the money we needed to continue pursuing the expansion plan that was now under way.

At times, I felt almost like Indiana Jones going after the Ark of the Covenant. Asked what he's going to do next as he gallops off on a horse, Indy mutters in reply, "How should I know? I'm making this up as I go along!" In a way, so it was with me. Eventually, with persistence, I got what I was after. Ripping up my own contract was an expression of faith that I'd lead the way, wacky as it might have appeared. And because I ripped up my own contract, I wasn't afraid to ask my colleagues to rip up theirs.

All but a few of them did, thankfully. A few years later, as our national strategy did unfold, their faith would be rewarded more generously than any of us had ever imagined.

Our third big ask was to our number one and most revered client, Clorox. The relationship dated to 1933 and had blossomed into as ideal a business partnership as one could imagine. Acosta's relationship with Clorox was the linchpin of its very first expansion out of Jacksonville in 1974. The Clorox brand also had a conspicuous presence in all but one of our more than two dozen subsequent expansions and acquisitions in the Southeast. And Clorox was the first client Acosta entrusted to me upon joining the business in 1983. Time and again, it seemed, "as goes our Clorox business, so goes our entire business."

In what couldn't have been more than a 90-day span, I knocked on Clorox's door not once, but twice. What I needed the first time wasn't money but Clorox's endorsement of our national strategy and its assistance to help us complete the transactions by using its influence with potential acquisition targets. "Frank, I need help, pure and simple," I said, speaking quickly into the phone to Clorox's then vice president of sales in Oakland, California. "You need to convince Kelley-Clarke that Acosta is the right company to sell to."

Phase two of our expansion strategy was acquiring a strong partner with market coverage across as much of the West as possible. Kelley-Clarke, Inc., fit our description to a T. Based in southern California just east of Los Angeles, Kelley-Clarke was clearly the "best of the West," with a presence from the Rockies to the Pacific Northwest. Unfortunately, Kelley-Clarke was also in the crosshairs of a rival company trying to expand just like we were. Worse, Kelley-Clarke's 13-member board was about to accept our rival company's offer. If that deal were to go through, our entire expansion could unravel just when it was starting to roll up.

Frank Tataseo, today Clorox's Executive Vice President – Strategy and Growth, understood my fears as well as anyone. He also understood the implications for Clorox. The company with which Kelley-Clarke was about to align was not a Clorox broker. Like their counterparts at Minute Maid, the Clorox sales executive and his ranking colleagues, Grant LaMontagne and CEO Craig Sullivan, studied our marketplace and drew the same conclusions. A consolidation of food brokers was likely at some point, so Clorox couldn't simply sit still and just watch—not when both Acosta/PMI and Kelley-Clarke were two of its most important brokers, accounting for 70 percent of its U.S. grocery business.

At the same time, the Clorox account was vital to Kelley-Clarke: Those millions in yearly billings represented almost 10 percent of its business, so even a few words from someone like Frank Tataseo might have an impact.

When I asked Frank for help, he wouldn't flat-out promise to deliver those all-important words, but he did commit to giving my plea ample thought. Evidently, he did. I cannot ascertain the precise words that were exchanged or when they were exchanged, or how. Let's just say that whatever the words were, it became clear to Kelley-Clarke president Charlie Frankowski and the company's other board members that accepting that other deal on the table would jeopardize the Clorox business.

"We'd like you to figure out a way to become part of the Acosta organization," is the gist of one comment that later made its way back to me. Kelley-Clarke's board apparently took this request into consideration. A few weeks later, I was pleased to report that Kelley-Clarke, Inc., rejected the other offer and had a renewed interest in resuming merger discussions with Acosta/PMI.

That's not to say phase two of our expansion was now home free. It wasn't, because now *we needed more money*. Although Kelley-Clarke was willing to be part of the Acosta/PMI organization, the ensuing negotiations were downright grueling and the actual terms a financial challenge. So back to Clorox I went, asking for more help.

"How much money do you need?" CEO Craig Sullivan essentially asked—quite nicely—when I brought the request to his attention in the spring of 1999.

Another $25 million would be ideal, I requested. "That could be a difficult sum to arrange," Sullivan explained. However, Sullivan did have the prerogative to approve a loan of $10 million.

"Ten million will be fine and much appreciated," I said gratefully.

But I still had to remain persistent and at times tenacious. As the numerous reservations uttered in and around the Clorox executive suite suggested, even my $10 million loan request looked, well, unreasonable. Initially, Sullivan himself was at least a little wary.

To begin with, what I was asking for was unprecedented. Clorox had never before loaned money against future commissions, which was the underlying condition of the loan being arranged. In addition, there were the usual concerns about our becoming dangerously overextended financially, as well as our ongoing ability to take care of business amid the zeal our expansion was generating, as the Clorox CEO put it. "It happens all the time in business," Sullivan counseled. "In the rush to expand, you can take your eye off the ball."

We weren't about to let that happen, I assured him in reply. So did Grant LaMontagne. The analysis that Grant brought to the discussions allayed those and other concerns and was invaluable. LaMontagne had been an important ally from the beginning. A career Clorox man who is today the company's senior vice president and chief customer officer, Grant also foresaw the consolidations that would reshape the business. He quickly concluded that it was in Clorox's best interest to help its key brokers as best and as often as it could. With the right kind of help at the right time, LaMontagne reasoned, what ultimately emerged might even give his company the benefits of a direct sales force without the ongoing costs. What's more, Acosta always performed for Clorox.

If doubts persisted, well, the $25 million vote of confidence we received from Minute Maid and Coca-Cola was sufficiently comforting. Twice, Clorox was there to support us, just as I had hoped. I would call on its help a third time about nine months later (more detail on that in Step 8), and our client would be there to help us once again. I believe in the Clorox Company and everything it stands for.

Minute Maid, Clorox, and our own shareholders placed big bets on our ambitious goal of national expansion. When we finally accomplished our goal in the fall of 1999, we were blessed with these brand endorsements and one more critical ally—one that anyone in business would savor.

One morning late in the fall of 1999, we learned that the CEO of Coca-Cola, Douglas Ivester, was heading to Chicago to deliver a speech and wanted to include a visit with Bob and me in his itinerary. A cynic might quip that a CEO like Ivester, who had an extensive financial background, may simply have wanted a face-to-face look at the guys his company had loaned $25 million. Minute Maid had consulted Ivester directly about the loan proposal and had gotten his approval. Since then, Ivester evidently hadn't lost track of our adventures.

After listening to us carefully for 20 minutes, Ivester first offered his perspective on how our expansion compared favorably with the Coca-Cola Enterprises consolidation, the bottling arm of Coca-Cola. But the thrust of his comments focused on how we had nearly built a bulletproof business that would be next to impossible to duplicate.

"Think of what you're creating and its overall value," Ivester urged. "It would take 20 years for a rival to try to do what you've done, if it could be done at all."

It's not every morning that you're praised by the boss of one of the most famous companies in the world. Memories of that meeting remain a great reminder—*and one more reason to never to be afraid to ask.*

What did I learn throughout this phase of my own career growth? Well, I learned a great deal. Practically speaking, Minute Maid and Coca-Cola really weren't risking all that much. Had we run into trouble repaying the $25 million loan, Minute Maid simply could have deducted portions of what we owed from the commissions it paid us monthly to represent its products—commissions that routinely lagged billings by as many as six weeks. Our business results were consistent. We produced quarter by quarter, which further eased any fears that may have festered in Atlanta at the time; then again, $25 million, although significant, was hardly an imposing sum to a company the size of Coca-Cola.

Minute Maid's financial support was not the only benefit we received. It was the encouragement and reputation of the respected and widely admired brands that accompanied those dollars.

Having not one, but two renowned brands in our corner jump-started our national expansion strategy at the most critical moment. Equally important was the strong belief of my fellow 60 owners that day in Chicago who said loudly and clearly, "Let's get it done, boss! We are with you, and we are willing to risk our retirement on the premise that, together, we can build a very successful national solution."

And we did! All of this occurred for three very important reasons:

1. *We built deep relationships at the highest levels within the organizations, and it was through these relationships that we were able to ask!*
2. *We had buy-in with key constituents to our vision. They believed, as we did, and viewed our strategy as integral to the industry's growth.*
3. *We established credibility and proved ourselves. We were seen as key partners who, day in and day out, maintained a track record*

of high performance.

Emerging from these reasons is a critical lesson: ***Unreasonable leaders build trusted relationships and are unafraid to ask!***

My not being afraid to ask for help—brazen as its recounting might at first appear—delivered huge benefits in addition to badly needed dollars. Because of the results of our actions, we knew three things:

We were on the right track. Cooper's reply was a welcome confidence builder, a real shot in the arm. It reaffirmed in a meaningful way that my thinking and our plan were both on target. It was also a precedent-setter we could use both to win more support and to silence naysayers—and believe me, there were legions of them.

We were in good company. Cooper, a veteran executive of Coca-Cola's management, had good reason to be confident about our expansion strategy – and not just because I was so dogmatically determined. Cooper had seen this strategy succeed once before.

Our strategy was a veritable mirror image of Coke's own plan that some years earlier had so successfully consolidated its bottling activities under Coca-Cola Enterprises. And because Coke saw its financial assistance to bottlers pay off so handsomely, the precedent existed for Cooper to be our emissary of sorts and seek the dollars we needed to help Minute Maid expand the distribution of its juices and other products. Especially significant was Minute Maid's willingness to assist us, as it never would have happened if I hadn't asked!

We would help each other. More significant still, my asking for $25 million wasn't as unreasonable as you might think. The replies it prompted showed why Minute Maid's executives had their own reasons to support the ambitious expansion plan Bob McCarthy and I were intent on rolling out.

First, Minute Maid saw in our plan a chance to take a competitive swing at its chief rival, Tropicana Products, Inc. In our world, Minute Maid vs. Tropicana was as intense a business rivalry as Coke vs. Pepsi or Ford vs. Chevy. Hell, it was Ohio State vs. Michigan, North Carolina vs. Duke, and the Red Sox vs. the Yankees. Getting a chance to align with the best company with the best plan and force your competition somewhere else was a major reason for its executives' support. Such an occasion was at hand for Minute Maid. It had been a significant client of PMI/Eisenhart in the Midwest since 1957, just as Tropicana had been a long-time Acosta client in the Southeast, and one of our most important. Relationships aside, some kind of realignment was inevitable—one that Minute Maid now saw as the chance to gain competitive advantage.

Representing brands that are direct competitors was strictly forbidden at the time. That we found ourselves representing both Minute Maid and Tropicana in mid-1998 was an unanticipated consequence of our merger, one that combined what had been distinct and separate operations throughout the Southeast and Midwest.

Because Minute Maid and Tropicana each generated significant revenues, we would have been just as happy to maintain both client relationships, if only for an interim period. Initially, in fact, Bob McCarthy and I even thought that we could erect some kind of internal "Great Wall" to address conflicting relationships where specific markets overlapped. Because we had some earlier success within Acosta doing that with other brands, we thought we could hold onto Minute Maid and Tropicana, too.

In truth, our fateful September meeting with Ralph Cooper in Houston was our second journey to Minute Maid's headquarters. Barely three weeks earlier, Bob and I journeyed to Houston to sell McWilliams and Saint John on how we could handle the Minute Maid–Tropicana conflict without having to resign either account, at least for the time being. Their reactions prompted the second meeting with Ralph Cooper and, in turn, the revelation that it really was time to pursue our ultimate objective: representing our clients nationally. Doing so meant resigning our Tropicana business and the hefty revenues it represented. But that was no longer as troubling a prospect as you'd think.

Tropicana repeatedly turned a deaf ear to our bids to represent its products nationally. Minute Maid, on the other hand, now offered us the chance to do exactly that. If a condition of Minute Maid's offer was resigning Tropicana, so be it. It was the proverbial offer Bob and I couldn't refuse, given all the plusses about to be dropped ever so nicely in our laps. Shall we shake on it? You bet!

In the final analysis, Minute Maid was like France's coming to the Colonists' aid during the American Revolution: helping the rag-tag Yanks was nice, but making life tough for their age-old enemy, the British? Well, that was *priceless*.

Our budding partnership with Minute Maid even came with an ironic twist. Years earlier, when I was an Acosta vice president, Mike Saint John alerted me about a rival broker in the Carolinas who was intent on stealing one of our key clients in the region. Mike's call helped us protect our relationship with Tropicana.

Along with attempting to outflank its number one competitor, Minute Maid saw that by helping Acosta/PMI, it also could help itself in a second way. If that reality hadn't been an overt discussion point during our meeting with Ralph Cooper, its implications were clear enough and hung above the conference table like an ever-present spirit. At scores of industry events and in informal conversations throughout the 1990s, I routinely talked about the future of the food brokerage business in general, and ours in particular, to many of the sales executives of our leading clients. Specifics of the scenarios shared might vary, but our consensus remained. The intertwined businesses of making, marketing, and selling food products and beverages were all steadily consolidating. Moreover, the pace of that consolidation was about to accelerate.

None of what these developments portended was lost on the savvy consumer packaged goods executives at Minute Maid, nor on those at parent company Coca-Cola in Atlanta; ergo, better to be proactive than reactive. Minute Maid always depended on its extensive network of local and regional brokers, yet these traditional market-by-market relationships quickly became an anachronism and an old-fashioned pain in the neck. As late as 1995, most manufacturers sold their products through as many as 50 food brokers around the country.

As supermarket chains consolidated, both individual promotion campaigns and overall marketing strategies were ever more complex and ever more difficult to implement with so many different agencies involved. Mix in more marketing channels, more cable TV channels, plus websites and all their links, and the challenge became ever more imposing. For Minute Maid, the solution was obvious. Less was more in every respect. Fewer brokers would make marketing life much easier, more effective, and vastly more efficient; just one broker would l.

Yes, it bucked industry tradition. But, as Saint John himself put it, "The risk of not changing was now worse than changing."

By the time Bob McCarthy and I came calling late in the summer of 1998, Minute Maid had decided it was time to pick its dance partner while it still had attractive partners to pick.

So which partner? Why, the strongest organization with the brightest future, of course, and if long-term objectives aligned, even better. To that end, neither operations chief McWilliams, nor sales VP Saint John were reticent about doing a little lobbying to promote their desired outcome and/or exercising some leverage wherever and whenever appropriate. Getting Bob McCarthy and me in front of Ralph Cooper was a case in point.

Given my conversations with them and the rapport we developed, I sensed that these influential Minute Maid executives felt we already had a leg up. Acosta/PMI now covered half the country, for one thing, and yearned to cover it all. Plus, we had a plan to do it. Moreover, Saint John and McWilliams also preferred our business model: a single corporate organization built via mergers and acquisitions. An alternative business model was emerging, but it was a loosely organized alliance, or confederation, of independent brokers whose daily operations could be much harder to control.

Saint John's enthusiasm was such that he embraced another slice of the Acosta/PMI vision: assembling a veritable dream team of brokers from around the country. On occasion, Mike even went so far as to suggest companies we might consider. As appealing as this scenario appeared, we had to acknowledge the same potential downsides that would later cause concern within Clorox.

First, could a modestly sized company finance the envisioned acquisitions without becoming dangerously over-leveraged and running into cash flow problems? Even a dream team of brokers could wind up living a nightmare without sufficient cash.

Second, could we direct our expansion without losing focus on our core business of representing clients and letting performance suffer? The $25 million loan from Minute Maid and the $10 million loan from Clorox helped address the former. As for the latter, only time would tell. However, our industry's long-standing tradition of 30-day contracts would always leave Minute Maid and Clorox an out if we didn't perform for some reason.

As it turned out, they needn't have worried. We performed, and in spite of some dicey moments, we had the stamina and resources to endure.

It's only natural now to look back and wonder what Acosta would have had to endure without the support Minute Maid, and subsequently Clorox, provided and what kind of company Acosta would have become. Furthermore, what if our shareholders had refused to eliminate their 10-year payouts and the banks had said, "No thanks, Acosta, you're on your own!"? I don't know. Nor do I want to know, frankly. It's far more enjoyable to recall all that did happen. Besides, it's my nature. My cup is almost always half full.

"We had a window of opportunity," remembers Bob McCarthy, who has since retired from our business. "We jumped in, and we did it."

And it all began because Bob and I were unreasonable enough on a Friday afternoon before Labor Day to ask a client for $25 million. Thank goodness we did!

Never be afraid to ask! If I had been afraid to ask, Acosta's bold expansion plan might well have remained dead in its tracks.

Food for Thought

Ask and it will be given to you; seek and you will find; knock and the door will be opened to you. For everyone who asks, receives; he who seeks, finds; and to him who knocks, the door shall be opened.

— Matthew, 7:7–8

Step 6

Set a Bold and Unreasonable Vision

It's essential to know and articulate your destination.

So, just exactly what did my company do to earn such enthusiastic support of Minute Maid and Clorox executives a decade ago—plus the $35 million in loans they arranged on our behalf? Well, as then H.J. Heinz Company's North American CEO Dave Moran publicly stated to describe Acosta's strategic importance to the H.J. Heinz Co., Heinz's relationship with Acosta is the most important relationship of all of its outside vendors. That's a pretty strong statement. The reason Moran, Grant LaMontagne of Clorox, Mike Saint John of Minute Maid, and all of our strategic partners feel that way is because of the valuable services Acosta provides.

We sell, merchandise, and help our clients market their most important assets: their brands! Along with selling, Acosta provides deep understanding of consumer trends, shopper insights, and category dynamics that lead to increased market share and growth of brands for the retailers we service. We are an extension of the sales management teams of the consumer packaged goods companies we represent, and because of our size, we provide the benefits of scale necessary for each manufacturer to market its products both effectively and efficiently.

We perform our services very well, too! Collectively, Acosta's annual billings now total more than $60 billion. Our consistent success through our more than 83 years in business is one of two factors that earned us the support of Minute Maid and Clorox. The other factor was our conviction to expand nationally, one that many of my peers deemed quite unreasonable.

Better that we direct the changes marching relentlessly toward our business and build a national company than wait and become victims of those changes and become part of a national company somebody else builds. This is the thought that kept rattling around in my brain more than a decade ago. To be a part of what somebody else builds? I don't think so!

That was the bold vision, one that I insisted complement and strengthen our number one task: to get our *clients'* products onto the shelves of our *customers*, and in the most advantageous positions on those shelves, so consumers in supermarkets and grocery stores throughout the land will snap them up, load them into their shopping carts, and whisk them home in droves each and every day. We live to see our clients' goods fly off our customers' shelves.

Our clients include many of the most familiar companies: Nestlé, H.J. Heinz, Sara Lee, Kellogg's, Campbell's, Ocean Spray, McCormick, and, of course, Minute Maid and Clorox. We also represent hundreds of other quality manufacturers of food and grocery products, some 1,200 in all. The more than 6,000 products we represent range from applesauce to baby food to canned goods to condiments to pet foods to spices … and virtually everything in between.

Our customers are supermarkets and grocery stores in the U.S. and Canada, giant multistate chains like Kroger, Safeway, SuperValu, Food Lion, and Publix, but also smaller regional chains, leading independent supermarkets, and now Wal-Mart, Target, and Kmart, too: almost anywhere you purchase food products—packaged goods in particular. Indeed, much of what's served on kitchen and dining room tables gets to those tables because of what we do.

Officially, Acosta is described as a sales and marketing agent, or simply SMA. Some would describe SMAs as middle men, but nothing could be further from the truth. We are *not* middle men! We provide services for a fee, usually in the form of a commission on sales. We do not take title of the goods and do not set pricing; therefore, we do not mark up the product as a middle man would. We actually reduce costs by providing a large-scale platform of efficient services that drives cost down, not up. We save our clients bundles of dollars by providing unmatched marketing services that help them sell more goods more effectively and more efficiently.

"I sleep better at night because you often don't," one client once told me. This means you will rarely hear our clients or customers assail Acosta. And you likely won't hear consumers say much of anything at all about Acosta. They have no idea what we do. Our Acosta brand resonates with the manufacturers and the retailers, where it should.

Even in our headquarter city of Jacksonville, Florida, Acosta is not a household name. Most residents who hear it, in fact, instinctively think of the Acosta Bridge, one of the downtown spans across the

St. Johns River. There is a connection, but it's distant. But even though Acosta isn't a household name, there's scarcely a household in America that doesn't benefit daily from the services our company provides.

For instance, it's no accident that Clorox is at eye level and gets more shelf space than many rival brands. More than 16,000 Acosta associates throughout the country work awfully hard to maintain that space and to win more prime space for the new products our clients develop. Acosta associates do their own developing—of both marketing ideas and shopper insights to help retailers and producers sell more goods to more consumers. As a matter of course, we participate in research to learn more about why shoppers select the products that wind up in their carts. The marketing services we provide all of our clients truly are extensive.

Perhaps my favorite example of Acosta's capabilities is a display you're likely to see as you walk into your favorite supermarket a week or two before the July 4 holiday: Grillin' and Chillin' Time features such products as Kingsford charcoal, a Clorox brand; Bush's baked beans; Vlasic pickles; Heinz Ketchup; KC Masterpiece barbecue sauce; Sargento cheese; Dixie brand paper plates, cups, and napkins; plus one or more Ken's salad dressings. Depending on where you live, a Grillin' and Chillin' Time display might also feature several more products. We are the conduit that brings all these brands together and garners the retailers' support to make sure proper inventories are on display—and at the right price for consumers to purchase and enjoy in their back-yards for this most magnificent holiday occasion.

Acosta was also the driving force in creating Aisles of Smiles, a yearly event that helps to generate charitable dollars for the Muscular Dystrophy Association from the grocery sales of 8,000 participating stores in 25 markets. In the past 20 years, this cause-marketing event has raised more than $67 million for Jerry's Kids. We are very proud of this accomplishment and the relationship we built with the MDA.

Grillin' and Chillin' Time and Aisles of Smiles both contribute to what really is a fascinating business. It's why I tell people, "Once you understand what we do, you'll never shop in a grocery store the same way again." By late 1996, not long after I had become Acosta's CEO, I came to understand a similar notion. Before long, sales and marketing agents won't be representing their clients in grocery stores the same way again, either.

A CEO's routine has to include thinking carefully about what the organization needs to become. Serene as it may sound, much of the time it's anything but. And it certainly wasn't a Grillin' and Chillin' Time display on my mind as I took the leadership reins of our company. "Potential doomsday" might have been more descriptive of my thoughts about the future of our business if we had adhered to the status quo. Acosta's 22-year transformation into a strong regional SMA was laudable, so laudable that others around the country emulated our expansion strategy. But we had no time to rest on our laurels, because having even a dominant regional presence became increasingly meaningless in the face of structural business changes swirling around us.

To begin with, food manufacturers continued to consolidate. As they did, they also started trimming the number of food brokers in their networks. The days when "N-E-S-T-L-E-S" made only "the very best … *chocolate!*" were long gone. "N-E-S-T-L-E-S" stood for all kinds of products, including pet food. Carnation, the company that had given me my first real job in 1976, was now a Nestlé company. So was Stouffer's Frozen Foods, while among Nestlé's rivals was H.J. Heinz Co. By the mid 1990s, Heinz had expanded its renowned 57 varieties to include pet food, too—enough of it, in fact, that Heinz stood as the number two pet food producer in the U.S.

The Clorox Company, meanwhile, made a lot more than bleach. Its repertoire of products included not only Kingsford charcoal, but also Glad bags, Brita water filters, household cleaners, and even STP and Armor All auto care products.

Having the brands we represented or could represent in the hands of fewer producers, who were at the same time slicing the number of independent sales representatives, was not good for several firms in our industry, not in theory at least. By definition, our market realm was shrinking. More importantly—and more ominous—the supermarket chains that sold all of these brands were busy consolidating, too. As they did, they expanded their geographic presence, often quite dramatically.

The same 45,000-square-foot Kroger supermarket you might stroll into in the chain's Cincinnati, Ohio, headquarters city was identical to the Kroger you'd find in Louisville or Atlanta ... and in plenty of other locales. In fact, you could shop in a Kroger store in 42 major markets across 31 states. Kroger was hardly alone. Almost everywhere we looked, we saw rival chains like Giant Eagle, Publix, Safeway,

SuperValu, Food Lion, Albertson's, and Ahold snapping up smaller grocer organizations and marching boldly into what for them were new markets. Wal-Mart, Target, and Kmart were fast becoming part of the mix, too.

"If both our clients and customers are consolidating," I kept asking, "what's the impact going to be on our business?" Pretty damned significant, I'd answer, and maybe life-changing.

Winning and losing clients among food producers was nothing new. In the 13 years I'd been with Acosta, we won far more often than we lost and we grew our geographic presence as we won. So although we couldn't dare be complacent, we had no real reason to fear these consolidations. But the more-startling consolidations among supermarket chains were another story, with a potentially dire outcome.

Losing a client was bad, but a client still could be replaced with another client. But losing *all access* to an entire chain of supermarkets because it had been acquired by another chain, which then had consolidated purchasing operations in some other part of the country? That could be catastrophic, and I was not about to let that happen under my watch.

What good was being a regional company if a Kroger or Food Lion should decide to consolidate all of its purchasing activity beyond our region? No good at all. Acosta wouldn't be able to compete for the sales that our clients hired us to make, because we wouldn't have any presence where the buying decisions would be made. The implications of this scenario were worse. If the retailer continued expanding—a very reasonable assumption—Acosta stood to lose more geographic territory each time if we stood still.

This very scenario unfolded within two or three weeks after our merger with PMI/Eisenhart in mid-1998 when Kroger announced that it was consolidating all of its buying operations in its home city of Cincinnati. Thankfully, a benefit of our merger with PMI was a modest sales office in Cincinnati. That office got bigger in a hurry and prompted subsequent changes in our daily operations.

Kroger's decision reaffirmed our decision to merge with PMI/Eisenhart, which was the first step toward national expansion. I was convinced more than ever that a national strategy was the only sure way to ensure our relevance and our survival as a business entity. The legendary jovial corner grocer "Mr. Whipple" with thinning hair, glasses, and maybe a mustache, who knew everyone and who lived a simple life around the corner in a three-bedroom home amid towering trees, was a wonderful, romantic notion. But it was not reality in 1996. Reality was fast becoming huge, multistate supermarket chains that sold huge volumes of goods produced by large manufacturers, so an SMA had better muscle up if it had any expectation of being part of this new reality, or it quickly might become the horse and buggy of the 21st century.

Acosta was the classic SMA and as big a player as there was throughout the Southeast. For many years, that worked fine and the rewards were bounteous. But it wasn't fine anymore. Acosta now risked becoming an endangered species, maybe even "the incredible shrinking sales and marketing agency." Not on my watch, I vowed. No unreasonable leader allows that.

Although I didn't need more evidence to support the conclusion that our SMA had to be national, I received some anyway in an exhaustive market research study in the fall of 1996. "The Rule of Three" was a featured topic of a conference I attended in Atlanta. Its title made both the study's thrust and conclusion easy to predict. All markets everywhere *inevitably* come to be dominated by three competitors—product or service notwithstanding. The only variable is time, contended the study's two authors, business school professors from Emory University and George Mason University. The authors further stated that all other competitors in a given market either "fall into a ditch" and struggle (or disappear outright) or wind up serving small niches of a given market.

Three major players invariably created "a certain balance of power," the authors further submitted, and reduced the risk of collusion that would ultimately harm consumers. A sound observation, I reasoned. So much so that, almost 13 years later, the research study remains in my files. Notably, its overriding conclusion is still valid today.

Painstakingly researched, "The Rule of Three" was loaded with powerful examples from a broad cross section of 17 American markets, including apparel, autos, cosmetics, pizza, publishing, beer, and breakfast cereal. As you can imagine, the last two especially caught my attention. The study also considered factors like geography, technology, and the impact of partnerships and mergers. It even factored in a business strategy then being championed by the likes of acclaimed General Electric Company's CEO Jack Welch: If a company can't be number one or number two in a given business, it's better off getting out of it.

Knowing what I knew from my 20 years in business, the conclusion of "The Rule of Three" struck me as being rock-solid and all but impossible to challenge. So was a closing suggestion of the study. All company leaders, "The Rule of Three" advised, "need to reassess their corporate positioning and strategic goals. For some, this will spell a once-in-a-lifetime opportunity to seize the initiative and firmly establish their companies on a larger stage."

The larger stage for Acosta was clear enough to me and inspired what was to be my rallying cry: "We've *got* to go national!"

Just what was so unreasonable about taking our cue from the clear-cut strategies of both supermarket chains and food makers, as well as some convincing research, and expanding our ever-strengthening capabilities beyond our 13-state region? Well, nothing, that I could see. For starters, Acosta had the necessary internal strengths. We had almost 70 uninterrupted years of experience in the business and the best people, technology, and systems; we knew our clients' needs, as demonstrated by our performance record; we grew solid research and market-analysis capabilities that we shared with clients and customers throughout the U.S.; and our track record showed that we could represent clients better than any other company. Perhaps most importantly, we already knew *how* to grow. Indeed, beginning in 1974, we essentially wrote the script that other food brokers followed almost chapter and verse.

Moreover, we had a proven financial formula *for* acquisitions: a comparatively modest down payment followed by annual payments usually over a 10-year period, plus a commitment to bring the acquired company's owners and key people into the Acosta family. Keeping everyone "engaged" in this way helped ensure continued success.

We even knew who our best prospective merger partners were. Having been active in industry groups like the National Food Brokers Association and brokers' councils sponsored by our manufacturer clients, we got to know food brokers from all over the country. This exposure gave us the chance to identify the best from the rest.

Meanwhile, supermarket chains also had reason to be supportive, thanks in part to the rise of Wal-Mart! As Wal-Mart's meteoric growth in the mid-1990s transformed mass merchandizing, Wal-Mart's methods also influenced all retailers. The benefits of "consolidation" were part and parcel of Wal-Mart's formula—just as they were of Acosta's expansion plan.

Acosta had one more competitive advantage: the ears of numerous leading manufacturers, gained from our long-standing relationships. I was hardly the only guy thinking about the future of our business, of course, or appraising it. The ability to share ideas and grasp the perspectives of ranking executives from companies like Clorox, Heinz, and Nestlé was invaluable to the vision rapidly forming in my head. The process had really started when I became president of Acosta in 1993.

For instance, Grant LaMontagne told me about the subtle but important shifts in thinking at Clorox. Although many sales managers still relished the leverage they enjoyed by having alternative brokers, many of them were beginning to see opportunities that thinning Clorox's network of 47 brokers would create. Taking complexity out of that network reduced costs and boosted effectiveness. Ideally, LaMontagne envisioned fewer brokers "performing as a transparent extension of our own sales organization," he explained.

Grant's ideas were almost mirror images of the ideas of Nino Cristofoli at Nestlé. Upon being named a Nestlé sales vice president in 1987, Nino had been asked to put together an SMA network to handle the company's ever-growing line of products. Having always had a direct sales force at his side, it was an unfamiliar task, but still one well within Nino's solid capabilities. By the time Nino finished, Acosta was among some 134 brokers representing Nestlé's three business units.

"But why not just one agent for each business line?" Nino asked occasionally. Not being tied to our industry's tradition, he was more willing to question it.

"Great idea!" I would answer as I outlined my vision. Nino liked what he heard and kept me in the loop on Nestlé's long-term thinking.

Minute Maid, too, was seeing ample advantages in trimming its number of SMAs. Being a major Tropicana broker then, Acosta did not represent Minute Maid's products and certainly wasn't in its inner circle. But annual industry meetings and conventions afforded me opportunities to informally share sales scenarios with executives of the major packaged goods companies. The consensus conclusion emerging from these and scores of other discussions was loud and clear. Consolidation among sales and marketing agencies was inevitable. "But not just yet," these same industry sales executives always seemed to add quickly and with conviction.

Why? Any number of reasons. Collectively, industry executives made my vision of a national SMA look as unreasonable as possible.

Start with the money. Even though our financial formula was sound and proven, we still needed significant cash for down payments. Start stringing together the number of down payments my plan required, and cash flow could become a problem, especially for modestly sized sales organizations like Acosta—as I was advised time and again. Borrowing the dollars was an unlikely option, too, because banks weren't familiar with the structure and details of the deals we typically arranged.

As a rule, manufacturers were just as wary. Yes, they had begun consolidating their own SMA networks. Yes, they all saw the logic in what I preached, often with evangelistic zeal. After all, they all had stakes in the eventual outcome, and they all wanted strong marketing partners. The trouble was, many of the same manufacturers also had long-term relationships with their sales representatives in regions and individual cities across the country. And they were apprehensive about ending such relationships.

Acosta's ties to Clorox dated to 1933. Although notable, this relationship wasn't unique. Minute Maid's relationships with a few of its brokers dated to the company's very first shipments in the spring of 1946. Bob McCarthy's father had been first a Minute Maid salesman and then its first broker in Chicago. In fact, in 1957, Bob McCarthy Sr. was handed 30 days' advanced pay to help him launch a sales organization to cover the Chicago territory.

Along with such loyalty came a suspicion. Will brokers be eager to consolidate solely to be able to sell a popular product and, in turn, fill their pockets with commissions? All too often, food producers feared as much. Raw avarice was not the key ingredient for a good partnership. Too, there was the age-old fear of giving an independent sales representative like Acosta too much power in the marketplace. This feeling was rampant, even among many of our own clients.

Another of my "unreasonable decisions," as I was told years later, happened in August 1997, when, to end an intense dispute over a client conflict, I risked resigning a portion of our Nestlé account. Fortunately, we never came to a parting of the ways. Nestlé was one of our biggest clients then and today is Acosta's single largest client. At the time, though, billings didn't matter. Nestlé wouldn't consider our representing one of its products in one region at the same time we wanted to represent a rival's product in another region. Nestlé's recalcitrance stood in the way of Acosta's expanding its own regional presence. Nestlé's initial refusal to accept my ideas for managing one of the conflicts that had become a nagging industry-wide problem exasperated me, so I played hardball, as Nestlé's Nino Cristofoli described it, and got people's attention.

In retrospect, then, perhaps I shouldn't have been terribly surprised, or so deflated, when 11 of our most important clients played hardball back a few weeks later. We convened a first-ever "advisory council" meeting in Tampa. National representation wasn't the sole reason for the day-and-a-half meeting we hosted, but it was a key topic on the seven-topic agenda, so we orchestrated the flow of the meeting carefully and picked the time to pop the question. Would you allow Acosta to represent your brands nationally, in all markets coast to coast, if we could build the best SMA in the country?

The individual responses to my question varied, but the words all said pretty much the same thing: "Not just No, but, No way in hell!" Among those telling me "No!" were executives from Clorox, Tropicana, Campbell's, Heinz, and Nestlé.

The refusals were a testimony to the times. Clients of every size, along with just about everyone else it seemed, vigorously told me "No way in hell!" as they continued to caution me that my plan was a recipe for disaster. It was, they said, too bold, too ambitious, too fraught with risks and ills, and simply too unreasonable.

Consolidate to a point, this line of thinking continued, "as long as we still can have the best broker in each market. That's what we want." As they assessed my plan, various food producers didn't see Acosta's being able to guarantee that. Nor did they want to risk severing ties with those firms who performed for them in given markets. One couldn't blame them, in at least one respect.

Acosta represented a newer generation of sales and marketing agent. We built our relationships on execution and performance—more scientific selling, one might say. We also ran a tight ship and didn't throw money around. It had been that way all along, thanks to Del Dallas. Del was the epitome of the class act. He had coined the phrase "People make the difference" and believed with all his heart and soul that the right people would separate Acosta from its competitors. Acosta was hardly the only SMA that fit this mold, but the stereotypical "food broker" was still fresh in the minds of manufacturers. Old-time brokers hadn't had the most spotless of reputations but wore gaudy wardrobes, drove big cars, and spent lavishly, especially when entertaining clients. As long as the brokers performed, their clients were willing to maintain relationships; because they represented food manufacturers only in select markets, the visibility was modest and manageable.

Many brokers themselves had little interest in change—including some top-quality companies and individuals. Their attitude was easy to understand. The lion's share of them made good livings and had long-standing business relationships and seemingly bright futures. So why rock this boat?

Just how much of a factor this profile was in fueling resistance to my national broker idea is anyone's guess, but it was out there, just the same, and it was one more reason why, in the final analysis, conventional industry wisdom continued to predict a long, slow evolutionary change among brokers, one that would take a good decade or more. No one could imagine what still was a fragmented business being dramatically restructured and turned on its head.

In turn, conventional wisdom decided that, in "jumping through that window" that Bob McCarthy was to refer to, we also would be jumping off a cliff. Let some of the dust of all the minor mergers taking place within individual regions settle, I was told. Absorb your expansions, enjoy what Acosta has achieved. As much as they respected my aggressive stance, they thought I should be content to grow more slowly and be safe. If I heard all this advice once, I heard it a million times, along with another bit that made me see red: "Gary, you've just got to be reasonable about all this."

Like hell I did! To be sure, I respected those opinions and those who expressed them. But reasonable? Not the way I saw it. From where I stood, *remaining regional* was the recipe for disaster. Acosta had to become a national company or risk facing its own demise. If that branded me unreasonable, so be it. It wouldn't be the first time. And it wouldn't be the last.

By the time the 1997 Association of Sales & Marketing Companies convention convened in San Francisco that December, I had been bouncing all these ideas around in my head for more than a year, along with other ideas about continuing to grow our business. Now it was time for action.

"We've got to go national! It's the only way," I blurted out to Acosta's Strategy Planning Group, a handpicked corps of seven or eight colleagues.

That's how one member of the group, Jack Parker, describes first hearing my long-term vision. I just "blurted it out," he says. As I spoke, Jack says, I emphatically slapped my hand on the table of the St. Francis Hotel conference room where we met.

Jack, now an Acosta executive vice president and head of strategic initiatives and business development, also recalls my declaration stopping the conversation cold for an instant while everyone absorbed what I was saying and its implications. Within a few seconds, though, I was explaining my rationale of how retailers were consolidating and how they would expect us to give them what I called "seamless execution" in all their markets—no matter where those markets happened to be.

"Only a national company could do that," I stressed, so the sooner we got on with national expansion, the better our chances. Moving both quickly and judiciously preempted anyone else from stealing our strategy. Before long, we were referring to it as our Pac-Man strategy, for we were convinced that the future was all about eat or be eaten. As I recall—or, at least, like to recall—we all got pretty excited that day in San Francisco, and pretty damned determined.

It always had been my nature to chase my conviction. I didn't have the inclination or the time to wonder about the irony that a guy like me wound up in northern Florida, eager to tackle a business challenge like this one. Now and then, though, I do wonder.

Food for Thought

People who dream and have a vision have something the average person doesn't have. They know what they want and those that possess a burning desire to succeed do succeed despite all handicaps. It is this burning desire, along with knowing exactly what you want, that will create a vision that will carry you over every obstacle that stands in your way.

This vision, this dream, this goal is invisible to everyone except the person holding it. It is responsible for every great advance and achievement in our lives. It is the underlying motive for just about everything we see about us.

It is the beautiful building where before there was an empty lot. It is the bridge spanning the bay. It is the landing on the moon. It is the young person accepting the diploma. It is a low golf handicap or a position reached in the world of business.

It really is quite simple ...when we are possessed by an exciting and worthwhile goal ...we reach it. For if you want it badly enough, you will get it.

– Napoleon Hill

Step 7

Execute the Vision, No Matter How Unreasonable

Executing the "Get National!" strategy when it needed to happen.

To me, the vision of Acosta I had shaped by early December 1997 was practical, logical, and natural. Acosta would be the first nationwide sales and marketing agency with full-service capabilities in every significant U.S. market and staffed by the very best people in the business. It also would offer economies of scale to help inspire new services and capabilities that would be available and affordable to every client and customer.

One other word helps describes my vision: *essential*. I saw no other option that could even hope to protect Acosta's standing as an independent business. I had concluded that a broker that stood still in its existing regional footprint would be very well equipped for a world that no longer existed. My vision was the culmination of a half dozen factors and experiences:

- Carefully watching my industry for 20 years
- Participating in and learning from Acosta's initial expansions throughout the Southeast
- Understanding the implications of consolidations taking place among food manufacturers and supermarket chains
- Absorbing the lessons of market research contained in "The Rule of Three"
- Accepting the responsibilities inherent in taking the company's reins from Del Dallas in 1996
- Being resolutely unreasonable

As I saw it, national expansion was simply a next step, the extension of what my predecessor and mentor had entrusted to me. And just about everyone I knew on the other side of Acosta's corporate walls thought my vision was not only unreasonable but also just plain nuts. Even Del warned me to be very cautious.

In retrospect, I suppose a San Francisco hotel meeting room was the ideal place to blurt out, "We've got to go national!" to my strategy-planning group. After all, isn't California supposed to be the source of all things new and trendy? The meeting room was ideal for a second reason, too. The very same 1997 Association of Sales & Marketing Companies convention we had flown to attend that week in early December was where Del himself was to be honored for his lifetime achievements and contributions. Somewhere amid that tribute, I couldn't help but smile and savor the irony. Del was now being saluted by his industry peers for achieving what his industry peers had once derided as being impossible to accomplish.

Did that reinforce my resolve? I think it did, even if I didn't think much about it at the time. Now I can't help but smile at and savor a parallel comparison. In the face of naysayers, Del Dallas grew a small, local company of 22 employees into a regional powerhouse of 2,000 employees that doubled revenues every three years throughout a 22-year span. In the face of more naysayers, my 14-year run as CEO grew Acosta's coverage from 15 states to 50 states, then north to Canada and even to a few points overseas. Our number of Acosta associates climbed from 2,000 to more than 16,000, and our annual billings grew from $5 billion to more than $60 billion. Not bad for a national expansion that we engineered in 15 months. I relish recounting how we did it every bit as much as I relish recounting the episodes that won us support from Minute Maid and Clorox.

The broad-brush description of Acosta's 15-month expansion reads almost like four paragraphs you'd find in a CliffsNotes synopsis.

In the spring of 1998 we approached PMI-Eisenhart in Chicago, started talking, and wrapped up the straightforward, non-cash, tax-free merger by that July. That both locked in the Midwest and led to our fateful meeting with Minute Maid in early September.

Then we headed west to California and purchased Kelley-Clarke. We reached an agreement in principle in February 1999, thanks in large part to the support we received from Clorox. We concluded the Kelley-Clarke acquisition in June 1999, giving Acosta/PMI, as we were then calling ourselves, representation in 39 states.

Next, it was "About-face!" We headed east to acquire Boston-based MAI Companies in August. That brought us market coverage in nine more states in the all-important Northeast, including New York

City.

No sooner was the MAI deal done than we did one last about-face in September 1999 and dashed off to Texas. There, we negotiated an operating agreement with the Luke Soules Company that included our purchasing the company outright in three years. Before September 1999 ended, Minute Maid had made good on its pledge. It had appointed us as its representative nationwide, the first coast-to-coast appointment ever given to a U.S. SMA. Just like that, Acosta had grown into a company with revenues totaling $480 million.

Glance at this synopsis and you could infer that our national expansion proceeded like clockwork, a finely tuned sales and marketing juggernaut rolling across the country like a fleet of unstoppable Sherman tanks, as if Acosta's destiny had been all but preordained. If only it had been that simple.

Our expansion *was* well planned. We thought so anyway, and I'll contend that the end result confirms it. But the expansion was nowhere near CliffsNotes simple and was vastly more deliberate. In fact, before giving any serious thought to expanding beyond our region, we spent the better part of two years studying and planning Acosta's long-term future and developing a five-year strategy process.

In November 1996, the strategic planning group I had assembled after becoming CEO in January was beginning to meet regularly, as it would for the next three months. Along with assessing what our business might look like, along with key trends, competitors, strengths and weaknesses, growth opportunities, and threats, this group also developed specific annual revenue targets as steps to attaining our overall goal of generating $190 million in revenue by the year 2000. For 1997, for instance, our target figure was $125 million.

Notably, this strategic planning group included both Jack Parker and Robert Hill, who was to succeed me as CEO on New Year's Day 2009. I was part of this planning group, too, but did not chair it. By design, I had appointed as chair another Acosta colleague, Mike Diaz, assisted by other members: Rod Crawford, Mark White, Roger McClung, and Eric Quinn.

The end result of the strategic planning group's effort was a five-year plan that was presented to Acosta's management committee at the end of January 1997. This plan was a good first step and formed the foundation for more detailed business planning developed during

1997—which culminated at that early December meeting in San Francisco with my blurting out, "We've got to go national!"

Without question, I wanted to continue—and accelerate—Acosta's expansion that Del Dallas so boldly launched in 1974. But, just as Del's expansion strategy had prescribed, I wanted the ownership and key employees of companies we would acquire to continue to thrive as contributing members of a larger, stronger, and ever more capable Acosta—to the point that I insisted they purchase Acosta stock and have a stake in the company's long-range performance. That would further ensure that these people were engaged and committed to the business. Before long, "Get National!" had become our rallying cry.

That I was intent on continuing what Del had started arouses an obvious question: Is that what Del himself would have done?

Absolutely, insists Peggy Dallas, Del's widow. There is no doubt whatsoever in her mind that Del, too, envisioned Acosta's someday becoming a nationwide organization, notwithstanding his cautious words to me. Del just would have gone about it more slowly and gradually, she believes, and without incurring any bank debt.

I agree with Peggy's observations. Del had a formula that worked for Acosta up until 1996. He very methodically stuck to his plan and grew Acosta to a wonderful position in the industry. What Del had had then that I didn't have now, though, was *time*. By 1998 we were absolutely convinced that we had to move and move quickly. This required new thinking and new risk taking.

Outwardly, it might have appeared I had plenty of time, as well as hordes of naysayers that would enable us to work patiently below the radar. Regional consolidations among brokers had become routine. But that's as far as it would go, at least for the foreseeable future, or so conventional wisdom declared. Moreover, still ringing in my ears were the blunt responses to the carefully orchestrated query I had posed to 11 of our key clients during the Tampa meeting we had hosted in early October of 1997: Would you appoint Acosta as your representative nationwide if we were to build the very best firm in the business in every market?

"Not on your life!" they all had chimed. Their blunt rejections should have shattered my vision of expansion then and there. Without manufacturers' support, expanding across the country couldn't happen. Even *with* manufacturers' support, there would be no guarantee of success. It had taken Acosta several years to become profitable in Tampa and nine years to become consistently profitable in Miami; how long would it take in Boston, or Denver, or Dallas?

Of course I was too unreasonable to accept "Not on your life!" Not when other noises were ringing in my ears while other episodes, along with some statistics, marched in front of my eyes. Collectively, these sights and sounds were flashing another strong message: Time's a wastin' pal! So get moving!

Let's start with the statistics. In 1997, one set of industry figures showed that the nation's top 10 retail supermarket chains accounted for a 30 percent market share of U.S. consumers' grocery purchases. By itself, that was a healthy percentage. By 2005, however, industry data was projecting that these same top 10 chains would account for as much as a 70 percent share of consumers' grocery purchases. The long-term implications of these numbers were ominous for a broker with only a regional footprint. More purchases controlled by fewer and fewer supermarket chains would require a national footprint with the capabilities to service every supermarket in America.

Supporting the numbers and the scenario were additional figures that had been reported in the February 1997 issue of *Supermarket Business*, an industry trade journal at the time. Between 1985 and 1995, there had been a whopping 7,154 food business mergers, including 599 among retailers and 1,322 among food brokers. The same article noted there had been "at least 100 more consolidations in 1996" and predicted that the pace of consolidations would continue.

Because those figures had been compiled by the Association of Sales & Marketing Companies (successor to the National Food Brokers Association), I knew they were valid. Our acquisitions were included in the totals of course, and the article briefly credited Del Dallas for being the primary originator of what it called mega-brokers. Interestingly—especially today—that was the lone reference to Acosta, other than a listing on a map within the article.

I couldn't have cared less about the mention of Acosta, however. What I cared about most were the words coming from the supermarket chains that were responsible for many of these numbers. What they were saying was making the statistics downright scary. In 1995, for instance, SuperValu, a wholesaler, had expressly told my future colleague Bob McCarthy that it was going to reduce its number of buying points from the 17 it had in place then to perhaps five, one in each of its major regions. The SuperValu folks had also made it clear to Bob that they expected brokers to take the hint and act accordingly. Super-Valu's decision foreshadowed what Kroger was to do in mid-1998—namely, consolidate *all* of its buying in *one* location: Cincinnati.

Closer to home was the mounting evidence of a companion trend: the often startling expansion plans of the supermarket chains. Jack-sonville-based Winn-Dixie had long been a regional chain and still was expanding. In the early 1990s, Florida rival Publix Supermarkets started following suit, despite a declaration from its founder and first CEO George Jenkins, "I left Georgia as a young man and have no intention of going back." Well, Mr. Jenkins changed his mind. In 1991, he opened a store in Savannah, the first Publix logo to appear outside of Florida. Publix logos on stores in Atlanta opened soon thereafter, fol-lowed by more store openings in South Carolina in 1993 and still more in Alabama in 1996. Many of these stores were cavernous, too—45,000 square feet or more.

Just about everywhere I looked and listened, I found evidence of ongoing consolidation and expansion among the retail sector of our business. Food Lion, Albertson's, Safeway ... everyone was on the move and within an economy that encouraged it. This was a structural change to be reckoned with. Retailers were the customers both of agencies like Acosta and of food producers, so never mind if there wasn't any enthu-siasm for a nationwide agency from the food producers. If the retailers wanted agencies with a nationwide reach, then those agencies that had a nationwide reach would win and win big. Those who didn't would lose just as dramatically. It was that simple. You could bet the farm on that, and I knew it, just as I knew that contentions about further con-solidation among SMAs being gradual were fast becoming delusions of folks whistling past the graveyard. *If I'm gonna whistle,* I told myself, *it's gonna be while I work on our plan to "Get National!" first.*

Before 1998 was more than a few weeks old, Acosta had identified the leading agencies in each region that we knew. We then narrowed those to a short list that we concluded would be the ideal merger part-ner in each region. Our criteria were always the same. We wanted only the best! This meant the best people, the best operating practices, and the most successful enterprises—the same basis Del Dallas had used. More often than not our target agencies represented Clorox brands and other products that we were representing in the Southeast. That was more than coincidental.

Being a Clorox broker was a badge of distinction in itself, because Clorox had high standards for its brokers. And, like many of our clients, Clorox had a "broker council" that met regularly during the year. The meetings afforded the brokers opportunities to compare business practices (within the parameters allowed by law), swap information on, say, health care and transportation costs, and develop good working relationships with each other. Because none of the brokers were competitors, a level of trust developed, too. These relationships became incredibly helpful in our planning.

In time, manufacturers recognized what we had been doing, but they didn't mind at all because they could see how our strategy would benefit their best long-term interests. Some even started lobbying me to approach certain brokers! After identifying these potential partners, we marked their respective locations on a U.S. map and delineated the regions in which they operated. More than once, our conference room looked like a scene from *Patton*, even taking on a war-room atmosphere from time to time. The atmosphere was apropos, too. We routinely talked openly about mobilizing and taking command of various territories. The talking points of our strategy to win each of these territories were to:

- Create the best selling system in the U.S.
- Provide top-tier excellence *in every market!*
- Utilize critical mass to enhance service levels.
- Leverage product portfolio with customers for business gain through superior customer teams.
- Provide the best systems for business/technological superiority.
- Retain a strong senior management team.
- Hire, retain, and promote the best people.
- Ensure financial stability.

By the spring of 1998 we were ready to make our first thrust. It would be into the Midwest and begin just as it should have: with another phone call dialed by Del Dallas.

We couldn't have designed a more ideal initial merger partner than the one already flourishing in suburban Chicago. PMI-Eisenhart was, as I stated in the opening pages of this saga, practically a mirror image of Acosta. Unquestionably the Midwest's leading agency, PMI-Eisenhart was the only viable prospective partner we identified in the region. It was a Clorox broker and had a long and successful history; a 1970 merger stretched the company's roots all the way back to 1917.

As that merger suggests, PMI-Eisenhart was no stranger to expansion. Indeed, the enterprise Del Dallas was calling on this March afternoon was itself the result of a 1996 merger that had united PMI, the Chicago agency founded in 1957 by Bob McCarthy Sr. with Eisenhart & Associates, founded in 1972 by Jim Eisenhart. Moreover, before the two had joined forces, PMI had made four acquisitions and opened two other offices, while Eisenhart had made four acquisitions of its own. Once united, PMI-Eisenhart had continued expanding across much of the nation's midsection much as we had rolled up the Southeast. By early 1998, PMI-Eisenhart was doing business in 14 states with northeast Illinois as its hub, just as Acosta was doing business in 15 states with northeast Florida as our hub.

Location was yet another jewel in PMI-Eisenhart's crown. Our "Get National!" strategy called for us to lock up the middle of the country first. Doing so, we reasoned, would give us a solid base of operations that would serve as a nearly impenetrable barrier to aspiring interlopers. First securing the nation's midsection would also put us in better position to expand to both coasts, in whichever order seemed prudent, and would virtually preempt someone from starting at either coast and marching across the country. That said, we already could see that Acosta wasn't alone in its thinking. In fact, three other companies were trying to "get national," too: Marketing Specialists and Crossmark, both based in Texas, and Advantage Sales and Marketing, a southern California firm.

Even PMI-Eisenhart's leadership had a striking similarity to Acosta's: Jim Eisenhart was retiring in early 1998 and had just passed the company's reins to Bob McCarthy, much like Del Dallas had put me in charge as Acosta's CEO in 1996.

"We'd like to come up and talk and share some ideas," Del said when he reached Jim Eisenhart. Del didn't say much more and didn't have to. He and Eisenhart were long-time business friends, having served together on the boards of several industry associations. Though he had been retired for two years, Del was happy to help flip the switch of Acosta's strategy and then let me take over—and perhaps it made him feel better about what I was intent on doing. It was a much appreciated contribution—and in my eyes a signal that, down deep, Del knew I was doing the right thing.

"Sounds interesting," Jim replied. "Come on up. Bob and I will be happy to talk." In short order, Jim and Del had arranged our first meeting at the Hilton O'Hare in Chicago later that month.

Once that first meeting began, it didn't take long to see that Jim and Bob also sensed that I was doing the right thing. As I laid out the broad strokes of Acosta's thinking and strategy, I stressed our ties and common interests and how starting quickly from the middle would give our combined enterprise a critical leg up. Jim's and Bob's heads nodding in agreement confirmed that our two companies had common perspectives, too.

PMI-Eisenhart's combined operation was not quite three years old and still digesting the acquisitions made in 1996 and 1997, Bob noted. In turn, any serious thoughts they had about further expansion had been on the back burner. "We're feeling pretty good about ourselves and our situation," he added, mentioning that they didn't envision any further expansion for a while.

It was a reasonable conclusion: PMI-Eisenhart's acquisitions of the past two years had stretched its sphere of operations across the better part of 10 new states, from Ohio and Michigan to the east to Oklahoma, Minnesota, and the Dakotas to the west. Taking care of a flourishing business in these states seemed like the right focus.

Still, Bob McCarthy concurred with my unreasonable thinking. He could read the tea leaves and discern the eat-or-be-eaten scenario our industry presented. And as PMI-Eisenhart's leader, Bob had to chart the company's future. Just as Del quickly bowed out of our conversations, so did Jim Eisenhart—on the very day that serious discussions began, Bob remembers.

Our customers, Bob stressed early on, "Wanted one face, a single point of contact that could service their stores everywhere they did business." What manufacturers might want, we both quickly agreed, wouldn't matter, especially with supermarket chains growing—and having Wal-Mart and Kmart in their midst.

It didn't take long at all for the question to become *how*, not *if*, Acosta and PMI-Eisenhart would join forces. Before concluding our initial meeting in Chicago that March, Bob and I scheduled a follow-up in Tampa, where serious discussions began.

The amicably arrived-at deal we struck was an exchange of stock, based primarily on the annual revenues our two companies generated—approximately $140 million for Acosta and $100 million for PMI. There was no cash involved in the deal at all. Accordingly, when all was said and done, Acosta principals held about 60 percent of the stock in the new Acosta/PMI Sales and Marketing Company, while PMI principals held 40 percent. I remember starting the discussions something like this: "Bob, you are not going to sell to me, and I am not going to sell to you, right? So then, the only answer is a true merger." Bob agreed to move forward.

Neither was there much hassling to speak of during negotiations. No merger is ever devoid of at least a little friction, and ours was no exception, but the friction was kept to a minimum, probably because the cultures of our two organizations were so much alike. We both thought very highly of our employees and rewarded them accordingly, and we both ran tight ships.

All things considered, our merger with PMI went so smoothly that more than once I had to stop myself from thinking, *This might not be so tough after all.* I knew better, though.

To begin with, merging with PMI-Eisenhart brought us face to face with that old industry nemesis: conflict. The same SMA couldn't represent competing brands of the same product, for obvious reasons, yet as mergers and consolidations accelerated in the 1980s and 1990s and rearranged all kinds of business relationships between brokers and manufacturers, following the rule was no longer simple. For instance, how much of a conflict was it if Acosta represented Heinz's 9Lives cat food in its North Carolina markets and Friskies, then owned by Nestlé, in Florida? In August of 1997, that was no hypothetical situation but a real-life dilemma created by one of our 21 acquisitions in the Southeast between 1990 and 1997.

Given where our industry was heading, my unreasonable nature started telling me this wasn't really a conflict at all. Different offices in distant locations managed by different representatives handled the respective brands and were each fiercely dedicated to them. They all just happened to be under the Acosta umbrella—but that was a *plus* for Heinz and Nestlé, as I saw it, because we performed equally well for both clients.

In Pittsburgh, that was the perspective the great H.J. Heinz Co. had begun to adopt back in 1997. That year, Heinz had decided to consolidate all of its business with one agency throughout the entire South. It was one impressive consolidation; its brands included Heinz Ketchup, Ore-Ida potatoes, Smart Ones frozen entrées, Heinz baby food, StarKist tuna, and 9Lives cat food. This was one big segment of business, and we wanted to grow with Heinz. Knowing Nestlé had publicly stated that a conflict of interest existed between the pet food brands, I moved forward and went to the Heinz interview anyway.

"Why are you even *here*?" I was asked initially by the Heinz management team. "Nestlé is going to declare this a conflict, and that will be the end of it."

"No, it won't be," I insisted. "Give us the business and your commitment, and Acosta will deliver and give Heinz its commitment, and let me deal with Nestlé," I urged. What's more, if Nestlé balked, I further declared, Acosta was with Heinz.

That was one ambitious and gutsy declaration, and everybody in the room knew it. Here I was, willing to walk away from our nearly $10-million-a-year Nestlé business to get a Heinz account worth $8 million a year. How unreasonable was that?

Not unreasonable in the least, I declared, because I was focused on the long-term implications of where our business was headed. So Heinz agreed to give it a shot. Instead of fretting about conflicts, its executives should focus on performance, I kept stressing. That's really what it was all about, anyway. Wasn't performance what Heinz wanted most of all? I asked. And if we didn't perform, we could be fired with 30 days' notice, anyway!

"Agreed," Heinz decided.

Nestlé didn't agree at all. Its executives were not interested in even considering my views on conflicts. Just as Heinz had predicted, Nestlé's official stand was essentially "It's a conflict. So, us or them! Make a choice."

"No! You make the decision to fire me," I replied in earnest, "because I believe strongly that I can get the job done for both companies. I am not walking away from you. I think you need to reconsider." I loved the Nestlé account and all the people with whom I dealt, I declared with conviction during one key meeting. I also appealed to my long-standing relationship with them, noting that I had begun my career with Carnation, now a Nestlé company. Even so, I explained, I was willing to risk our long-standing relationship because I believed I could convince Nestlé management to allow Acosta to represent both brands. Just give me the chance, I asked.

Throughout these discussions, though, I kept asking myself, "Gary, who'd you rather have as an ally? Someone who acts like he's willing to hurt you or someone who's said he wants to help you?" It was a big bet, and my final answer was what I related to Nestlé vice president Nino Cristofoli: "I am accepting the Heinz business. Now the ball is in your court."

"Damn, I was afraid of that," Nino muttered when I told him. He was another industry pal, and one who then was trying to reduce the number of brokers Nestlé had to deal with. So Nino himself sounded willing to give my idea a go and let Acosta's performance dictate whether we kept the Friskies pet food account. For good reason, too. Nino didn't want to have to even think about replacing us. But Nestlé's West Coast headquarters was overruling him, he told me, and forcing the question.

But I wasn't going to blink now—unreasonable as I appeared to be —and by now this situation was hot news on the industry grapevine. If acting on my conviction meant losing the Nestlé pet food account and the hefty billings that went with it, so be it. I was convinced my stand was in Acosta's best long-term interests, and I still held hope that there was a way to hang on to both Nestlé's business *and* Heinz's business. Of course, that's how I always thought. Hell, I wanted everybody's business all the time.

I got the chance to make one last appeal to Nestlé the very next week and grabbed it—although I had to interrupt a December family skiing vacation in Utah to do it. Nino had found me a sliver of an opportunity to plead my case to his West Coast bosses, "but you've got to be in Los Angeles tomorrow," he said.

I sailed off the slopes in an instant, hurried to Salt Lake City, and boarded a flight to LAX. At the dinner meeting that had been arranged, I presented my case: Focus not on conflicts but on *performance*. Establish your goals and metrics, and then let us go to work. If we don't perform, fire us!

As we talked, I also inserted remarks about how my proposal reflected Acosta's long-range plans. And Nestlé said OK. They would give us a six-month trial. That's all we'd need, I assured them. And it was. Today, Nestlé remains Acosta's single largest client.

"One of the best demonstrations of salesmanship I ever witnessed," Nino says.

The Heinz-Nestlé affair was one of our more celebrated struggles we've had over conflicts, but it was fairly typical, too. Every time we completed an acquisition—and there have been upwards of 100 of them, all told—we had to review the portfolio of the business that came with the merger, then proceed accordingly. And the portfolios could be pretty thick. We didn't win all of the struggles, and those we lost cost us millions. They were battles lost in pursuit of winning the overall war, I always concluded, casualties we had to endure along our relentless march to "Get National." In the final analysis, having to confront conflicts was ultimately a good thing; it wound up whisking Bob McCarthy and me to Houston, where we forged our alliance with Minute Maid in 1998. Without Minute Maid … well, I don't want to think about how our national expansion might have fared.

Conflicts afforded Acosta another priceless benefit: an opportunity to build relationships, gain a perspective into industry "politics," and articulate my emerging vision of Acosta all at the same time. As I think back in time, I remember that one especially memorable episode erupted early, not long after I had been named a regional vice president in the mid 1980s. It, too, involved the Nestlé Company.

Watching carefully the consolidations and expansions that the supermarkets were engineering, Nestlé decided to do some consolidating of its own. Naturally, we presented Acosta as being uniquely qualified to represent three Nestlé divisions throughout Florida, and we seemingly won the appointment. It was a huge step forward, one on which I worked hard, and would direct as head of Florida operations. In fact, Nestlé's business would be lucrative enough for us to resign our account with a direct competitor. Of course, we couldn't resign that existing account until this new deal was done.

But suddenly, this new deal was coming undone. An executive within Nestlé's Stouffer's Frozen Foods division was trying to reverse the decision. It made no sense, because it contradicted Nestlé's own consolidation plan. It prompted a call out of the blue from my pal Nino Cristofoli. "Typical corporate politics," he said, explaining how the case was nothing more than a case of some miffed vice president trying to flex his muscles. Sit tight, Nino advised. "We'll get this settled Monday morning at a meeting we've called in Jacksonville."

"Nino, I hope so," I replied nervously. "We're going to resign the other business at 10:30. That's $2 million we're walking away from, so I'm practically betting my future with the company, here."

Nino again urged me to sit tight, for good reason. Participating in the Monday meeting would be Nestlé chairman and CEO Tim Kroll, who thought enough of the situation to arrange for a telephone conference from Catalina Island off the California coast, where he was vacationing on his boat. A savvy veteran of corporate politics, Kroll knew what was happening. "We made a decision and a commitment and we're going to honor it," Kroll directed at that meeting. The crisp words coming through the speaker phone left no doubt; Nestlé's appointment now *was* a done deal.

"Somebody played a king, but Tim played the ace," summed up former Nestlé executive John Pritchard, who watched everything unfold. Tim's presence and Nino's, too, reminded me of how important relationships were and how important it was to nurture them. For one thing, I had maintained my good ties to Carnation after leaving the company, which had come in very handy when Nestlé had later acquired Carnation. Moreover, I had hired John Pritchard during my early years at Carnation! John had gone on to build a terrific career there, one that kept flourishing after the Nestlé acquisition—so much so that Ken's Salad Dressing ultimately hired John away to become its president.

The Nestlé incident was "as politically driven an episode as I've ever seen," John says now, and one decided on the strength of relationships more than anything else. It was an up-close-and-personal glimpse of corporate politics I've always remembered. Might it have contributed to our saving Nestlé's pet food business a decade later? I think so, without a doubt.

But neither relationships nor lessons from conflicts seemed to help at all when we headed west to purchase Kelley-Clarke, Inc., in late 1998. "Get National!" was fast becoming out of reach, or so it seemed. Expecting to negotiate directly with Kelly-Clarke President Charlie Frankowski, I immediately was told I would be talking at all times to not just Charlie but also the 13 members of the company's board. That didn't prove to be all bad. As talks proceeded, I managed to win a few confidences and wound up with a mole or two among those 13 directors; it did help our cause.

What was all bad, though, was learning that Kelley-Clarke had another suitor. Publicly traded Marketing Specialists, one of three other firms trying to "get national," was dangling a combination of stock and cash before Kelley-Clarke's board. The stock was thinly traded and of very limited value, which was to be affirmed in a few years; at the time, though, the overall package was appealing to Kelley-Clarke—dangerously appealing, from my standpoint.

Acosta's offer, by comparison, had scant appeal, its fairness and future value notwithstanding. The proposal I presented on November 12 was consistent with most Acosta offers. We would purchase only the assets of the company, not Kelley-Clarke stock; put down only a modest percentage of the purchase price (the cash to come from the Minute Maid loan I'd arranged about 60 days earlier); then arrange for seller financing to cover the rest of the purchase. In retrospect, it was the biggest test of Del Dallas's age-old acquisition staple, and it wasn't faring well.

Kelley-Clarke rejected the offer out of hand, triggering exhausting rounds of negotiations that were as grueling as any I can remember. That Kelley-Clarke was willing to be acquired was evident, but not so evident was by whom—Acosta or Marketing Specialists.

The trips I made to California for the acquisition have blurred into an endless trek, but I'll bet there were as many as 10 trips in less than four months. One proposal beget a counteroffer, then another proposal, then a revision. We sweetened deals, adjusted provisions, added this, and deleted that. I noted how much stronger Kelley-Clarke would be as part of Acosta than it would be as part of Marketing Specialists. At one point I even agreed to have Acosta assume more than $35 million in employment contracts. But nothing I suggested had any impact on the Kelley-Clarke board as a whole.

Neither did appealing to Charlie's ego. "The combination of Charlie Frankowski, Gary Chartrand and Bob McCarthy will result in the strongest management team in the United States, and will attract significant new business," I wrote. That flattery went nowhere and left me sprinkling my sentences with phrases like "these guys are impossible to deal with." I had other words in mind when Charlie called in mid-January.

"You've got to be kidding me," I practically snapped when Frankowski told me his board was on the verge of accepting the Marketing Specialists offer.

If there had been another viable option in the West, we might have just walked away. But there wasn't another viable option. Kelley-Clarke was the best of the West, a $140 million enterprise with operations from Denver to the Pacific and offices right where we wanted them. We just had to have it, period. Our whole "Get National!" strategy depended on it.

That's why I finally appealed to Clorox for help. It was about the only leverage I had left. While Kelley-Clarke was a Clorox broker, Marketing Specialists was not; I knew in my gut that Clorox would not want to live with that kind of combination. Exactly what was said, by whom and when, I'll never know. The outcome was all I cared about.

Even *after* that consultation, though, we weren't out of the woods. Beginning in mid-January, we had another month of calls, memos, faxes, and revisions. It wasn't until February 19 that I could report to Acosta's owners that Charlie and I finally had signed a letter of intent. The agreement was unusual by Acosta's standards, including both a higher down payment and the purchase of stock. The combined $35 million in loans from Minute Maid and Clorox and the $30 million loan from NationsBank made the deal possible. It was more cash up front than we had intended, but at least the tentative deal was done and was to close within 120 days. I've never ever been a clock watcher. But until mid-June 1999, I counted down the hours and minutes until Kelley-Clarke was officially in the fold.

Acquisition number three, by comparison, was as heavenly as it was efficient. The deal was done in approximately 60 days. MAI-Alper was one of two prominent Northeast firms with offices from Virginia to Maine that generated annual revenues of $100 million. Based in metropolitan Boston, it wasn't our only option, but it was easily our first choice. MAI-Alper and Acosta were similar in many ways and had equally similar operating principles. I had become well acquainted with CEO Vic Del Regno and his designated successor, Jack Laurendeau, and had the utmost respect for both men. They were solid professionals in every respect—and here was yet another instance of a CEO (Vic) getting ready to retire, albeit in 1999. MAI was not a Clorox broker, but our two firms had numerous other common clients. All in all, it was a great fit.

Initially, MAI was a little cautious. For a time, Jack especially had envisioned the company remaining independent. It was understandable, too: MAI operated in the one section of the country whose supermarkets weren't being dramatically realigned by major consolidations. "I could see what was happening elsewhere, of course," Jack says, "but still wondered if we might weather the storm and be left alone."

As they wondered what moves to make, MAI-Alper's leaders began casual conversations in the spring of 1999 about being part of something larger, though not at first with Acosta but with rivals Advantage and Crossmark. Del Regno even recalls a few notions surfacing about MAI making its own national run. Interestingly enough, such notions were spurred in part by suggestions from a few major manufacturing clients such as Tropicana, which by then had gotten wind of our negotiations with Kelley-Clarke. Tropicana was just looking out for its interests, you might say. "But by then we never seriously considered doing anything like that," Vic remembers. The train was already going too fast and on tracks taking some very interesting twists.

The retail landscape in the Northeast, if still more fragmented, was also uncertain. Both Del Regno and Laurendeau knew that size suddenly mattered even more and that ties of some kind to a national organization certainly would help ensure MAI's future. In the final analysis, Vic and Jack sensed that the train was about to leave the station and, feeling a sense of urgency, wanted to be sure to be on board. Acosta represented the best option and had the best operating plan, which Vic and Jack could readily discern.

Just to be sure, though, I received a little affirmation. My pal John Pritchard spoke to Jack on Acosta's behalf. "You owe it to yourself to at least talk," John urged.

Jack agreed, and the talking that began shortly thereafter quickly led to a purchase agreement that included a payout for all MAI shareholders over eight years. The amiable negotiations worked out well for Acosta, too, in large part because the agreement did not include a cash down payment. It was a good thing, because we didn't have any cash for a down payment. We had used all our cash to purchase Kelley-Clarke.

After the closing, Vic retired and Jack became a key Acosta executive and a close confidante of mine; he is now Acosta's vice chairman and remains my close friend. My ties with Vic still bind, too. Eight years later, just after we made our final payment, he sent me something very special—a gold coin and a note that read:

Dear Gary,

It's official! I have been informed along with all other MAI Alper shareholders that we have received final payment from Acosta. I want to thank you personally for all your hard work and dedication to your "Bold Vision." I would sincerely appreciate it if you would accept the enclosed memento as a small token of my appreciation and acknowledgment that Gary Chartrand's word is: As good as gold.

I had the gold coin and Vic's handwritten note framed and hung them on a wall in my office, where they still hang today.

Fortunately, we also didn't need any cash up front to acquire the final territory of our "Get National!" strategy. Barely one month after we closed on MAI, in September 1999, we were in Texas and New Mexico, thanks to a two-phase agreement with Luke Soules, a $40 million Texas-based agency. Joe Soules, Luke's son, was a tough negotiator but a fair businessman. I loved sparring with Joe because he made us think differently. Joe and I remain good friends.

Phase one of the Soules acquisition was an operating agreement that became effective in November. We operated as one company, but Acosta and Luke Soules each handled their own expenses for the next three years, until we acquired the company outright in 2003. Why the arrangement? There were tax advantages for the seller, pure and simple.

For all practical purposes, though, Acosta and Soules were one company. The mission of "Get National!" had been accomplished. There was even a bonus. In November, we also brought a Denver-based agency, McFerren, Speakes and Gustafson, into the family. It hadn't been critical to our strategy and really hadn't been on our radar screen, but it was a solid and well-run company and was destined to contribute handsomely to Acosta's future, thanks to the guy at the helm who came with the deal: Jamie Gronowski.

Jamie certainly personified our "get the best people" imperative. He had decades of experience and had been an executive with Kelley-Clarke before joining McFerren in 1982. He had become president of the Denver firm in 1990. Like Jack Laurendeau, Jamie had once had notions of "weathering the storm" and being left alone in the Rocky Mountains. But also like Jack, he had heard the train whistling and decided to get on board. Finally, he did!

It took a lot to convince Jamie and his fellow owners that aligning with Acosta was in their best long-term interests—and it took a lot of meetings. It was like pulling teeth. We courted McFerren, Speakes and Gustafson for more than a year and had to cope with competing offers throughout. The other primary suitor was Advantage, our large, capable California rival whose own national-expansion strategy was also then well underway. At one point, Jamie was on the verge of accepting Advantage's offer. He felt that Advantage was offering a sweeter deal, and one that would give him more freedom and autonomy.

"Before you commit, just get on a plane and meet me in Chicago," I pleaded in the summer of 1999. "You owe it to yourself and your company to hear me out."

Jamie agreed, and we met a few days later at the O'Hare Hilton, where I had Bob McCarthy and Jack Laurendeau waiting with me. "It was the full-court press," Jamie laughingly commented when he first saw us. Yes, it was. But I wanted Jamie to get a firsthand look at the Acosta team that we were just about finished building.

Comparatively speaking, what Jamie ran was just a small company in the Rockies. But it was a jewel of an operation, and I was relentless … and unreasonable once again. If we had the chance to become stronger still, I wasn't about to ignore it. In conversations that were congenial throughout, Bob, Jack, and I convinced Jamie and his colleagues to review their options one last time.

"We literally went up into the mountains near Dillon, Colorado and thought it over," Jamie recounts. Soon after they came down, McFerren, Speakes and Gustafson agreed to be part of the Acosta family. We were delighted then, of course, and in time would be more delighted still.

But that was among the tales still to come as 1999 faded. Acosta now had revenues of $480 million and, as a nationwide company, was clearly the industry leader. We'd done it! My impossible, unreasonable dream for Acosta had been realized in 15 often wild and crazy months. I guess I should remember how we celebrated that New Year's Eve, but it's gotten lost in all the other memories, and there really wasn't time to celebrate, anyway.

Suddenly, we were like the car-chasing dog that had caught one. It was time to make good on our pledge to deliver the very best service in every one of our markets, new and old. It was time to leverage the myriad business portfolios now in our laps, time to grapple with all the details inherent in the addition of Minute Maid as our first national client and the departure of Tropicana, and time to confront more headaches and crises than I could have imagined. I had thought the hard part was over, but the game was just beginning. Before long, I was gaining new insights into some time-honored advice: "Watch out what you wish for, you just might get it."

Food for Thought

The longer I live, the more I realize the impact of attitude on life. Attitude to me is more important than facts. It is more important than the past, than education, than money, than circumstances, than failures, than successes, than what other people think or say or do. It is more important than appearance, giftedness, or skill. It will make or break a company. It will cause a church to soar or sink. It will be the difference in a happy home or a home of horror. The remarkable thing is you have a choice every day regarding the attitude you will embrace for that day. We cannot change our past. We cannot change the fact that people will act a certain way. We cannot change the inevitable. The only thing we can do is play on the one string we have, and that is our attitude. I am convinced that life is 10 percent what happens to me and 90 percent how I react to it. And so it is with you.

—Chuck Swindoll, "Strengthening Your Grip on Attitudes"

Step 8

Stay the Course, Even When All Seems Impossible

The challenges can be unreasonable, too.

When you're an unreasonable leader with an unreasonable vision, you have to be prepared for unreasonable challenges and dilemmas. My colleagues and industry peers have frequently credited me with nationalizing the SMA business, and I am proud of that accolade. But that achievement brought with it the startling transformation of Acosta itself. Becoming an enterprise that did business from coast to coast triggered a multitude of tasks. As much as we had thought we were prepared for anything and everything that could conceivably accompany our "Get National!" expansion strategy, the situations and surprises that erupted in the wake of our expansion still felt like shots from out of the blue.

By November 1999, Acosta was indeed the national company I had wished for, only what we now had to tackle sure as hell hadn't been on my wish list. You could say that Jack Laurendeau was looking for some words of wisdom—and words of encouragement, too—when he called in the fall of 1999, not long after MAI-Alper had become part of the Acosta family. "I need your help," Jack began.

"Sure. Fire away," I replied.

"Help me explain to my staff why this merger is good for us," Jack said next.

At least his good nature and sense of humor were still intact. There really wasn't any panic or sarcasm in Jack's voice, for we had already become the close business partners and friends we remain today. Still, I could recognize a plea when I heard one. At the moment, it was hard to find anything good in the situation that our new partner in the Northeast was confronting.

Within 90 days after joining Acosta, MAI had lost two of its top three clients, as well as some staff members whose jobs had been eliminated by the merger. As anyone could understand, Jack's fine team was a little shaken. That the MAI operation would have to resign its Tropicana account had been a foregone conclusion. As promised, Minute

Maid had appointed Acosta as its nationwide representative in September, just about the time we began doing business in the Northeast as a single entity. To the MAI folks, however, welcoming Minute Maid was, at best, a consolation.

Tropicana had been generating more revenues—as much as $5 million more a year. The Northeast was one of Tropicana's best overall markets; its products outsold Minute Maid there by a wide margin. This made MAI one of Tropicana's most prized brokers, and one that Tropicana certainly didn't want to lose. Tropicana reacted to the resignation almost as if it were being betrayed. To a degree, perhaps it was.

Years earlier, Tropicana had helped establish MAI in the always-critical New York City market. Tropicana had even gone so far as to turn its direct sales force over to MAI as MAI entered the New York market. The personal relationship that Tropicana then developed with the man directing MAI's New York operation, Kenny Rice, was so tight that one of Tropicana's sales executives had been the best man at Kenny's wedding. In forcing a professional parting of the ways, our merger had triggered more than the usual emotional fallout. That was only for openers. Jack and MAI were also reeling from an even more damaging consequence of our merger: being fired by the Gerber baby.

Gerber, like every other maker of food products, had been watching our "Get National!" strategies unfold very carefully; it had a dog in this fight, too. Gerber marketing executives especially wanted to see how the conflicts that were bound to arise would affect product distribution—principally because Gerber recently had shifted from selling direct to relying on independent agencies like ours.

By then, too, our three rivals, Crossmark, Advantage, and Marketing Specialists, had their own expansion marches underway. Our whole business world was rife with uncertainty. Rather than wait around, Gerber became proactive quickly—far too quickly from Jack Laurendeau's perspective. In a heartbeat, Laurendeau saw Gerber's legendary trademark transformed from that cute and cuddly little baby face to a little fire-breathing monster crawling away in a huff—and taking $10 million worth of annual revenues with him.

"Why should we sit around and wait for you to resign us? We can see what's going to happen. Acosta is aligning with Heinz throughout the country. It's only a matter of time before Heinz appoints Acosta in the Northeast," Gerber essentially told Jack. So Gerber pulled the trigger first and terminated our relationship. There was only one major problem with this approach for Acosta: Heinz was happy with its agent in the Northeast and decided to stay with that agent. Ouch! This was a classic guilty-by-association assumption, because Acosta was representing Heinz everywhere in the U.S.—except the Northeast.

Gerber was the second major client MAI had lost over a conflict created by our merger. I imagine it gave somebody at Gerber a little "it's payback time" satisfaction, as well. Gerber had had ties with several of our other recently acquired merger partners, most notably PMI-Eisenhart. As a matter of fact, Gerber had once wanted Acosta to represent its brand in the Southeast, but our fast-evolving relationship with Heinz had preempted that, because among Heinz's products was its own brand of baby foods. Those bits of history had now come full circle, and there wasn't a thing we could do about the situation.

As if that wasn't bad enough, our MAI contingent had been counting on acquiring the Clorox line after the merger, but that wasn't happening yet either. According to Grant LaMontagne, Clorox needed time. In the Northeast, patience was in short supply. Our new partners were seeing key clients leaving, jobs going away, revenues falling off the table, and not enough new clients and products to compensate for the losses. No, these were not happy times in Boston.

Whatever words I might come up with, Jack was all ears. To be sure, he never wavered, not an inch. Jack was savvy enough to anticipate that some short-term pain would precede the long-term gain, yet he still had to be able to counter promptly any "this isn't what we signed on for" grumbling that showed signs of erupting.

I don't recall the exact words of assurance I offered. Essentially, I reaffirmed that we weren't going to let our Northeast operation be hung out to dry. We absolutely would not hold anyone there responsible for consequences Jack had no control over. If the operation wound up running in the red for a time, we'd somehow cover the losses. In the meantime, I further assured him, I'd keep after Clorox. In truth, we had been pressing both Grant LaMontagne and Frank Tataseo to appoint MAI as its Northeast representative even as our merger was being completed. Our campaign had included a dinner meeting in late August 1999 at a Chicago restaurant—a meeting in which, I noted in a confidential memo, "we will have four hours to convince Clorox why we are the best solution in the Northeast." At that meeting, my memo had concluded, "we need to throw a knock-out punch."

It wasn't that our punch had missed that night but that Clorox simply couldn't move as quickly as we had been counting on—our relationship notwithstanding. For one thing, Clorox's existing agency was doing a solid job. Indeed, Clorox might have preferred that we acquire that firm, not MAI. And Clorox still wasn't quite as enthusiastic about national representation as, say, Minute Maid was. So it took a number of additional weeks before my unreasonable persistence finally paid off and convinced Grant and Frank to take what they still call today "a leap of faith." It took an abrupt leap from Jack Laurendeau himself, too.

"We've got our chance to wrap up Clorox!" I told Laurendeau hurriedly over the phone. It had to be after 11 p.m. in the East, but my call couldn't wait, as I was about to explain.

Jack was delighted, of course, even at that hour. Then he heard why I had called so late.

"We have to be in California tomorrow morning, Pacific Time," I said. "But you can make it. I checked the flight schedules."

Jack could make it, barely. He had no more than about five hours to arrange his cross-country flight, pack, and get to Logan Airport for a 6:30 a.m. departure that would get him to Oakland by midmorning—if everything was on schedule. Thankfully, the meeting's excellent results made Jack's return flight less hectic and a lot more satisfying. He was bringing home at last solid evidence to affirm why the merger with Acosta just might be good after all: our second national agreement that gave us the Clorox account in the Northeast.

As Rick Nist headed out west a little more than a year later, another of my colleagues had a different challenge on his hands.

Rick had joined Acosta when we acquired his Pittsburgh agency in 1996. After peering into the future, he had concluded that it was time to give his $14 million regional firm, McClay and Associates, a better future. Upon joining Acosta, Rick had become a vice president, stayed in Pittsburgh for a time, then moved to Cincinnati to head our first national team created to serve Kroger. From day one, Rick had proven himself as both an able guy willing to tackle new challenges and a troubleshooter. More importantly he believed in what we were doing and wanted to be a part of building the best sales force in the industry.

By 2000, there was plenty of trouble with the operations at Kelley-Clarke in the West. The company that had given me fits during our negotiations in late 1998 and early 1999 kept giving us more fits.

Kelley-Clarke associates didn't have a good understanding of how Acosta wanted to run the business. Initially, Kelley-Clarke had operated fairly autonomously as our merger agreement generally suggested. Before long, though, I could see that such freedom was becoming increasingly problematic. As a member of Acosta's executive team, Rick could see it too. Because his oversight responsibilities as the Kroger Team leader had grown to include our West Coast operation, he volunteered to go west and, as we called it, "Acosta-cize" Kelley-Clarke.

I kept Rick's offer in my head and then took him at his word during a break in our February 2000 board meeting on a Tuesday morning in Salt Lake City. "Can you fly to Los Angeles and start looking for a house? I need you there now," I said.

Rick readily agreed and asked how soon. By that Thursday, he and his wife, Pam, were in LA house-hunting, which tells you how badly we needed him out West. That first visit proved to be an omen of what he had volunteered for: Rick wound up swapping his home back East for a home in southern California that was one-third smaller and cost almost three times as much. He got a second glimpse of the challenge at hand the morning he first walked into Kelley-Clarke headquarters. The operation that Charlie Frankowski, Kelley-Clarke's president at the time of the merger, had been directing had been given new responsibilities. Among them was a new national assignment of heading up our strategic channels business, including Wal-Mart. In turn, Kelley-Clarke's LA office had become the headquarters for Acosta's Western Region and consisted of two sites: one where the executives were located, the other where the rest of the associates worked. That communicated elitism to Rick, and he was determined to show quickly that elitism was anathema to Acosta's thinking and way of doing business.

Rick began his first day as the new division president in California by arriving at the executive suite, from which, presumably, he would work. Rick's newly designated office was right next to Charlie's—and also close by the office of an assistant Charlie had decided he wanted Rick to work with.

Rick's reply was cordial but crisp. "Thanks for the suggestions, but I've already decided that I will work out of the other building," he said, "where the work really gets done." Rick also summarily declined Charlie's suggestion for an assistant and immediately selected his own assistant—from among staffers he didn't know at all.

"All I did was look quickly around the room, point to the person who was to be my new assistant, then ask her, 'How would you like to work with me?'" Rick remembers. "I know she was wondering what in the world she had done to deserve this." Rick had selected well, though. Joyce Eckart proved to be, in his words, "an incredible person," who embraced the new work ethic. Joyce was his assistant until he retired from Acosta in March 2009.

It wasn't as if this new order of things needed an affirmation, but one came anyway. Not long after they relocated, Rick and Pam Nist attended an industry meeting in San Francisco. While Rick took care of business, Pam joined a spouses' tour of nearby Napa Valley wine country. En route aboard the tour bus, she couldn't help but overhear a conversation in the seats immediately in front of her. "Don't worry about this new guy from Cincinnati," one voice said. "He won't last out here, and everything will get back to normal."

As graciously as she could, Pam leaned over the seat, introduced herself, and said, "Ladies, we're not going anywhere."

Rick and Pam didn't go anywhere, of course. But many of Kelley-Clarke's existing managerial corps did go. By Rick's count, the turnover among them was about 76 percent. About four months after Rick's arrival, Charlie decided to retire to pursue other interests.

Charlie's departure, and the departure of the others, reflected the contentiousness throught which we had to work at our West Coast headquarters. There was a whole new mind-set and culture to develop. We had to make the operation much, much more efficient. Kelley-Clarke had done its own expanding before we had acquired it, but the end result was a confederation of independent entities—plus a heavy load of debt we wound up having to pay off. On one occasion, I had to call and ask Rick to take some $2 million out of salaries. The operation in the West was that inefficient.

None of this was fun, but it was necessary, as just about any executive who's experienced similar struggles will attest. Early on, it taught me an important lesson: *Get the people out of your organization who won't buy into the new strategy!* I saw some of the excessive opulent behavior firsthand several times, particularly when I attended one meeting the West Coast managerial staff had arranged before Rick arrived. *Opulent* doesn't really describe what Acosta had paid for: fancy hotel overlooking the Pacific Ocean, about the most expensive dinner menu one could select, plus all the requisite extras. Most alarming of all was the attitude the scene suggested.

"I hope you all are enjoying this evening," I had finally said, "because this is the last of these dinners you'll see Acosta host." We simply could not afford this type of spending, I explained candidly and crisply. It didn't make me the most popular guy in the room, but I couldn't have cared less. It would have been apropos if someone had dubbed it the last supper. We sure as hell didn't need to spend money like this; as was slowly becoming painfully obvious, we didn't have it to spend.

It wasn't the best of late-winter Sunday mornings for Jamie Gronowski, who in 2001 was still based in Denver at the firm we had acquired not quite two years earlier. He woke up feeling grumpy and almost sorry for himself, Jamie remembers, in part because he was wrestling with assorted dilemmas unrelated to business. The gray Colorado skies matched his mood. And because it wasn't football season, there wouldn't be a Broncos game later in the day that might help brighten his spirits. My phone call only made Jamie's mood darker.

"How are you?" I asked quietly.

"Actually, kind of rotten," Jamie replied.

"Me, too," I had to admit. Naturally, Jamie asked why. "Because," I continued slowly, "I'm not sure we can make payroll tomorrow."

Nothing signals a business crisis like doubts about being able to pay employees. But I knew I had to give my Denver colleague a heads-up—on a Sunday morning, no less—because I *wasn't sure*. That's how precarious our cash flow situation had become by the early months of 2001, and it was mighty scary.

"Do we have any contingencies or options?" Jamie asked, almost by instinct. A veteran of our business who had run his own very successful operation before it joined Acosta, he knew all too well what we might be facing.

Not really, I told him. We had tapped out our credit lines with the banks, and there were no angels with deep pockets in sight. "It all hangs on what accounts receivable roll in on Monday," I finally said.

Now I was the one eager for any words of wisdom. But there weren't any to be had. All Jamie and I could do was try to identify the clients who were likely to have checks in the mail, do a quick tally, hope that the math worked, and trust that Monday's mail would include the envelopes we were counting on.

The seeds of our cash flow problems that finally came to a head in 2001 had been sown as we had launched "Get National!" but it's far too simplistic to blame expansion as the sole culprit. In truth, our troubles erupted from four distinct sources, none of which is hard to understand:

- Upon the careful inspection that only hindsight provides, several of our acquisitions had turned out to be nowhere near the cash generators we had projected. PMI-Eisenhart and Kelley-Clarke were among them. The speed at which we had expanded in 1998 and 1999 may suggest to some that because we were in a rush, we had become careless. But each of our mergers and acquisitions had received ample due diligence. Moreover, with the exception of Kelley-Clarke, Acosta had purchased only the assets of the businesses, expressly to avoid subsequent surprises that outstanding obligations can spring.

- Long-standing financial obligations to both Acosta's retired owners and the owners of acquired firms who decided to cash out quickly mounted—at a time when we needed more and more cash to run a rapidly growing business. Even though a number of our purchase agreements afforded us some flexibility to stretch out payment schedules based on business conditions, there wasn't nearly enough flexibility to make the kind of difference we needed. In addition, we felt it was paramount to honor our obligations, lest the industry grapevine begin crackling with rumors that Acosta's bold expansion plan was taking down the company; it is a good thing Twitter didn't exist then.

- Losing clients over conflicts created by our mergers dried up some key revenue sources. And although we gained plenty of new clients to replace those we'd lost, we still encountered what I'll call payment gaps. It took even more than the normal four to six weeks between billings and receipt of commissions to get fresh dollars flowing into our revenue streams, yet we still had a payroll to meet twice each month. More than once I muttered, "If we could all just skip our next paychecks...."

- Simply put, we had growing pains. Almost *all* our procedures and systems had to be overhauled: new accounting system, new software for this, new software for that, a bigger and more sophisticated ordering system, vehicle management and maintenance policies, human resources policies, in-house legal counsel … you name it, we needed it, and we needed it yesterday. Now and then we had to replace poorly performing people, too. It all took a toll.

Individually, each of these challenges would have been disruptive but manageable. Arriving practically all at the same time, these challenges compounded one another to produce one unreasonably monstrous and often terrifying trial by fire. Almost a decade later, many of us occasionally still marvel at how we survived those days. We've come to call them "the tough times," and they surely were.

"Tumultuous" might be the best word to describe a good many months of 2001, if not all of them. That's the word Sandy Ramsey has used, and her perspective is well worth respecting. As our corporate controller who joined us in early 1998, Sandy was constantly in the trenches, expertly dealing with all the details. She had her hands full.

Of course, we all did, though. To begin with, the mailman did bring us the checks we so desperately needed on that Monday in 2001. There may not have been a more thankful man in America that day than I. And I'm pleased to say that although we had some close calls, especially in 2001, we never ever missed a payroll, nor any scheduled payment to any former owner. Our cash flow began to improve significantly. In no time at all, however, those achievements would seem insignificant, if not moot, for close behind the mailman was a parade of absolute chaos. As Sandy also says, "You can't make this stuff up."

As you'd expect, our lead creditor, Bank of America, was more than interested in Acosta's situation, but although Bank of America was becoming concerned, our relationship at that point remained generally cordial, and we at Acosta were never flat-out running scared. That's in large part because Sandy always kept the bankers aware of our situation. When finances get lean, she said, that's rule number one, and it helped a great deal.

Aware of our mounting cash flow woes, Bank of America advised us to find private equity. Not eager to tempt fate again, I readily decided to take that advice. Clearly, we didn't need to take on any more debt that we'd have to pay down later. Without too much hassle, and with the help of Bank of America's capital markets group, we prepared the requisite private placement letter and found the deep pockets we needed: a private equity firm out of New York. But in the midst of trying to close that deal came the biggest shot out of the blue.

It would be a stretch to say we were *shocked* by the collapse of Marketing Specialists Corporation as Memorial Day approached in 2001. The preceding February, its executives had approached us about a merger proposal. We had declined to listen. As a practical matter, we couldn't have afforded to consider it, because we had neither cash nor credit to acquire what had become one of three major competitors. More importantly, we had known we'd be buying badly damaged goods.

Marketing Specialists had had its own national strategy, but what had emerged was a national enterprise with pockets of weakness, especially in the West and Midwest. There was no firm central command to speak of at Marketing Specialists, so costs had begun spinning out of control; tales abounded about how the company entertained lavishly in Las Vegas and at the Super Bowl, for instance. Worse, Marketing Specialists had gone public, which had subjected it to all the intense short-term pressures. For a time, its operating partner had been a Wall Street guy who had struck more than a few clients as being a bit arrogant and not terribly knowledgeable about the business.

By late May 2001, it had become common knowledge that Marketing Specialists was hemorrhaging and at the brink, yet its failure still shook our industry to its core. The death spiral began with a default on some loan payments. Marketing Specialists' banks then pulled the revolving credit facility, leaving it unable to fund its end-of-the-month payroll. A Chapter 11 filing quickly followed on the Thursday before Memorial Day, and total financial implosion was soon to come.

Food producers across the land were practically in a panic. Literally overnight, the 5,700 Marketing Specialists employees in 65 locations around the country who had been serving as the producers' de facto sales forces and retail representatives effectively had vanished.

For Acosta, the timing couldn't have been worse. Bob McCarthy, who was in Atlanta that week, recalls his initial reaction being quite succinct: "Oh, shit!" Bob knew Acosta didn't need this kind of mess on the horizon when we still had our own crisis to wrestle with.

My own reaction was a little different; I was carefully pondering how best to respond to a request I had received that same Thursday morning from Marketing Specialists president Jerry Leonard. He had asked me to call him. Before calling Jerry Leonard, I called Drew Prusiecki, who had joined Acosta as our first-ever in-house legal counsel the preceding August. Acting carefully and properly was paramount, given the situation.

"What do you suggest, counselor?" I asked upon telling Drew about what I had called "an interesting phone message."

"Let's call Jerry together and see what he has in mind," Drew said.

When we reached Leonard, he briefed us on the Chapter 11 filing and then said he wanted to come see us—and bring with him his chief operating officer, his chief financial officer, and his bankruptcy attorney. Jerry also made it a point to say he was speaking on behalf of his company's board and legal counsel.

"Jerry, Acosta has no interest in discussing what I think you have in mind," I replied. After some cordial words, we ended our conversation. That was the end of that, I concluded. But the next morning, Friday, Jerry called again. This time his focus had shifted to "protecting the interests of Marketing Specialists' clients," he said, as well as— Drew and I instinctively knew—protecting his company's receivables. They were the only assets Jerry had left to try to protect. His employees were now at liberty to seek employment elsewhere since they had been terminated—and, incidentally, they had not been paid for the preceding two weeks of work. By now, the free-for-all scramble by clients to find new representation had begun. Acosta had a unique and critical role to play, Jerry then stressed, asking us to reconsider our refusal to meet.

After a short huddle, Drew and I agreed to meet in our offices the next morning. After we hung up, I had the enviable task of alerting my key colleagues how they'd be spending at least the beginning of their Memorial Day weekend.

The closer we got to Saturday morning, the more my sentiments echoed Bob McCarthy's earlier reaction. *Just as we're starting to feel like maybe we can see a little daylight at the end of our tunnel of turmoil, we're suddenly having to think seriously about doing an about-face and rushing headlong into the breach of a full-blown train wreck.* How much of a wreck? Marketing Specialists' 2000 annual report showed a net loss of $365.5 million on top of a $21.6 million loss in 1999. The company had negative cash flow and negative working capital, plus an auditor's opinion that expressed doubt about the company's ability to continue. The day after its Chapter 11 filing, Marketing Specialists' stock price fell to a nickel a share. This was just what we didn't need, but here were the company's head honchos knocking on our door again. The reasonable response would have been to ignore the knock or open the door slightly and bark, "Go away!"

But, of course, I wasn't going to be reasonable. I couldn't be.

As rotten as the situation was, we couldn't ignore it. There *was* an obligation to service those clients that trusted and relied on the agency business model. Many of our clients, Nestlé and Heinz among them, relied on Marketing Specialists in other parts of the country, and they needed our help. In addition, there were those 5,700 employees who had been stiffed on their last paychecks; they were good people who needed jobs. And at least once, I couldn't help but recall "The Rule of Three" presentation I'd heard in late 1996, especially references about "falling into the ditch." For better or worse, we had to sit down with Jerry Leonard and company.

"We stick to our guns and stay the course!" Drew was now advising me firmly. "They'll be back."

My legal counsel and I were alone behind closed doors in my office. A critical moment had arrived, and we needed to confer. In our boardroom nearby were the members of the team I had assembled for the hastily arranged Saturday meeting.

What had begun cordially had quickly turned into an exhaustive, occasionally contentious, and, from our perspective, *ludicrous* ordeal. Marketing Specialists' opening proposal had called for Acosta to buy Marketing Specialists' entire book of business, at a suggested price of $300-plus million! We couldn't throw that idea off the table fast enough. The firm had effectively terminated all its employees and was in breach of its contracts with all its vendors. It was out of business!

Talks pretty much went downhill from there, but ever so slowly. It was one hell of a way to spend what turned out to be the entire Memorial Day weekend. We had our executive team on hand, plus the Marketing Specialists executives, plus assorted lawyers, all trying to figure out what to do and ensure that whatever we did was legal and proper. There were more options than you might imagine, too, with most of them focused on Marketing Specialists' outstanding receivables.

By Saturday, we had reached a stalemate over the essence of what we had proposed: Acosta would agree to create a $4 million fund to pay the wages owed to approximately 1,700 Marketing Specialists employees. In return, Acosta would be able to hire these employees, including some covered by noncompete agreements. There were other provisions on the table, too, but they weren't deal breakers.

Marketing Specialists demanded a $10 million fund. No, $4 million, we repeated intently. Soon thereafter, Marketing Specialists threatened to walk out and go back to Dallas, prompting Drew and me to excuse ourselves to confer privately.

"Don't do it!" Drew said again, holding firm as the two of us assessed the situation. "They've got no place else to turn. They have no business. It's gone! They *will* be back."

On board for barely 10 months, Drew Prusiecki was experiencing his first real test and was knowingly putting his career on the line. Bumping up our offer to something closer to the $10 million being demanded was being suggested by some of my colleagues. Also being suggested was that I counter, just to move off $4 million.

As much as I respected those colleagues' views, I went with Drew's opinion. It might have looked unreasonable, but I knew it was the right thing to do. Drew's thinking was sound; it recalled what my Minute Maid pal Larry McWilliams had once told me during a round of golf: "The good people and the good clients will come to you." Let's find out if that's true, I was now saying to myself. Besides, we didn't have the $10 million being demanded; hell, we didn't really have the $4 million, either, but I'd figure something out, I told myself.

"Our final offer is $4 million," I announced to Marketing Specialists once we reconvened. As Jerry Leonard had threatened, he and his team got up from the table and walked away—and then returned the next morning, Sunday. Marketing Specialists had reconsidered, our team was told. The most sleepless night Drew Prusiecki had ever endured hadn't been for naught.

Marketing Specialists' about-face decision kept us working through the remainder of the holiday weekend. The end result of our effort was the agreement that enabled Acosta to immediately hire 1,700 Marketing Specialists employees. Along with covering their two weeks of back pay, we also paid their health care premiums, to keep them current. We wanted these folks to be productive right away. They had endured enough traumas already. They wouldn't be nearly as effective, we reasoned, if they were worrying about medical bills and lapses in coverage.

Over the next 12 months, our lives were to be stressed once again, and all of us worked day and night to service the clients that decided to move to us. The stress also ignited a pretty wild 30-day period. I don't know if *exciting* is the right word, but everyone everywhere rallied to the cause. We had to grab as many fax machines as we could find to process new orders from all of our offices throughout the country. Within a week, we had ordered and received 900 laptop computers from Dell. It was something to behold, and incredibly gratifying. Other than details and legalese, about all that was left was figuring out how to pay for it.

Of all our "tough times" actions, what we crafted proved to be as dramatic as it was effective: a confidential "emergency request" I made to about 30 of our largest clients—and, yes, it was yet another unreasonable plea, but these were unreasonable times. So just like in Houston in 1998, I had nothing to lose. For an interim period, I asked each of these clients, "Would you send Acosta by the middle of each month a 'prepayment' of a portion of the commissions due us, based on our invoices? You could then make whatever adjustments are necessary as part of your final commission payment, to be sent as you normally would."

It certainly bucked industry practices, I allowed, but it would be incredibly helpful. "If you had direct sales forces, you would be paying people twice a month anyway," my reasoning proceeded. "For now, I need you to treat Acosta as you would your full-time employees."

Because the request had been a result of the Marketing Specialists affair, we first reached out to its former clients who also were our clients. A dozen or so of them came to our rescue and complied with our request. Among them was Ken's Salad Dressing. Its president, my former colleague John Pritchard, really went to bat for me. In his eyes, another of my unreasonable requests amounted to receiving advances against our commissions—no big deal, really, and a smart move, he said.

Just as I had hoped—and had counted on in preparing my appeal —John and others grasped how assisting Acosta was in their best interests. They were simply helping a key partner weather "tough times." Surely, adjusting accounts payables procedures was a piece of cake compared with facing whatever consequences might befall them should Acosta run into more severe difficulties.

Enough of our clients agreed, thank heavens. Chalk up another achievement that being unreasonable can bring. In this instance, though, it also brought an annoying epilogue to *L'affaire de Marketing Specialists*. About the time we thought the mess was at last behind us, we still got sued ... for "interference," some lawyer claimed. I still claim we had grounds to counter. "Just who interfered with whom?" we had reason to ask. But we didn't counter; we finally settled the damn thing some five years later. No good deed goes unpunished, I guess.

Meanwhile, we still had the private equity deal with the private equity firm from New York to close, but after monitoring how we spent Memorial Day weekend, the firm was getting cold feet and wanted to renegotiate the tentative agreement we had struck. We tried to convince the firm that we could handle all this turmoil, but these New Yorkers just did not want to be part of it.

We weren't about to mess around haggling over revised terms or getting dragged into still more *negotiations*. We both just sat still, let the tentative deal lapse, and went our separate ways.

Today, this private equity firm will candidly admit its blunder. For that matter, so will a Jacksonville private investor. This investor actually did make a modest investment, but soon he, too, got antsy and wanted his money back. OK, we said—a reply this investor now sorely regrets. Had he hung in there, he would have reaped such a multi-fold return on his investment that even the word *bonanza* would have been inadequate to describe it.

But we had no reason to gloat at the time, because we found we still were a long way from being out of the woods. Indeed, the light seemed further away and growing dimmer. With the private equity deal gone sour, Bank of America was becoming increasingly tough. For one thing, Bank of America felt it was entitled to "finder's fees" despite the fact that what it had found had since disappeared. *Fees for what?* we demanded. So now we were in another crunch with Bank of America that was getting testier by the day.

Why I then needed to leave town I don't recall. What I do recall is how positively splendid it was to wind up on a flight seated next to a guy from GE Capital! You bet we chatted—casually at first, and then far more seriously. Without a whisper to the Bank of America folks, we were soon engineering a deal to have GE Capital assist us in our continuing search for cash.

You can imagine Bank of America's reaction to learning of Acosta's intent to terminate our relationship to retain GE Capital. Furious? Yes, indeed, and then some. Bank of America exerted just about every pressure and pulled every legal lever it could find to thwart us. The jousting that ensued was painful and pricey, but we managed to pull it off anyway.

Had enough of our "tough times"? Sorry, but there's more. Not every dilemma was as dramatic as cash flow crises, coping with a competitor's demise, or the soap opera-like odyssey to find an equity investor. Even so, we couldn't get very far without resolving even the less-dramatic dilemmas. Besides, as often as not, we had to deal with these tasks at the *same time* we were in crisis mode.

Our old accounting system, for instance, was woefully ill equipped to handle our new volume of business; you could almost say it was something molded out of QuickBooks. So we began the Request For Proposal process to replace it with a much more sophisticated product. We closed on a deal with Oracle and then began the painful process of implementation.

Ordering systems became another nightmare. We had to expand, integrate, and update all at the same time—without the technological wizardry we take for granted today. Both PMI and Kelley-Clarke, for instance, had older, less efficient systems than did Acosta; a few of my Acosta colleagues might say my description is charitable. Not only did we have to bring those systems up to snuff, we also had to integrate them into Acosta's system, which needed overhauling itself.

In fact, if it had been up to Sandy Ramsey, we might have walked away from the Kelley-Clarke deal altogether. Deeply involved in the due diligence stage of all acquisitions, she was forever finding nettlesome problems we had to solve. For instance, Kelley-Clarke had something like 30 bank accounts all over the place. And it had scores of partners who departed after we merged in July 1999, and they had to be paid for their shares of the old company.

"Oh, by the way" annoyances is what Sandy started calling the rash of nettlesome chores we confronted, because that's what she often first said in bringing them to my attention. It got to the point that Sandy all but became the reputed Acosta "doomsday naysayer," yet that was part of her job, and she performed admirably throughout all our ordeals. Sandy still does, too, as Acosta's senior vice president of finance and its treasurer.

There was something else Sandy recommended we address: our

very corporate structure. Almost from the moment we united with PMI, Acosta had essentially grown out of the legal structure we had had in place for so long. In many respects, the restructure was a routine chore. But in the midst of everything else we had to tackle in the trenches, it became still one more pressing headache.

Before we could create the appropriate corporate structure, though, we first had to conduct a formal audit—another routine task, one would think, and normally, yes, but not when you're mushrooming from a $140 million company into a $480 million company in 15 months and having to restate two or three years' worth of operations of both your own firm and those of your new partners.

The first firm we hired to conduct the audit simply couldn't get it done. The situation was a matter of the firm's partners promising more than they could deliver. The second time around was more successful, but we barely had time to notice; by the audit's completion, we had become embroiled in too many other problems.

Forever looking for capabilities to make us better and stronger, in 2000, we launched a logistics subsidiary we christened Enable. Our overall goal was creating a better and faster way to get smaller orders of goods from clients to retail customers. Because these orders were what truckers call partial loads, their deliveries often were delayed. We thought we had a nifty solution, especially because Enable's business plan included harnessing the skyrocketing capabilities of the World Wide Web.

Well, we thought wrong. Our new venture got ample resources, time, and enthusiasm—maybe too much. Two or three of our ranking executives, including Mike Diaz, devoted most of their waking hours to Enable. It didn't matter. The subsidiary proved to be far too capital intensive, especially as troubles mounted later that year and in 2001. And although we had envisioned our new idea as a service that would complement our core business and assist both clients and customers, the clients and customers perceived Enable almost as a competitor and an intrusion.

Comparatively speaking, Enable is barely a footnote of Acosta's history. It serves as a reminder that even the best of organizations isn't immune to missteps. We allowed ourselves to be distracted at a time when we couldn't afford to be and to appropriate dollars that would have been far better spent elsewhere. Don't ask me how much. I don't like to think about it.

At least the Enable situation didn't cost us our senses of humor. By the time we pulled the plug, we'd given our subsidiary a new name. What we had once called Enable we now called Unable.

Recounting these ordeals is apt to startle the majority of people familiar with Acosta, and that's the wonder of it all. We always performed, no matter what. The lion's share of our people remained focused on Acosta's core business and delivered as promised to clients and customers. That's why we always were able to put our best foot forward and keep all the turmoil pretty much out of sight and behind the closed doors of a handful of executive offices.

If someone had wanted to snoop around and dig deep enough, no doubt he could have uncovered evidence of our trials, tribulations, and close calls. Greg Delaney still likes to tease us about the mess he found upon arriving in 2002 to become our chief financial officer—a mess he helped clean up in a hurry, too. A few other veteran colleagues and confidants might liken us to "the dog that caught the car it was chasing" as we coped with the rapid growth that "Get National!" brought. Bonuses were meager now and then, too, or not paid at all, such as in late 2000 and into 2001.

We couldn't avoid layoffs, either—although a good portion of them resulted from duplication of services the mergers created. Briefly in early 1999, Acosta had three chief financial officers—one in Jacksonville, a second in Chicago, and a third in St. Louis—all because of sorting out the union with PMI-Eisenhart.

All things considered, however, Acosta kept humming along. We made the most of new technologies that appeared, added expertise as we needed, and weren't shy about acting on new opportunities—no matter what crisis might have been raging down the hall. If we lost clients along the way—and we did—we replaced them with many more new clients.

There is a mighty fine line between extreme success and failure, and we tiptoed along that line for quite a while, longer than I expected. But with every step, we kept our sights on our ultimate goal. The vision never left us. "We can make it!" was our mind-set each and every day. No matter what was being thrown at us, Bob McCarthy likes to say, we always had some version of a Def-Con 4 plan to wield.

We always had our senses of humor, too, and could keep crises in perspective. I don't remember where we stood on negotiations with Marketing Specialists on Memorial Day, for instance, but I still had lots of barbecue brought in for lunch from the best barbecue purveyor in Jacksonville: "Bono's BBQ, a great Southern tradition!" I declared.

An old rule of thumb holds that many ventures collapse just as they're on the verge of success, because people simply give up. We weren't about to give up. We never stopped believing, nor did our people in the trenches. We never stopped being unreasonable.

For me, the tough times really were no different than my days behind the plate with my baseball team back in New Hampshire, throwing out base stealers with my supposedly weak arm; no different than going eyeball-to-eyeball with muscle-bound, football-playing fraternity brothers who thought they were above the rules. I never blinked then, and I never blinked in 2001.

My longtime Ponte Vedra Beach pal Ernie Bono all but swears that Acosta was blessed with divine intervention. Nothing else explains how we endured the tough times, Ernie insists. My own Catholic faith tells me that Ernie is right; God had to be watching over us during these tough times. How else could have we prevailed?

What I know for certain is that throughout our ordeals, I also was blessed with incomparable earthly support from my Acosta associates. These tough times proved to all of us just how important it is to believe in your vision and to never lose faith in each other. People working together by putting their hearts and minds together can indeed accomplish just about anything they set out to achieve. Acosta is proof of that.

Food for Thought

It is not the critic who counts; not the man who points out how the strong man stumbles, or where the doer of deeds could have done them better. The credit belongs to the man who is actually in the arena, whose face is marred by dust and sweat and blood; who strives valiantly; who errs, who comes short again and again, because there is no effort without error and shortcoming; but who does actually strive to do the deeds; who knows the great enthusiasms, the great devotions; who spends himself in a worthy cause; who at the best knows in the end the triumph of high achievement, and who at the worst, if he fails, at least fails while daring greatly, so that his place shall never be with those cold and timid souls who neither know victory nor defeat.

— *Theodore Roosevelt*

Step 9

Get the Culture Right!

Nothing is more important to uniting your people.

If I ever asked Ed Luccione what motivated him to say what he said during our inaugural September 1999 management meeting in Chicago, I forgot what he told me. But I'll never forget Ed's observation. It was classic: "I feel like I'm part of an Italian cycling team," he quipped, with just the right dash of disdain.

Ed looked like part of an Italian cycling team, too. Then again, so did everyone else in the room, thanks to the rash of inscriptions stitched on the sleeves and front pockets of the 200 golf shirts we had purchased for the occasion. The motivational wrinkle that provoked Ed's comment proved to be money well spent. It's just that the wonderfully profound consequences beginning to unfold weren't the ones any of us anticipated.

With our national expansion essentially completed, we brought our executive teams, managers, and owners to Chicago for our first companywide meeting. As the summer of 1999 faded, it was an ideal way to wrap up our "Get National!" campaign: convene to not only celebrate our achievement and enjoy a firsthand glimpse of the organization we created but also to let new colleagues get better acquainted with each other, ignite some esprit de corps, then march forward as the proud, unified organization we had become.

Proud? Yes, indeed. But *unified*? Well, not exactly. Not yet. Perhaps you've noticed that my recounting of this particular episode has so far avoided any mention of our unified organization's name. It's purely intentional. Upon gazing at all the logos adorning the shirts on display in Chicago that September afternoon, one could have concluded that we weren't quite sure ourselves what our unified organization's name was, although our legal name was Acosta/PMI. Not to offend anyone, we had had all the logos stitched onto our shirts.

Ed's own gaze, for example, might well have first focused on "MAI Companies" because the Mid-Atlantic operation he was directing from

Philadelphia had been part of our Northeast merger partner. But colleagues from our operation in the Midwest might have instead first gazed upon "PMI," which had been Acosta's first major merger partner. And colleagues from the West Coast would instinctively have searched for "Kelley-Clarke." And as I looked around, my own eyes were naturally first drawn to "Acosta" itself.

That the shirts were all black made Ed's Italian cycling team quip ever more appropriate, I had to admit with a slight smile. More importantly, there soon was to be a method to Ed's bit of mischievous but masterful madness. "If we're now one company," Luccione continued, *"then why don't we act like it? Why don't we start with one name?"*

Whether this respected elder statesman of our business was posing a question or presenting a recommendation, it was a damn good one. So damn good that we actually began pondering it several months earlier, notwithstanding what the black shirts suggested.

One national sales and marketing company needed one name; that was a no-brainer. But *what* name? There was the rub. As I was to write in a letter to all of our associates a few weeks thereafter, there was "equity, tradition and strength" in the names of each of the four companies that "Get National!" united, and loyalty, too. So despite far too many hours of discussion and analysis with peers Bob McCarthy, Jack Laurendeau, and Charlie Frankowski—plus others—we still had not decided what to call ourselves going forward.

But with our September meeting fast approaching, we had to settle on something. Out of both raw necessity and a sense of respect for the "equity, tradition and strength" of the four names—as well as lingering loyalties—we settled on having the golf shirts we all donned in Chicago feature *all* the logos of the merger partners. It was indicative of the mind-sets of those assembled, because throughout the meeting, each of the four companies' representatives sat pretty much as blocs. There had been little mingling.

That hadn't escaped Ed Luccione's attention, either, and it was all the more reason for him to goad us to decisive action. Before we adjourned our September meeting in Chicago, we announced that, henceforth, our unified organization would be Acosta. It was the logical choice, Jack kept stressing as the four of us huddled yet again during a break in the agenda. "And you've been the guy who's led the charge," Jack added forcefully, "so it's got to be Acosta." Charlie and Bob agreed, and that was that.

In hindsight, our foot-dragging paid a pair of dividends. First, we could show our assembled company leaders that we could respond to a suggestion and act quickly. Second, and more importantly, I couldn't have orchestrated a better burst of momentum to help kick-start a *process* to announce our new corporate name. To me, it was a very important challenge we had to tackle. Ensuring that what stood behind the Acosta name and logo was, in fact as well as fancy, one proud and unified organization. The unifier was to be the culture of the *new* Acosta.

Ed Luccione's comments—totally unexpected and unscripted— really helped us roll up our sleeves and tackle the critical process of defining, articulating, and reinforcing just what Acosta was to be as a company, what its values would be, and how it would behave. Culture is really unfinished business, which is why we deem it a *process*, rather than a *project* or *campaign*. Throughout our company, we're still work-ing as hard today on nurturing culture as we did when we began the creative process a decade ago.

Notably, the action Ed urged us to embrace was one that we kept postponing almost from the moment we launched "Get National!" At some point when Del Dallas and I met with Bob McCarthy and Jim Eisenhart in Tampa in the spring of 1998, someone asked, "What shall we call ourselves?" Del had immediately replied, "Acosta!" But I could see then that didn't sit well with Bob, who was justifiably proud of what PMI-Eisenhart represented, so it didn't sit well with me either. At the time, I gave little thought to names anyway. I just wanted our first deal done. Once it was done, we officially christened ourselves "Acosta/PMI," but as other deals followed, that name became ever more outdated. "No big deal," we kept saying; we can wrestle with a name later.

Yet implicit in Ed's observation in Chicago was a plea to do more than adopt a name, and it proved to be serendipitous. A key theme of my closing remarks to my colleagues that same afternoon was "the power of one." Ed provided me with the ideal introduction to the ideas I wanted to share about our company's culture.

I put tons of thought and energy into my words. For one thing, culture wasn't something to be left to chance. Here was my chance to present my vision of what the power of one could be. You never have a second chance to make a good first impression, so I didn't dare squander it. I wanted to send our Acosta team out the door bursting with the fiery enthusiasm of an NFL team about to kick off a Super Bowl.

Now that we knew who we were and had "created the best-selling system in the United States," I began, it was time to "create future possibilities that we cannot yet imagine." The cornerstone of Acosta's future was not people per se, I stressed, but the *right* people armed to the teeth with optimism.

"Optimism is nothing more than confidence in oneself and in the future. Optimism is faith in action. Everything is going to be OK. I may not know exactly how, but everything is going to work out just fine. It means looking for the good side of a situation or of people," I continued, warming to the opportunity at hand. "Optimistic people can and do make the difference, and that's why optimistic people are the right people and the right people are our most important asset."

Each of us in the room is a unique individual, I then submitted. Our uniqueness was an important attribute and something we dared not take for granted. Next, I recounted some age-old advice: "Watch your thoughts; they become words. Watch your words; they become actions. Watch your actions; they become habits. Watch your habits; they become character. Watch your character; it becomes your destiny."

In serving clients, customers, and each other, we could choose to be positive or negative. The choice was obvious, I insisted. Being positive would enable us to make a difference uniquely. As the saying goes, if we weren't part of the solution, we were part of the problem.

Next, I challenged my colleagues with the ideas of two British literary luminaries. First was Robert Louis Stevenson, who said, "The person you are today and the person you are capable of becoming is the only reason for your existence." Second was George Bernard Shaw, who, when asked while on his deathbed who he might like to be if he could return to life, replied, "the George Bernard Shaw I could have been but was not." (I did not relate what's now my favorite Shaw observation, that all progress comes from unreasonable people.)

I wanted to ignite what was possible in each one of us that day. I reminded everyone that the greatest tragedy in life is not death but rather "the death of what is inside of us while we are still alive." My intent here was to urge everyone to use his or her own power of one to always give his or her very best effort; never leave anything on the table, so to speak. A thoroughbred that runs just a second or two faster in a race than other horses is worth millions more, I reminded everyone.

I also stressed how important it was to always have a sense of humor, because it helps one remain optimistic and keep things in perspective. "I've met very few successful people in life who didn't have a good sense of humor," I said. By the same token, I had seen precious little achieved by pessimists consumed by negativity, I continued. In making that point, I all but commanded my assembled colleagues to avoid pessimists at all costs. "You see, most people have it backwards," I explained. "They think, 'If I achieve something, then I will feel important, then I will be worthwhile.' That's backwards! The people in this room say, 'I'm important. I'm worthwhile. I have special gifts and talents that are unique to me, that can make a difference. Now, *watch* me achieve!' And that's what makes all of us in this room different!" I emphasized, reaffirming my focus once again. "That's why we achieved the success we enjoyed in the past, and that's why we will continue to grow and lead the industry and achieve great things together."

Day in, day out, I observed, we can find whatever it is we're seeking. If we choose to look for negatives like mediocrity, cynicism, pessimism, bitterness, prejudice, and resentment, "then we are going to have a good day," I noted, "because there is a lot of that out there. On the other hand, if we are looking for generosity, patience, kindness, understanding, love and—most importantly—optimism, we are going to have a *great* day! Because that's all out there, too! The decision is totally up to each one of us."

Acosta and its associates were poised to make a significant difference, I said in closing. One company filled with the right kind of motivated, optimistic people did indeed have an unlimited future. "It is our responsibility as leaders," I reminded, "to motivate and inspire everyone that they *can* and *do* make a significant difference in our future success by positively applying their special gifts and talents."

Executive Leadership 101 instructs that employees take their cues from the guys at the top. That's why I worked so hard on the send-off thoughts I shared with my colleagues that day in Chicago and why I have reprinted a portion of them here. As we were off and running as the country's first national sales and marketing company, I wanted everyone to depart knowing exactly what kind of culture I thought Acosta ought to create. Do I think my words were influential? I believe they were! I'd contradict myself if I didn't. But as you read on about Acosta's culture, you can judge for yourself.

As leadership guru Stephen Covey likes to urge, let's start with the end in mind. Acosta's culture looks toward a destination that hasn't changed since we established it in 1999 and shouldn't ever change, really, because we're on an unending journey:

"Positively, The Best Sales, Marketing and Service Solution Globally."

Likewise, the same seven core values that we identified a decade ago to guide us along our journey remain in place as the foundation of our company's business practices:

People: People are our most important asset.
- We show dignity and respect to all people.
- We embrace diversity.
- We exhibit leadership with humility.
- We listen to, encourage, and support each other.
- We cultivate an environment that attracts, develops, and retains the very best.

Integrity: We exemplify the highest degree of ethical behavior.
- We practice open, accurate, and timely communication.
- We are honest and trustworthy.
- We honor all commitments to our associates, clients, customers, and shareholders.
- We uphold and operate within the letter and spirit of the law.
- We protect our reputation.

Results: We have the passion, pride, and commitment to succeed.
- We operate with a sense of urgency.
- We relentlessly pursue our objectives.
- We reward excellence and superior results.
- We are all accountable for the bottom line.
- We take ownership in providing solutions.

Trust: We are in the business of building trusting relationships.
- We are passionate about honesty.
- We speak our minds with sincerity.
- We are confident in our abilities.

- We do what we say we will do.
- We do what is right.

Teamwork: *We believe in the power of one.*
- We use a collaborative process.
- We do what is best for the total company.
- We practice systematic problem solving.
- We engage cross-functional resources.
- We give recognition to others and celebrate success.

Innovation: *As change is always present, we will progress through a combination of creativity, common sense, and visionary leadership.*
- We are empowered to demonstrate initiative and take appropriate risks.
- We continually strive to exceed our previous performance.
- We learn and improve from our successes and failures.
- We strive for simplification in business processes.
- We expect continuous learning and education.

Balance: *We support the personal and professional development of our associates.*
- We keep a perspective on what is important in life.
- We demonstrate good community and corporate citizenship.
- We cherish a good sense of humor and an optimistic attitude.
- We encourage a caring and enjoyable atmosphere in the workplace.
- We honor the sanctity of "family" in our lives.

The culture that our destination and core values helped create is evident in our success and continued growth. Because we made it important, we did become the one company we all envisioned.

Here's why I can attest to it. No matter how many Acosta offices you visit, you're apt to walk away with the same conclusion that Jamie Gronowski drew after visiting some 30 offices in 2008: "They're essentially all the same," he declared. "The faces and the personalities differ, of course, but there's still the same atmosphere, the same pace, and the same optimistic attitudes."

Just a coincidence? Hardly. This reality reflects the unifying effect that culture can have and how dramatically culture contributes to a consistent, effective, smooth-running and fast-reacting operation. Acosta's culture is not just words on paper but a real lifestyle. It's why I shake my head at the large number of companies that still dismiss culture as fluff—especially when times are tough—and give it only brief lip-service attention. In those companies, after the initial fanfare and slogans, the consistent support that a culture needs withers away, and it's back to business as usual: it's simply unreasonable to keep up the emphasis because it's similarly unreasonable to expect *every* employee to embrace a company's culture.

Maybe so, but I expect employees to embrace the culture anyway. I was—and am still—as unreasonable about expecting the enduring commitment by all of our people as I had been about molding one national company. Indeed, this very expectation itself is part of Acosta's culture. I've never settled for anything less, for I know from our own experiences in Jacksonville how important it is for associates to embrace a culture.

Not long after Acosta began expanding in Florida and then into the Southeast in the late 1970s, we coined a new phrase. Once we completed an acquisition, we began to "Acosta-cize" it. That meant more than doing the usual nuts-and-bolts tasks of adding employees to payroll and a health care plan, incorporating fresh revenues and costs onto a profit-and-loss statement, and sending copies of procedures to a new location and legal filings to a requisite secretary of state office. "Acosta-cize" also reflected how we conducted ourselves as a company, the high standards we set, the optimism we always tried to express, and the *passion* we felt for serving our clients and customers. It was about living the core values in everything we did.

It was critically important for every new member of our company's expanding family to embrace all that "Acosta-cize" came to mean. Their doing so is what drove our success and won their commitments, because there's never been an acquisition anywhere at any time that hasn't ignited at least some discomforting change—lots of it, as often as not.

Assuming that we could "Acosta-cize" the giant enterprise that our "Get National!" strategy created as we always had was out of the question, however, and foolhardy. Our company was now simply too big and vastly more diverse. To try to Acosta-cize it would have been almost like the tail wagging the dog. Far worse, our new colleagues might well perceive us as an elitist, insensitive, and arrogant bunch of brutes from Florida ruthlessly trampling on what had been successful businesses themselves. That kind of perception would breed only disunity and perhaps mutiny.

Those glimpses, plus my own grasp of organizational dynamics, told me that what we finished building in 1999 could fall apart in a heartbeat if we didn't integrate the associates of the newly acquired companies into Acosta just as fast as we possibly could. Just the sheer numbers of them, some 10,000, suggested that, were we to dawdle, the old attitudes and procedures to which people were accustomed could become entrenched, to the point that raw inertia and foot-dragging would wreck anything we might try to instill.

As I saw it, culture-building was anything but fluff; it was strictly business. Being the best-selling system in the U.S. and providing top-tier excellence in every market, as we promised, depended on harnessing all the advantages that our new economies of scale portended. That harnessing required unity and a common sense of purpose, which only a single culture could mold.

Why is the culture of an organization so vitally important? It is important because the culture becomes the DNA of the organization. Anthropologists use the concept of organizational culture to describe how members of groups understand their world and their place in it. It is best conceived as the patterns of actions, the words, the beliefs, and the behaviors that shape what is at the very core of the organization. The culture shapes the employee experience, which impacts the customer experience, the business partnerships, and, ultimately, the success or failure of an organization.

There was another reason for fast action for defining the culture. Although Acosta's national expansion had been the first one out of the gate, it wasn't the only such expansion. Nor was our business model the only one on display. The organizational structures that our primary competitors stitched together are best described as alliances or confederations, with not as much central control and more autonomy exercised by its respective members. They each were different enough from Acosta's operating structure to invite comparisons and, in turn, more than casual scrutiny by both grocery manufacturers and supermarket chains.

Naturally, I felt strongly that our model was infinitely better.

You wouldn't expect otherwise. I couldn't have flatly predicted Marketing Specialists' meltdown then, but I saw lots of flaws in what our competitors built. Without common practices and some central direction, economies of scale are never achieved. Though our expansion had brought us ample respect, a lot of people remained curious about what we had built, whether we could control it effectively, and what our long-term viability would be.

"It looked almost like some kind of Roman empire, that's how huge it appeared, especially given its creation in 15 months," quips Vic Del Regno, MAI's former CEO. But how Acosta's appearance was being described didn't bother me all that much. In a way, it was flattering. My sole concern was about how our greatly enlarged company *performed*. Acosta had to be judged as the unquestioned industry leader in every respect—not just as the first national sales and marketing company but also as the best! I was flatly unreasonable about that.

All things considered, we had to get busy and start acting just as Ed Luccione wisely suggested in Chicago: like one company. Fortunately, the wheels already had begun turning toward that end.

Given our desire for speedy results and lightning-quick decisions, you're apt to snicker at how we began to identify both our destination and our values: with a committee—lots of them, actually.

Of course I've read, heard, and seen all the disparaging words that *committee* provokes—snoring men with gaping mouths, women looking bored to tears, puppies sleeping, and such. In this situation, though, we had no option but to form our Culture Committee, plus 15 supporting regional committees. Truth be told, I also assembled other committees in 1999 to help build unity within other functions.

I formed these other committees because, as had become evident at our Chicago meeting, Acosta was now a veritable melting pot of firms from all over the country. By the third quarter of 1999, the original Jacksonville-based Acosta negotiated, at minimum, 75 mergers and expansions dating back to the late 1970s. We also opened many new offices in distant cities. Each of the companies that joined us during our national expansion—principally PMI-Eisenhart, Kelley-Clarke, and MAI, and subsequently Luke Soules—were themselves all products of assorted mergers and expansions. All told, the number of individual organizations represented at our gathering in Chicago could have been as high as 200 or more! As best we could, we needed to ensure that the

scores of ideas, attitudes, work habits, perceptions, and mind-sets per-
colating within our melting pot would get due consideration in some
way.

The Culture Committee and the structure around it proved to be
the quintessential tool. Looking back, I cannot imagine any other way
we might have collected and assessed the wealth of information we
gathered. It's fair to describe it as a grassroots effort. Notably, the Culture Committee remains in place today and continues to serve Acosta
well. Officially, the Culture Committee came to life on July 19, 1999,
when I announced its formation. The Kelley-Clarke acquisition had
closed by then, and we already were well along in the due diligence
phase of our MAI acquisition, which essentially made us a national
organization. So the timing was right. The committee's standing members each represented one of Acosta's four major regions:

- Greg McDonald represented the Central region, the old PMI,
  and would become our national chairperson.
- Brian Baldwin represented the Western region, the old Kelley-
  Clarke.
- Mark Henney represented the Northeast region, the old MAI.
- Jack Parker represented the Southeast region, the former
  regional Acosta.

Notice the words *old* and *former* in the four preceding points; it's
by design. We used the words in the announcement of the committee's
formation, to help drive home our quest for a *new* culture. I served as a
member of the Culture Committee, too, to emphasize my personal
commitment to the culture-building process and to represent Acosta's
executive committee. Besides, it was a process I wanted to be directly
involved in, and I was curious to see just what would unfold.

Creating Acosta's culture was a grassroots effort in every respect.
The Culture Committee itself convened for three face-to-face meetings in different locales and conducted numerous conference calls for
the better part of a year. And I couldn't even guess the number of individual conversations and email messages. In addition, once the committee and its mission gained momentum, our four members
representing regions established regional committees and convened
more meetings to generate and react to all the ideas, collect feedback,
and "check the pulse" of the organization along the way. In all, there

were 40 such meetings devoted to our culture. They brought 50 more Acosta associates into the process and represented 400 man hours of invested time. Those are the hours we could count; there likely were many more hours of informal conversations, too, before a final presentation was made to the board of directors on September 11, 2000.

More preparation followed before we finally introduced our culture to the entire company during the first two weeks of December 2000. That included a three-day conference of all committee members in November in Chicago, just to make sure we had our ducks in a row. Our participants represented geographical areas and various company functions, a veritable cross-section of the new Acosta: business managers from various locales and offices, as well as members of staff departments like human resources and administration. There were representatives from senior management executives, too. That was a must. To the degree possible, we wanted associates in every nook and cranny of our company feeling like they were involved and able to make a contribution. I was thrilled to see so many people involved. Then again, it's part of my nature, I guess.

"Chartrand can *never* do it alone," Jamie Gronowski likes to mutter with a teasing grin. "He always has to have help, and he knows it." I plead guilty as charged. But why not get help, especially for this process? Hell, the very foundation of the national expansion strategy we'd just bet the farm on had been to align with the very best agencies led and staffed by the very best people in our industry. We'd have been fools *not* to solicit their ideas and consider carefully all that was suggested.

There were scores of ideas and suggestions to consider—enough that we could chart a true work stream of activities. Creating Acosta's new culture was a challenge because we needed to create three parts:

1. A new destination or vision for the *new* Acosta;
2. A core list of values and operating principles; and
3. Strategies and tactics to support, nurture, and reinforce Acosta's culture so it would be forever viable and a guiding beacon to all employees, including Acosta's executive corps.

To begin, I challenged the Culture Committee with the question "If we were starting from scratch, what kind of company would we want to create?" We were about to declare what Acosta stood for, I said, and what we embodied was absolutely critical to the organization's long-term success. "It's what we will live every day, and what we stand for."

The words helped us frame both our destination, as we defined our overriding objective, and the core values that should guide our journey. Job one was to define *culture* itself, to be absolutely certain that everyone involved knew exactly what we were trying to create and — equally important—that everyone had a single, consistent definition of what we created after we started pushing the culture throughout the company. That was essential.

We defined *culture* as simply "a powerful, persuasive influence on human behavior" and started from the sound premise that a culture of some kind is woven within every company, by design or by default. Culture is apparent in the ways people behave in and outside the office; some ways are acceptable, others are not. Behavior that appears repeatedly demonstrates people's values, and among these repeated behaviors, some actions are dominant.

Along with actions and behavior, we paid particular attention to those individuals whom others admired; accordingly, we dubbed these associates "heroes" and made it a point to examine in detail their behaviors and the values they demonstrated. We further concluded that behaviors rarely change without there first being a change in underlying assumptions, beliefs, values, and attitudes.

The Culture Committee's activities also included several other actions:

- Examining the cultures that already existed in specific regions of the company. We relied on surveys, general observation, anecdotal data, and the specific opinions of various Acosta associates. We found numerous common threads throughout our four regions, too. That was encouraging, for it affirmed that, by and large, the expansion partners we selected were sound choices.

- Performing a tried-and-true SWOT analysis that focused not on Acosta but on creating Acosta's new culture itself—the strengths, weaknesses, opportunities, and threats. Among the strengths, for example, was a culture's value as a recruiting tool and the competitive difference it gave us. Not taking the culture seriously and failing to reinforce it at every opportunity were among the weaknesses. Shaping behaviors that ensure consistent results was one of three opportunities, and not becoming passionate about culture and treating culture as a project were two threats.

- Gathering a wealth of information. The Culture Committee tapped a variety of sources, including consulting firms like the Partnering Group and Answerthink (since renamed the Hackett Group), the Food Market Institute, articles from *Harvard Business Review* and *Fortune*, and other pertinent articles members could find. Among the articles was an essay on managing by values by Ken Blanchard, author of *The One-Minute Manager*, and one by Tom Peters on making work fun.

- Studying other companies. In the spirit of benchmarking that U.S. business embraced beginning in the mid 1980s, the committee examined companies' best practices such as Disney's branding prowess; Nordstrom and FedEx customer service practices; Southwest Airlines, which stood as the number one employee-rated company; Clorox's ability to transform a culture; Meijer's culture, which declared that supporting and developing employees are its management's first responsibility; Minute Maid's stressing of team in everything it does; and Sargento's overall excellence.

This study of other companies' best practices unearthed a best practice that we expressly embraced, what we called "branding the destination" that our culture seeks to reach. It's best illustrated by citing some examples:

The Coca-Cola Company strives "to put our product within arm's reach of desire." Publix envisions its supermarkets being "where shopping and working are a pleasure." Ritz Carlton is staffed by "ladies and gentlemen serving ladies and gentlemen." Subway succeeds on the strength of its "sandwich artists."

Our Culture Committee used these and similar statements as templates to help it articulate the destination that Acosta's culture should seek—"Positively, The Best Sales, Marketing and Service Solution Globally." Our destination statement became our branding declaration. Some organizations define this as their "vision," but the objective is the same. The overarching goal that gets you up in the morning to forever strive, but never quite achieve; the gleam of light that's always in the sky just over the hill, never seen but always present, and always worth pursuing. This branding effort certainly was in keeping with our business, and we thought it would help promote our new culture in its entirety.

Once our destination was firmly in place, we focused on identifying and articulating what became our seven core values that were to guide our operations and personal conduct. Even though I am not giving that phase of our process a lot of attention here, we put as much time and effort into identifying our core values as we had identifying and shaping Acosta's destination. Culture Committee Chair Greg McDonald puts it best: "What were the values and ideals for which we'd fall on our swords?"

Greg's is a strong statement, but such was our devotion to our new culture. I don't recall how much we spent promoting the culture with all the pencils, mouse pads, posters, and such, but we thought it was worth every dime. And I've lost track of the number of hours I spent videotaping comments about culture. It was a full-blown internal marketing program of its own, all to make the culture "mainstream Acosta."

Just to show you how serious we were, we put together a Culture Toolbox to help ensure the success of what we rolled out in a two-week period beginning in early December 2000. Prepared for those who would present Acosta's new culture to their peers in a series of "town hall meetings" in our offices all over the country, the toolbox was an inch-plus-thick manual bound in a hardcover three-ring binder. It was divided into 12 (count 'em!) distinct tabbed sections such as defining the culture, cultivating the culture, communicating the culture, walking the talk, and marching to the beat of our values and principles; plus ways to share results and celebrate success. We tried to leave no stone unturned, including even suggested meeting agendas.

At the back of the toolbox, notably, were provided the names of 22 "cultural ambassadors," along with their photos, telephone numbers, and email addresses. The four members of the Culture Committee were among the ambassadors, but so were other associates of various ranks representing every region of the country.

There were smiles tucked in the toolbox, too, such as a statement by Woodrow Wilson: "If you want to make enemies, try to change something." And there was a version of the renowned illustration of Uncle Sam pointing his finger, but this time asserting, "The Acosta Change Champion Program Needs ... YOU!" In this case, we had recruited Uncle Sam to help promote an awards program we created, yet another activity to drive home the destination and core values and help make the new culture stick.

We continued to demonstrate our commitment after the rollout with town hall meetings. We tracked reactions with surveys so we could better gauge reactions and respond to any questions or concerns that arose—"temperature checks," as my colleagues called them.

In a way, I made another contribution of my own by restructuring Acosta's executive management team in the same general time frame. To further help drive home our being a national company and drive away lingering reminders of "the old days," the new structure that I announced in June 2000 focused not on regions but on key functions: Bob McCarthy became President of Client Services, Jack Laurendeau became President of Retail Services and Customer Teams, and Charlie Frankowski became President of Diversified Channels. The restructuring also designated a Chief Financial Officer, a Chief Strategy Officer, and an Executive Vice President of Human Resources.

These were substantive changes and came with critically important responsibilities that would help us respond to our clients and customers. Somehow I also managed to avoid leaving egos in shambles—for the most part, anyway. Cynics might disparage that we really "drank the Kool-Aid" when it came to culture. Yes, we did. Better still, as I write these words, the "Kool-Aid" has tasted good for almost a decade and nourished us every step of the way.

As proud as we are of Acosta's culture, and as determined and comprehensive as we were in introducing our culture, it's not for everyone. No culture ever is. We've had to endure our share of painful reminders of that truth, too.

A number of such reminders erupted at Kelley-Clarke in California, as I've already indicated. For a time shortly after he arrived, Rick Nist felt like one man against the world. I know there were plenty of times during the next two years when Rick pondered essentially the same notion that Jack Laurendeau pondered in Boston—namely, "Tell me again why this is going to be good for us."

Rick persevered because he felt he was doing "some of the best work of my life," he remembers. Of the 70 company shareholders on the payroll when Nist arrived on the West Coast in early 2000, all but three wound up leaving. Initially perceived as a hired gun from the East, Rick had to win over people almost one by one—at the same time he had to reduce our payroll, on more than one occasion, no less. It couldn't be helped. He was confronted with a sorely inefficient operation, "one that had never been put together," he says. In turn, there were overlap, costly excess, and positions that weren't needed.

So Rick looked extra carefully for associates who seemed at least willing to listen. He found one in Terry Quinn, who had been one of the 70 Kelley-Clarke shareholders. Rick did as much listening as Terry did, acted on Terry's advice, and guided the introduction of our culture accordingly. Over time, the Acosta culture took hold. As it did, the operating margins of the offices under Rick's direction soared and are still double what they were before his arrival.

"Terry Quinn is what I call an untitled leader," Rick says now. "I still remember the time another guy who hadn't been a believer finally approached me one day. 'Maybe this stuff makes sense after all,' he said. Turns out he had been talking to Terry Quinn."

Rick had another ally in Brian Baldwin, from day one. A nine-year Kelley-Clarke veteran when it became part of Acosta in 1999, Brian was already familiar with our company, had admired us from afar, and had no difficulty adapting to what we were trying to introduce. He embraced our culture effort right away and then came to Rick's rescue. "We had to deal with some tough questions, especially early on when we had layoffs. I became the culture preacher, which I could be because I didn't have to do any of the layoffs like Rick did," Brian says. "I'd sit with people and ask them if they had gone to our website and read about the values we identified. Those values were what I called our 'guardrails' and would make Acosta a good place to be, I said. And we'd keep talking. On the other hand," Brian adds, "if people hadn't made any effort to find out about our values and what we were doing, I knew I was wasting my time."

Brian preached so well in California that he became the region's representative on the Culture Committee. Now he is one of Acosta's executive vice presidents and head of our Wal-Mart team in Bentonville, Arkansas—a locale that he likens to "an island that needed to be integrated into the mainland company." Brian remains fiercely proud of his contribution and calls it "the cornerstone of a billion-dollar company. Nothing I've ever done comes close to the satisfaction it gives me," he says.

My colleagues needed to have tough skins and stand tall as we developed Acosta's new culture, and both Brian and Rick are role models of the kind of colleagues I was lucky enough to have standing alongside. Brian used an interesting analogy both on the West Coast and in Bentonville: Consider Acosta a train that was about to leave the station, "and you're standing on the tracks. Now you have a decision to make," he'd begin. "You can jump on this train because you want to be here and be part of what Acosta is building. That's great. Welcome aboard. Or you can jump on some other train heading in another direction. That's OK, too, if that is your choice. But just don't keep standing on the tracks and do nothing," Brian would conclude, "because if you stand there long enough, I have to make a decision."

Brian had plenty of those conversations, and his was an ideal way of looking at the situation. As I concluded early on, departures would be inevitable and, although they could be painful, they were still good in the long run. If people weren't going to embrace our new culture, they wouldn't be happy and should leave; otherwise, they'd hang around, grumble, and spread ill feelings. We didn't need that, especially during the tough times.

The challenges we faced on the West Coast—and elsewhere, too—taught me to appreciate the practical wisdom of "getting the poison out early." You risk sabotaging your efforts if you don't.

To be sure, not everyone who departed could be assailed as "poison." Some otherwise congenial, capable people simply had a hard time accepting what we were introducing and tried to dig in their heels for a time—for any number of reasons. For example, Acosta had always been what Greg McDonald calls "plain Jane." We drove white Fords, never even considered reserving spaces in the parking lot, faithfully flew coach, served modest box lunches during meetings to save time, and were diligent about saving dollars when and where we could.

How diligent? Well, part of the Acosta lore is the tale of a visitor's attending a meeting at our Jacksonville headquarters sometime in the 1980s. Stepping into the men's room during a meeting break, the visitor noticed the "Please turn out the lights as you leave" sign. Upon departing, the visitor dutifully followed directions, only to hear, "Hey! What the ##@@ are you doing?" and realized the men's room still had another occupant. After he heard that story, Bob McCarthy always made it a point to listen carefully whenever he visited an Acosta men's room.

Not everybody who had become part of the Acosta family was as diligent or as committed as Bob McCarthy. Some were accustomed to old practices where they worked and weren't interested in adjusting, so we parted company.

Now and then, too, introducing a new culture required being sensitive to the strange bedfellows mergers can connect. Among the sales and marketing firms our "Get National!" strategy brought us in 1998 and 1999 were a few that had been in Acosta's sights in the '80s and '90s but wound up being acquired by other agencies—agencies that subsequently became part of the nationwide Acosta. We had to make sure the associates of these firms were fully invested and comfortable, too. It wasn't anywhere near the challenge that the Kelley-Clarke situation represented, but we didn't dare take these locations for granted or treat them in a way they might infer as being deprecating or discriminatory.

Even when it's introduced properly and nurtured carefully, culture still won't insulate an organization from bizarre personnel problems. Amid all the trauma we had to endure in 2000 and 2001, one of our higher-profile employees managed to get himself entangled in a fairly serious mess that he tried for a long time to keep under wraps. That's because the mess he was in had the potential to put our entire enterprise under a cloud of suspicion. So, of course, I finally was alerted to the situation. What I confronted blatantly flew in the face of integrity—one of our core values—and yet it happened anyway. Go figure. Fortunately, the company itself wound up steering clear of problems, and Acosta parted company with the individual in question.

That episode reinforced my belief: If I have to choose between an associate who makes the numbers but won't live the culture and an associate who doesn't make the numbers but lives the culture, my choice is the guy who lives the culture. For the time being, at least, it's better to hold onto that individual who doesn't make the numbers and try to help him achieve the desired results. Ideally, of course, you want someone who both lives the culture *and* delivers the numbers.

That combination can be hard to find, though, in part because Acosta's culture isn't for everyone. Without question, and really by design, Acosta is a "work hard, play hard" company. That's another observation from Sandy Ramsey, and from others, too, for that matter. Your very best shot every day is what's expected—like the football coach who expects his players to get up a little dizzy after every play.

Our expectations are high all the time, "in a way I think that's almost scary to some people," Drew Prusiecki adds. "So, no, the culture here is not for everyone." No, it's not, I have to agree. But Acosta's culture sure works wonders for those it's for!

That's another hefty assertion. I'll back it up with a reminder, and three illustrations that you could label defining moments. First, the reminder: We created Acosta's culture and put it in place during our tough times years of late 2000, 2001, and early 2002. We didn't put off the process or suspend any of its phases because "we first had to get our house in order." Nor did I ever consider doing that. Without our culture's destination and core values to guide and support us, I am convinced we could not have overcome all the difficult episodes we had to live through.

Always striving to live up to our standards helped us keep our associates committed and energetic in more ways than I can ever recount. I know Acosta's culture has nurtured relationships with clients. Indeed, we typically begin presentations to new clients by speaking first about Acosta's culture. And culture was the "x-ingredient" in absorbing 1,700 Marketing Specialists employees in mid-2001. "Hang in there. Here's where we're going," we said again and again, "and we'll get there!"

We did get there ... because we demonstrated that we really were what we said we would be.

During a final conference call late during the summer of 2000, just before the final presentation to Acosta's board of directors, the Culture Committee asked me one last time if I, as the CEO, truly meant it when I said that associates had every right to hold executives accountable and to "call us out" if someone wasn't living up to our high standards.

"I'm absolutely behind you! It starts at the top," I said. "We *will* live these values."

I had a chance to affirm it early, thanks to a situation Brian Baldwin saw approaching. "I see a train wreck coming," Brian was telling me in a phone call. He realized that a clause in the contract governing one of our acquisition agreements was about to trigger an action that would have a significantly negative financial impact on a great many people. Yes, Acosta had every legal right to do what the clause called for, "but it's going to hurt a lot of our people, and it's not in line with our values and what we said we'd do," Brian continued. If there was any way to modify the action, Acosta should, he was urging.

In turn, I arranged a conference call with appropriate senior managers so Brian could state his case and explain the consequences of what he saw happening. In doing so, he really stuck his neck out, especially when he pointedly asked us to try to change or alter the pending action. Brian's request prompted as pregnant a pause as I ever heard. It was the kind of interminable silence that can make one think his career is going down in flames right then and there. "OK, Brian, what do you propose instead?" I finally asked.

Clearly well-prepared, Brian offered several suggestions—adjust this, adjust that, and move a date. It would show that, while doing as we should to protect the company, Acosta still put people first.

After another long pause, I asked two of the other executives on the call if what Brian proposed would work for them. It did. "Good call, Brian," I said in reiterating that we were going to do as he suggested.

That's illustration number one. Living our culture became increasingly easier from that point forward. Actions always speak louder than words, and that action spoke volumes.

I am particularly proud of illustration number two, which occurred in 2003, when Acosta negotiated an equity ownership agreement that gave Berkshire Partners, LLC, a significant minority interest in the company. The quick and convenient action would have been for all of our managers who were owners of stock appreciation rights to sell their entire stakes to Berkshire. It would have given them sizable checks and a good return and made them happy. They would have been delighted to sell, too, because they weren't in the position to see the entire picture.

But I could see the entire picture, and so could Acosta's inner circle executives. Long term, we knew our managers would each be far better off retaining a portion of their respective stakes and taking immediate smaller payouts. It would make for more complex and more drawn-out negotiations for all concerned, but it was the right thing to do. And that's what we did. These people had no voice at the table, only the values we had agreed to live by.

Our industry took notice of what we did, too. My third illustration shows as much. It also shows how solid an investment Acosta's culture has proven to be. When we launched our culture process in July 1999, I was continuing to negotiate with McFerren, Speakes and Gustafson, the Denver firm that Jamie Gronowski headed. As I earlier explained at the end of Step 7, acquiring that firm became like pulling teeth. That's largely because the final offer Jamie weighed from

Advantage included more dollars and more autonomy—factors our southern California competitor really stressed. Such things were mighty tempting to guys who had run their own show for so long and cherished their independence. But in the end, neither dollars nor autonomy were the deciding factors. What was? Jamie says it best: culture!

"As we thought it over during our final retreat—literally on a mountain top near Dillon, Colorado—we asked ourselves, 'Who would you want to be in a foxhole with?' Our answer was Acosta," Jamie says. "It was all due to the culture and the fit. And that was the difference, not the money."

Need I say more?

Food for Thought

There are three kinds of problem people who will prevent your team from winning:

1. Participants who give an all-out effort but don't pull in unison with their teammates. These people are doing their own thing. If they were musicians, they'd be off-beat, they would be out of sync with everyone else.
2. Participants who hold onto the rope but do not pull. These people are team members in name only. They take but they do not give. They want all the privileges but none of the responsibility.
3. Participants who pull in the opposite direction. These people work against their teammates and are poisoning the team with dissension.

You can't afford to be a problem. You have to part of the solution. Groups of people either pull together or pull apart. There's no in-between.

— Anonymous

Step 10

Make Serving Others Important to Everyone in Your Organization

With success comes responsibility.

Unless you look and listen extra carefully to the Jerry Lewis Telethon each Labor Day weekend, you probably wouldn't associate Aisles of Smiles with Acosta. It would be nice if people did, but it doesn't upset us. It's consistent with the behind-the-scenes relationships we have with our clients and customers.

Besides, making a big splash for ourselves wasn't the objective in the first place, and it never will be. Having said that, over the past 20 years, the Aisles of Smiles cause marketing program has raised a little more than $67 million for the Muscular Dystrophy Association and, of course, those we know as Jerry's Kids.

In fact, Acosta is a proud and long-standing principal sponsor of Aisles of Smiles, and our direct support has helped raise $50 million of that $67-plus million. Moreover, you'll find the very roots of this outstanding cause marketing program on our company's family tree. The original idea was crafted by a Kelley-Clarke associate in California, who then convinced the company to get behind his idea and help it grow. There was never any question about our continuing the support once Acosta acquired Kelley-Clarke in early 1999. We not only supported it; we expanded the program into what is now a national relationship.

Aisles of Smiles is a classic example of the charitable activities our company enthusiastically supports both locally and nationally. As I see it, supporting our communities is a responsibility of success. Imagine what could be accomplished in this country—and how much more appreciated America's free enterprise system undoubtedly would be—if every American business and its employees embraced this idea in their own backyards. That's where the lion's share of our community service takes place.

Supporting the communities where our associates live and work is an integral part of Acosta's culture. That's what we envisioned in 1999 that makes it especially gratifying to all of us who helped craft our culture. It demonstrates our culture's staying power. Community service is so much a part of Acosta's culture that I can tie the broad range of activities our associates support to each one of our seven core values.

- Community service certainly helps and supports *people*, both our associates and those we serve outside our company—a real win–win–win for our clients and customers as well as for Acosta.
- Community service contributes to our corporate *integrity* and helps strengthen our reputation.
- Our ability to support community service comes from the *results* that Acosta generates each year.
- Our community service helps affirm the *trust* we want to instill among everyone we touch as a company and our sincerity of purpose.
- It goes without saying that community service builds *teamwork*, an important special sense of purpose, and esprit de corps.
- Community service also has enabled us to demonstrate the *innovation* that has been so vital to Acosta's growth and success.
- Finally, community service activities not only enable us to demonstrate corporate citizenship but—and equally important —also help us make good on our pledge that our associates will be able to maintain a healthy *balance* in their lives as they work.

All told, community service is incredibly rewarding, beneficial to everybody, and fun. It's made Acosta a more successful organization in every respect. Is it a coincidence that our bottom line has grown at the same time we rolled up our collective sleeves on behalf of our communities? I don't think so.

You could just as easily link each of our core values to the Aisles of Smiles campaign itself. It's hard to imagine a community service endeavor better suited for Acosta. Collectively, we raise significant dollars for a very worthy cause by leveraging the very tasks we tackle daily. At the same time, we're helping our clients put their best feet forward, while also boosting both sales of their products and overall store traffic —which benefits retailers. It's truly a natural for us, with an ideal concept that is ever so simple. Participants, which, along with Acosta, include manufacturers of food products we represent and upwards of 75 retail chains like Albertson's, Jewel, SuperValu, and Winn-Dixie, each pay a participation fee to the Muscular Dystrophy Association (MDA) and donate a portion of brand sales to MDA. In return, the brands of the manufacturers receive special ad placement and point-of-sale materials that link the brands to MDA's cause. Sales of the brands are then promoted with in-store point-of-sale displays and with newspaper advertising and public service announcements on television and radio.

Today, Aisles of Smiles is a month-long event that kicks off August 1 and culminates with the MDA Labor Day Telethon hosted by renowned entertainer Jerry Lewis. I'm pleased to say that Jerry knows about our involvement and has thanked us personally many times.

Believe it or not, the telethon has aired for 43 uninterrupted years and draws some 60 million viewers to the 200 stations that televise it to virtually every locale in the land. In some of the locales, the event's promotion also includes golf tournaments and other special events, dedicated fundraising "galas," and celebrations of all kinds of themes.

Hank Lautrup wasn't interested in such fanfare back in 1984, just in some dollars to help his son and others' sons and daughters. Hank is the Kelley-Clarke associate in southern California who started the Aisles of Smiles Campaign not long after he and his family received the devastating news that son Timmy had muscular dystrophy. But rather than despair, Lautrup got involved with a local MDA executive committee, while Timmy started being treated at an area MDA clinic and attended MDA's summer camping programs.

As Hank observed the types of events and money being raised by sponsors such as 7UP, Anheuser-Busch, and Harley-Davidson, he wondered why his own company, Kelley-Clarke, couldn't create a program of its own that would raise money supporting MDA while also serving as a mechanism to boost sales of its clients' products and enlist support from other SMAs.

There was no reason at all, as it turned out. That single notion prompted Hank to propose the merchandising event that was soon christened Aisles of Smiles. Launched in 1985, the program generated $50,000 in its first year. From that modest origin, the program has grown to become the $5 million annual fundraising event it is today. Acosta has played a role in that growth, too. Early on, MDA and Aisles of Smiles officials relied on a three-inch-thick Food Brokers Directory to muster support. Now they can tap into our network and our relationships with more than 1,200 manufacturers and essentially every supermarket chain in the land. As we like to say, "Everyone smiles with Aisles of Smiles."

Hank was no longer with Kelley-Clarke when we merged in early 1999, but a great many people are in his debt. Aisles of Smiles is cause marketing at its finest. Retailers benefit from increased traffic and sales, the brands of participating manufacturers get a spike in sales activity,and shoppers get great deals. Ultimately, of course, it's Jerry's Kids who benefit most. Aisles of Smiles raises funds for life-saving research and supports clinic and patient services for more than 250,000 children and adults stricken with muscular dystrophy, which is actually a series of some 40 genetic disorders that continue to defy efforts to cure them. At least there's been ample progress in extending lives.

The value of supporting Aisles of Smiles and programs like it ought to be self-evident. Even so, here are some numbers from a 2004 Cone Report to reaffirm it.

- 91 percent of Americans have a more positive image of a company that supports a cause.
- 86 percent of Americans would be more likely to switch to a brand(s) associated with a good cause.
- 80 percent of Americans can name a company that they believe to be a strong corporate citizen.
- 77 percent of Americans believe that companies have a responsibility to support a cause.

We've also tracked the performance of supermarket brands during August, when the promotion is in full swing. Sales lifts, as we call them, have jumped anywhere from 33 percent to a whopping 148 percent! No one should need any more evidence to understand why Aisles of Smiles has the support of such clients as Bayer, Clorox, Gorton's, Heinz, Minute Maid, Nestlé, and Welch's.

Just the same, such evidence has come in handy for our own use. We used it as motivation, along with the enduring and obvious success of Aisles of Smiles, and challenged ourselves to replicate that success. Since 2006, Acosta has lent its support to a second national cause marketing campaign. The Shop to End Hunger program directed by Feeding America (formerly America's Second Harvest) is another natural for us.

To date, Acosta has helped raise more than $9 million to combat hunger, which gnaws at an estimated 25 million low-income Americans a year, including nine million children and three million senior citizens. That's flatly unacceptable and gave Acosta one more unreasonable goal: We want to see *every* retailer in America participating in Shop to End Hunger in some way. There were 20 major chains involved in 2008; that's good, but there can be and should be a lot more.

The program is built around essentially the same concept format as Aisles of Smiles. It is a merchandising event with a participation fee; retailers and manufacturers also donate a portion of their brands' sales to the campaign, which uses the dollars to support food banks around the country. Retailers already on board include familiar names like Albertson's, Food Lion, Kroger, Jewel, Safeway, Target, Wal-Mart, and Winn-Dixie.

Our company's support of Shop to End Hunger dates to 1994 when what is now Acosta's Metro New York office supported Check out Hunger, a forerunner to Shop to End Hunger. That campaign, too, leveraged in-store promotions and lots of creativity. It grew to be an effort that our entire company would embrace and turned out to be contagious, and mighty ambitious. By 1999, for instance, a corps of Acosta associates was teaming up with Winn-Dixie and a local television station in Charlotte, North Carolina, each November to create the annual Winn-Dixie Holiday Can Tree. It was some tree—16 feet in diameter and soaring 40 feet tall in the center of the Carolina Mall.

Some 71 food manufacturers each donated 150 cases of products—10,650 cases in all, plus another 1,300 cases of donated green beans. Acosta associate John Pittman used our space technology computer software to design the structure, which took 35 people a total of 306 man hours to build; 10 of the 35 were Acosta folks. All told, the effort raised $40,000 for America's Second Harvest and inspired a second tree to be built in Greenville, South Carolina. My colleagues also helped dismantle the tree after Christmas.

That Holiday Can Tree exemplifies our community service efforts. Individual Acosta associates and local offices pitch in all the time and in all kinds of ways. Whoever said "all retailing is local" could have observed the same thing about community service. I can crow all I want about corporate commitment, but it's our individual associates who do the heavy lifting. Acosta associates have not only donated to

MDA campaigns but also walked, run, ridden, bowled, and even swum for MDA. They have exerted themselves in the same ways for scores of other charitable causes and campaigns. Here's but a sample of the organizations and causes our 16,000 associates working in 65 offices across the U.S. and seven Canadian provinces support:

American Diabetes Association
Brain Injury Association
Susan G. Komen Breast Cancer
Children's hospitals
Depression& BipolarSupport Alliance
Dreams Come True Foundation
Easter Seals
Fight Against Hunger
Humane Society
Juvenile Diabetes Research
Learning Center for Deaf Children

Make-A-Wish Foundation
March of Dimes
MDA Foundation
Multiple Sclerosis Association
National Heart Day
Race for the Cure
St. Jude Children's Research Hospital
Toys for Tots
United Way Foundation
Various local food banks

Naturally, I think it's an impressive list. By and large, each of our offices and its employees determine the charities and activities they want to support. What's more impressive is what many of our individual Acosta associates do on behalf of their respective choices. As it is, we routinely devote pages of our internal newsletter, *News From Around the Company*, to community activities and, on occasion, devote entire issues of our company magazine, *Spirit*, to recounting how we support our communities. Moreover, one of our seven annual Chairman's Awards is presented to the individual associate or team that best exemplifies the balance that community service provides.

Take a look at a few of the creative ways my colleagues have and continue to "walk the talk." In many instances, you'll see the ties to our business; that's certainly not coincidental.

Hot stuff. The chili cook-off that our Grand Rapids office created serves up fun and good food while raising money for the city's Juvenile Diabetes Research Foundation. Associates pay $10 to enter a recipe, while colleagues and guests pay $5 to taste what's cooking. An enterprising bunch, the office also got a crew of buyers from Spartan Stores to judge the entries on appearance, flavor, and heat. The effort doesn't raise a huge sum ($2,800 in 2008, for instance), but it's still much appreciated and raises awareness along with cash.

Ride 'em, cowboy! In February, associates in our San Antonio office contribute time and talent to the famed San Antonio Stock Show and Rodeo, a 59-year-old event that benefits Texas youth. Our associates are among 4,000 volunteers who help raise millions of scholarship dollars and provide an opportunity for young men and women to learn about agriculture and livestock. In 2008 and 2009 the event raised more than $8 million. To date, the Stock Show and Rodeo has raised $96 million in commitments to education.

Shear Delight. Yes, I spelled it right, at least as far as some of our Calgary, Ontario, associates are concerned. They shaved their heads on behalf of a fundraising effort for the Children's Make-A-Wish Foundation in 2008. As volunteers at Calgary's famed Stampede, they also contribute in other ways, such as wielding scoops in serving barbecue on opening day of the annual rodeo event. The barbecue event typically supports charitable causes like the Children with Cancer Foundation.

Denim for Dough. This idea dates to at least the spring of 2002, and maybe earlier. Like just about everyone, our Minneapolis associates loved casual Fridays—so much so that they were willing to use it to generate a little cash. Wearing jeans on Fridays would, henceforth, cost $2, our gang there declared, with the money raised going to the Make-A-Wish Foundation. In less than two years, they had raised more than $8,600.

Variety is the spice of … In our Marlborough, MA, office, it's the spice of charitable activities. First, there's an annual charity golf tournament—we're sales people, remember—that's become a signature community event. Our associates also fill goody bags that are sent overseas to thank our American soldiers and then fill more goody bags in support of the community's youth baseball team. In addition, associates in this office collect weekly for jeans day and each year collectively designate a cause. The causes have included assisting a cancer victim. Since this Jeans Day effort started in 2002, more than $75,000 has been collected.

For Jerry's Kids. As you'd expect, many, many individual Acosta offices and regions support the annual MDA campaign in various ways. In New England we present an annual golf classic that draws 250 participants to golf, dinner, silent auction, and loads of fun that further strengthens our relationships with clients and customers. In 2008, the event generated $108,000 in donations to New England MDA branches. Across the country, Acosta's southern California office in

Brea—where Aisles of Smiles began—hosted a silent auction and barbecue that raised more than $13,000 for MDA. And our Dallas location raised $2,600 to send four children to MDA summer camp.

Teamwork to a T. Because members of one of our Jacksonville teams were new to town, they decided that community service would help them get to know the community. At the invitation of a city homeless shelter, they first volunteered there. It was so satisfying that they kept volunteering at Ronald McDonald House, a children's hospital, and then a retirement center, which wanted Acosta to help with an ice cream social. Somewhere en route, the team got the idea to involve its customer, a Winn-Dixie division, and some of our manufacturer clients. The team is still active, regularly visiting the retirement center and elementary schools, where it hosts coloring contests and fun-fact quizzes.

Pedal Power. For the past half-dozen years, 29 Acosta associates in Toronto have climbed aboard a big bike to ride on behalf of the Heart & Stroke Foundation. And when I say big bike, I mean it! It's designed for 30 people. Colleagues who don't ride showed up to cheer them on. This, too, is an enterprising office. One November, the guys in marketing all grew mustaches to help raise funds for prostate cancer research.

Educate for Success. We're very proud to also support the free enterprise system itself. In 2001, one of Acosta's divisions began assisting Students in Free Enterprise (SIFE), the worldwide organization of college students and business leaders that now operates in 41 countries. SIFE promotes business as the best tool "to create a better, more sustainable world," as its mission states, and it's one mission we are delighted to support with all of the enthusiasm that we can generate. I am one of the many directors on the SIFE board, as are numerous ranking food industry executives. It was a hard-working little sales company, too—including the President and CEO of Campbell Soup Co., Douglas Conant, who first got me involved in SIFE.

Helping Children Heal. In the Boston area, Acosta associates have long supported the Jimmy Fund, a cancer relief fund for children, and one year arranged to have the Kingsford NASCAR simulator on hand for young patients to drive. In Jacksonville, Florida, we similarly support the Jay Fund, which assists the families of children stricken with cancer and was launched by Tom Coughlin when he coached the NFL's Jacksonville Jaguars.

Yes, all of these efforts help enhance our image and raise our visibility, but that value, however you choose to measure it, pales in comparison with the camaraderie and pride that such efforts develop among associates. Time and again we've heard, "It makes it fun to come to work at Acosta." What never ceases to amaze me is something best described by our vice chairman, Jack Laurendeau, a little more than five years ago. Writing in *Spirit*, Jack noted the grassroots involvement of our associates and their enthusiasm. "No one makes them volunteer their time," Jack observed. "They choose to make the effort because they believe in the charities they support."

You could say our community involvement starts at home, by assisting our associates internally. In 1997, we started our Leadership Development Program. It is a two-year program that helps our most promising recruits learn all about the three major phases of the consumer packaged goods world—retailing, marketing, and sales, in that order. The development program continues to pay huge dividends and helps make Acosta a company that people aspire to join. LDP, as we refer to it, accepts about 50 associates per 24-month period and assigns each participant a mentor to further ensure success.

And we don't just herd everyone into one location. Acosta now has 15 Career Development Centers at strategic locations all over the U.S. and Canada: in places where you might expect them, like our Jacksonville headquarters and in or near major cities like Boston, New York, Chicago, Minneapolis, and Los Angeles; but also in Bentonville, Arkansas; Cincinnati, Ohio; and Grand Rapids, Michigan. That's also where you'll find major retailers Wal-Mart, Kroger, and Meijer, respectively.

Community service also means paying attention to the little things that can be ignored easily. To do our part to ensure food can be grown, for instance, we're among countless companies paying more attention to our environment. You'll see more fluorescent lights in our offices, for instance, and ENERGY STAR qualified appliances. We're also paying closer attention to the tire pressure on the cars our associates drive and both the thermostats and light switches on the walls of our buildings.

I suppose a case could be made that all of these wonderful gestures just happened, that they are a natural consequence of hiring quality, hardworking, generous, and caring men and women. Maybe, but I doubt it.

The catalyst for all these activities is really Acosta's culture and the time and effort we have spent for more than a decade nurturing and continually reinforcing it. Our culture and its seven core values are strong influences. One of our core values—balance—helped inspire one last idea. Eating dinner with your family, too, is another natural for a company in the food business. But it's a worthy idea for any company.

What we designated as Family Day is part of the nationwide A Day to Eat Dinner with Your Children campaign. Started in 2001, the movement promotes good eating and good health and reduces substance abuse among children and teens. Its inspiration comes from Columbia University's National Center on Addiction and Substance Abuse. The center's research concludes that the more often kids eat dinner with their families, the less likely they are to smoke, drink, use drugs, and make poor decisions.

These findings make sense to us, so we also provide sponsorship support to A Day to Eat Dinner with Your Children. We're in good company, too. The Stouffer's division of Nestlé is the title sponsor, and Coca-Cola is the presenting sponsor. Safeway's Foundation, the philanthropic arm of the retail supermarket chain, also supports the movement, as does General Mills. In 2008, President Bush, all 50 state governors, and the mayors of 800 cities also endorsed the idea.

At first blush, it may not sound like more than a token gesture at best. On a Monday in September, we allow employees to leave work two hours early to spend more time with their families and, of course, prepare and eat dinner together. Still, it's meaningful. Growing up in New Hampshire, I took for granted enjoying dinner with Mom, Dad, and my brothers every night. It was a way of life. It should be that way for everyone, every day.

One more thing should be for everyone, too: Each citizen should have a quality education.

Food for Thought

Is anybody happier because you passed his way?
Does anyone remember that you spoke to him today?
The day is almost over and its toiling time is through;
Is there anyone to utter now a kindly word of you?
Can you say tonight in parting with a day that's slipping fast,
that you helped a single brother of the many that you passed?

Is a single heart rejoicing over what you did or said?
Does the man whose hopes were fading now with courage look ahead?
Did you waste a day or lose it? Was it well or sorely spent?
Did you leave a trail of kindness or a scar of discontent?
As you close your eyes in slumber, do you think that God will say,
you have earned one more tomorrow by the work you did today?

– John Hall

Step 11

Never Stop Being Unreasonable.

One more unreasonable goal—we must fix public education!

When I arrived at the University of New Hampshire in the fall of 1972, I aspired to be a teacher and coach. That aspiration wound up manifesting itself in a much different way for the past 30 years. That "fire in the belly" that dedicated teachers possess in one way or another has never stopped burning inside of me. Today it burns ever more intently—and yes, it's fueled in large part by the same unreasonable attitude that drove my career with Acosta. In 2006, that fire rousted me to resume pursuing my aspirations for public education in a more overt and traditional way. In September 2006, with the strong and sincere support of my wife, Nancy, and our children, Jeff and Meredith, we founded The Chartrand Foundation with a desire to help reform public education in Acosta's headquarters city of Jacksonville, Florida.

Naturally, we think our mission—to substantively change our urban neighborhood schools by empowering educators, students, and the surrounding community—is distinctive. We continue to pursue it, and not just with financial contributions. We also rolled up our sleeves and involved ourselves by seeking proven ideas that we find from various sources and investigative efforts, then putting them to work in a grassroots effort with one simple goal in mind: a quality education for all.

At first glance, one might want to describe our foundation as another noble effort to dip our toes into the water to help to solve a monumental task, except we are intently serious in our quest to make a difference here. We are determined to give children—particularly children who live in disadvantaged neighborhoods—a better public school education than they currently receive. We aim to close the achievement gap and prepare all kids to participate in our democracy.

Collectively, we're failing many of our kids! There's no other way to say it, and the consequences are all too apparent. For decades, we've heard all kinds of talk about failing students and failing schools and inadequate teachers. The landmark federal study "A Nation at Risk"

161

was written in the spring of 1983—more than 25 years ago! "History is not kind to idlers," the study's authors warned then.

From where I stand, there has been a lot of idling all over America, so the Chartrand Foundation decided to focus on grassroots solutions and transform what we contend is a system that is wrought with inequality. All over the nation, urban schools are disadvantaged and are failing our kids. The Chartrand Foundation wants to turn all of our schools into first-class institutions of learning. An unreasonable goal? I don't think so. Fixing our public school system is not only possible, it is essential. Our continued successful way of life depends on it.

To me and my family, this is the ultimate responsibility that comes with success and being able to live the American Dream. I believe with all my heart that we have an intrinsic duty to share our success with as many as we can and to help others succeed. Ask our son Jeff about our family's motivation, and you will hear a more impassioned rationale. As the seeds of this idea started to grow amid family discussions sometime in 2005, Jeff recalls my saying over and over how we had an opportunity to make "a tremendous impact on our city," one that would pay dividends for generations.

The more the four of us talked, the more excited and committed we became. "I think we even surprised ourselves a little," Jeff now says. Soon thereafter, we became determined to, as my son says further, "make the most of everything God has blessed us with."

For Jeff, who serves as executive director, The Chartrand Foundation is, in his words, "a spiritual expression." Those are the right words, too. Although we don't wear our faith on our sleeves, we're serious about it. And all of us love being around people and working together for a common good. I remain grateful for Jeff's enthusiasm and dedication and also for our daughter, Meredith. Our children are motivating in their own right. Notably, both of them also aspired to teach, and they both spent a few years in classrooms after graduating from college. Their enthusiasm and commitment is essential, as well, given the critical importance of the challenge and its imposing degree of difficulty.

Let me frame it this way: Though freedom is abundant in America, it is not universal, as odd as it may sound. Inequalities still exist, I submit, because the same American Dream my family and I have been able to enjoy is out of reach for far too many young people.

Remember my contention at the end of Step 10 about "something else everyone should enjoy"? That something else is a solid, basic education. That's out of reach in far too many urban classrooms. Too many young men and women have no real chance to pursue their dreams, because they leave school without the fundamental skills and knowledge they need to make their way in our world and become contributing citizens. Take a look at the following chilling statistics, and you'll quickly understand why I call greater private sector support of public education an imperative and a quiet crisis with which we have to come to grips and fix.

- The graduation rate in Duval County among financially disadvantaged children is 47.3 percent—that's right, *more than half of these children don't graduate*!
- The school district's official 69.6 percent graduation rate is one of the state's lowest.

"Just plain lousy and unacceptable," I said when I first saw these statistics, which come from the Duval County School District. These numbers are not anomalies but snapshots of a frightening trend that continues unabated and continues to jeopardize the futures of the school district's approximately 123,000 students. After looking at the numbers again and pondering their implications, a study by Johns Hopkins University concluded that most of Jacksonville's high schools were little more than "drop out factories."

The Chartrand Foundation aspires to bring focus, attention, funding, and in-kind resources to three critical areas of need:

- Public education reform.
- Early childhood initiatives.
- Support for parents and families in Jacksonville's urban core.

What we envision when we close our eyes and dream is a world where demography is not destiny. We want to take *disadvantaged* and all it stands for out of the education equation. Our goal is to ensure that every young person's destiny is driven not by demographics but by that young person's determination and desire to pursue a career—*any* career, regardless of street address, the amount of money in one's pocket, or family circumstances.

In addition, it is our hope that everyone in Jacksonville and the First Coast region of northeast Florida who has been blessed with financial resources will join us in a philanthropic movement to create equal opportunity for all. Together we can make this a reality. Nancy, Meredith, Jeff, and I sincerely believe that.

If there was some sudden epiphany that might explain why, when, or where the idea and thrust of our foundation took root, I cannot recall it. Neither can Nancy, Jeff, or Meredith. It just evolved as we talked informally, so maybe it's best to conclude that it's in our genes.

In a roundabout way, what we created was somewhat similar to what I did back in San Francisco in December 1997 when I blurted out, "We've got to go national!" Acosta realized in 1997 that going national was essential for our continued success as a company. Well, guess what? My family has come to the same conclusion about public education reform: Our continued success as a nation depends on it.

Jeff is ideally suited for the task of executive director, if I do say so myself. He grew up in Jacksonville, Florida, so he knows the city. He graduated magna cum laude from New York University and headed to the classroom. In 2003, he became a teaching fellow in Brooklyn's Bedford-Stuyvesant community, where he taught fifth-grade special education. In 2005, Jeff moved back to Jacksonville, both to teach and to begin work on the establishment of our foundation. By then, he had seen firsthand the inequities and disparities of our public education system. It motivated him to leave the classroom and build a career in education philanthropy. Along with directing our foundation, Jeff has gotten active in several community activities that complement and support our cause.

Meredith is the Foundation's director of Early Childhood Initiatives and is just as well suited for her role as Jeff is for his. She graduated from Florida State University in 2003 after earning a Bachelor of Science degree in family and child sciences. Shortly thereafter, Meredith followed her brother to New York, and then into a classroom. She taught art at a Montessori School for children ages 18 months to eight years old. She came home in 2006 to help us launch the foundation. She's since married but remains as devoted as ever to improving the lives of Jacksonville's children.

Meredith helps our cause in other ways, too. She currently serves on the board of the Healthy Start Coalition and is co-chair of the Black Infant Health Community Council's subcommittee for Philanthropy and Political Will. She is also a Big Brothers and Big Sisters of North-east Florida volunteer and participates in Jacksonville's Junior Achievement chapter and in Take Stock in Children, a program sponsored by Communities in Schools.

Both Jeff and Meredith serve on the foundation board, along with Nancy, who is Board chair, and Sandy Ramsey, Acosta's Senior Vice President, Finance and Treasurer. Are Nancy and I proud parents? Do you have to ask? Of course we are. But make no mistake: Jeff and Meredith work hard to make a difference; they are not mere figure-heads – far from it. They're engaged, and just as determined as the old man, and not afraid to speak out as necessary. Neither of them will accept the status quo, because they know this will not fix the system.

Just as I was finishing writing these words, Jeff offered an observation that generated Editorial Page comment in *The Florida Times-Union*. He forthrightly observed that Jacksonville's "New Town Success Zone" needed to strengthen its planning in order to replicate the successful Harlem Children's Zone effort in New York. Since both our children represent our foundation on the New Town Success Zone initiative, Jeff wasn't just talking off the top of his head—and the editorial board concurred with his perspective.

Jeff's willingness to speak out is one reflection of our family's collective determination to make our schools better. There are others, and I am proud of them all. Jeff put his classroom experience to work in less than six months after we established the foundation. He created a school-to-school partnership called Inspire.Create.Achieve. in which we brought to 26 of the district's schools relevant, real-world experiences in the arts, civics, and sciences.

Early on, our foundation also contributed $1 million to bring to Jacksonville Teach for America, an effort that could be described as a Peace Corps for urban schools. Founded by Wendy Kopp, TFA has more than 8,500 recent college graduates teaching in public schools across America to tackle the achievement-gap disparity that exists in our urban schools. We joined with Jacksonville Jaguars owners J. Wayne and Delores Barr Weaver, who donated $1.2 million, and then together we raised another $3 million in additional support—in less than five weeks. We're told it was a record for the program, which enabled the school district to deploy a special corps of more than 50 teachers into some of Jacksonville's toughest and most challenged schools for a two-year period. The next year, another 50 teachers were brought to Jacksonville to double our efforts. These energetic and dedicated young folks are making a real difference in Jacksonville. God bless them!

These early achievements notwithstanding, at first glance, it might not appear that we've made much of an impact yet, but we've been encouraged enough to launch other ventures and keep plugging away. Most worthwhile achievements are never easy, and public education reform is no exception.

I'm active myself in scoping out programs with a proven record of success that could be replicated in Jacksonville. One with which I have been especially impressed is the Knowledge is Power Program, or simply KIPP. It was founded in 1994 in Houston by two committed teachers who took what they learned in two years with Teach for America into a fifth-grade classroom in the inner city. Today there are 82 KIPP public schools serving 20,000 students in 19 states and the District of Columbia. Let's look at a sample of KIPP's track record.

After four years, fully 100% of eighth-grade KIPP students outperformed respective district achievement averages on state tests of reading–English and math proficiency. These same students performed at the 80th percentile (i.e., the top 20 percent) in math and the 58th percentile in reading. And more than 85 percent of these students from the original KIPP academies went on to pursue college educations.

These students are not handpicked, "cream of the crop" top performers, either. KIPP is a charter school with open enrollment; however, there is a selection process. Parents and the children must sign a contract and commit to spend more time in the classroom. More than 90 percent of the students are from African-American or Hispanic households, and more than 80 percent are eligible to participate in the federal government's free or reduced-price lunch program. Don't tell me that not all kids can learn! They can!

These kids achieve because KIPP offers a rigorous academic environment. Its five pillars of operating principles are high expectations; the commitment of both students who choose to participate and their parents; more time on task—until 5:30 p.m. during the week, plus a few hours on Saturday; powerful leadership from principals who have the freedom to reallocate dollars and change staff if needed; and a focus on results and a refusal to accept any shortcuts. Notably, students also study almost year-round, except for a three-week summer vacation.

I was impressed enough that I agreed to serve on the KIPP board in Jacksonville and helped lead a coalition of KIPP advocates to bring the charter school to Jacksonville. We will open our first school in northwest Jacksonville in July of 2010.

The kind of results I just described are what we need to see routinely in our schools throughout our community, and every community, for that matter—and not just because the majority of the students from KIPP programs go on to college. As unaccustomed as I am to the idea of being reasonable, here's an instance where it's required. As much as we might like to think otherwise, not each and every U.S. high school graduate will march directly to a college campus. What we want to do is create the opportunity for each child to make that choice by preparing them properly for making that choice.

I realize that some kids may not want to go to college. Others cannot afford it, scholarship assistance notwithstanding. Still others feel a calling to military service and the outstanding training that comes with it. Whatever the reasons, they're not college bound. But does that make them bad kids unworthy of guidance, encouragement, and support? Of course not! Nor does it make them unworthy of the intense education and training of KIPP, Teach for America, and the similar kinds of initiatives our foundation is championing. *All* young people need to be better prepared to determine and pursue their own futures, whatever they may be.

These experimental efforts to revolutionize public school education deliver another benefit. They show students all the possibilities that our big wide wonderful world really does offer. That's encouragement in itself, and it helps young people make better choices, about careers and about life. There's no question about that, as results to date illustrate.

We need better educated and more knowledgeable students everywhere. They grow up to be better citizens who are willing and able to contribute to society, whether they're doctors, lawyers, CPAs, business executives, or the commanders of 18-wheel rigs that haul freight from a producer to a distribution center. All things considered, day in, day out, regardless of the professions people choose, we all add more value when we are educated.

Somewhere along the way, a demeaning and dangerous notion has taken root in American society: that it's almost OK for anyone not going to college to remain ignorant and not to be held to the same basic high academic standards as those headed off to, say, law school. Why? That very notion is the epitome of ignorance! Without smart, well-trained citizens, our very democracy is at risk. We only can imagine what our economy might be like today had we heeded the plea to overhaul public education so evident in "A Nation at Risk" back in 1983. A recently completed study by the consulting firm McKinsey equates the current achievement gap in America to that of a permanent national recession.

So, we have a very special opportunity facing America today. The public simply must get engaged and encourage positive change in our public schools for *all* our children—with a special emphasis on poor and disadvantaged children. Back in 1983, we were told that we were in the throes of "unthinking, unilateral, educational disarmament." Twenty-six years later, we have a long way to go before we can lay this concern to rest. We must all understand that to secure the nation's investment in student achievement, we first must have a knowledgeable and informed public, one with the will to invest in and *demand* excellent public schools. To do otherwise is ignorant, complacent, and downright unacceptable.

Now, unfortunately, we can only imagine what might have been had we mustered the public will back in 1983 to fix our public schools. I don't think we have another 26 years to get this done; by then, it will be too late. We need to roll up our sleeves in every community across this great country and see how public education ought to be, not how it is. If we make this commitment and set a bold agenda, we can solve this dilemma. Why? B*ecause all kids can learn! Don't let anybody tell you they can't!*

We never know what we're going to do when we grow up. Not in my wildest dreams did I ever envision winding up in Jacksonville, Florida, helping to build a company like Acosta. When Mike Keohane first approached me, I barely knew what a food broker was, but I had been blessed with a good education, so I could grasp the opportunity Mike and Del Dallas offered.

I have been blessed beyond my wildest dreams and have earned more rewards than I could have possibly imagined. And though I could simply wander off to the golf course, I just can't do that. I'd be mighty uncomfortable in no time at all. So I'll be unreasonable one more time: Improving public education is America's greatest imperative. When schools are the center of the community, student achievement increases, parents and neighbors become more involved in students' success, and community pride and safety increase. Fix our schools, and we'll fix our communities.

It will take an unrelenting effort and dedication, just like the challenge we faced at Acosta to "Go National!" I'm not sure where improving our schools will take us and what will be required, but the task is certainly worth pursuing. Indeed, it's one that must be pursued, unless we are willing to live with the "two Americas" that the nation's critics often cite. I'm not. Neither is Nancy, Jeff, or Meredith.

The goal of the Chartrand Foundation is to make the public schools in our neighborhoods vastly better—all of them. We'll do all we can to achieve it and look forward to the day when everyone is rallying to this cause. If some say that's unreasonable, I say no, it's not; it's essential for our survival as a free nation.

Food for Thought

Service is the virtue that distinguished the great of all times and which they will be remembered by. It places a mark of nobility upon its disciples. It is the dividing line which separates the two great groups of the world—those who help and those who hinder, those who lift and those who lean, those who contribute and those who only consume. How much better it is to give than to receive. Service in any form is comely and beautiful. To give encouragement, to impart sympathy, to show interest, to banish fear, to build self confidence and awaken hope in the hearts of others, in short—to love them and to show it—is to render the most precious service.

– Bryant S. Hinckley

Step 12

Take a Look Back to Gain Perspective

Understand why it all worked and what was critically important to accomplishing the unreasonable mission.

Hearing the declaration "It's OK to be unreasonable" can sound like a contradiction. For one thing, it sounds contentious and inconsistent with what we expect the successful role-model business executive to deliver: leadership, direction, vision, praise, inspiration, motivation, encouragement, teaching, coaching, cheering, consensus building, and reassurances as necessary. Being *unreasonable* seems at odds with all of these desirable skills—and far more characteristic of the nasty, autocratic, unsuccessful boss we know and loathe as "that old SOB."

But it's not really, at least not from my perspective. From all that I have experienced, being unreasonable is an attribute, among the desirable qualities of a business executive, as I have tried to convey.

But first an acknowledgment: In my 26-plus years with Acosta, I have no doubt that on at least a few occasions, someone, somewhere described me as "that old SOB." Like any CEO, I've had occasions to be—shall we say—unpleasant. It comes with the territory. For example, Drew Prusiecki, our company's general counsel and secretary, can well recall the time not long after he came aboard when I abruptly cut short a meeting by angrily telling him and several colleagues to "get the hell out of my office!" Something said at a critical time in a discussion had exposed my dark side. Within a few minutes, I had calmed down, called Drew back to my office, explained why I had erupted, offered some words of assurance, and quickly put the matter behind us. We laugh about it today. Drew and I have great respect for each other and remain good friends.

That episode is among the exceptions to the rule. Most of the time, I demonstrated my unreasonable nature with a bright smile fueled by boundless optimism. Why not? It's been fun, all things considered, and incredibly satisfying. Achieving what conventional wisdom labels impossible always is.

"C'mon, Gary, be reasonable!" I'd been told time and again. "You just can't expect …" whatever it was I happened to be expecting or striving to achieve at the time.

"Sure, I can," I'd cheerfully reply in so many words. "It's what we need to do, because it's the right thing to do—which is why we're going to do it, come hell or high water."

That's what unreasonable leadership is all about. By and large, there is nothing inherently unpleasant about it, either. It's my way of describing one's determination, holding fast to convictions, maintaining focus, mustering the support of colleagues and clients, being a good communicator, and remaining undaunted no matter what. Being unreasonable helps you tune out the naysayers, ignore the odds, and overcome the obstacles in the path, no matter how imposing they may be.

Being unreasonable is a mind-set as much as anything and is the common thread that weaves throughout Acosta's 83-year history, in particular the history of our expansion that began in 1974. Del Dallas was being unreasonable long before he ever heard of Gary Chartrand. Hy Albritton and L.T. Acosta might well have been unreasonable, too, in their own ways.

Being unreasonable is a mind-set that's critical to success. As unreasonable as I was about building Acosta into a national company, I didn't dare adopt a different mind-set after that goal was reached. I've been just as unreasonable ever since about driving Acosta's continued growth. Good thing, too. What the quick or casual glance at our expansion saga often misses is that the true heavy lifting came *after* we had negotiated our mergers and completed our major acquisitions. Nothing that ordained our success was cast in stone. It was up to us to earn it. If we got careless, we could squander everything in a heartbeat.

Had we not remained unreasonable and resolute, or had we become the least bit complacent, who's to say we would have endured those tough years? One of our competitors did not. We were able to adapt and handle the disruptions, the chaos, and all the surprises because we never stopped insisting on success. There was no other option—unreasonable as our stand may have seemed on occasion.

Indeed, Acosta's performance validates what management consultant and author Dr. Richard T. Pascal contended in his 1990 book, *Managing on the Edge: How the Smartest Companies Use Conflict to Stay Ahead.* As a business leader recounts a seminal accomplishment, it's common for that leader to infer that there was some kind of formula or detailed game plan that guided him or her virtually every step of the way when, in fact, there was no such formula at the time, not even a whisper of one. The leader simply did what he or she thought ought to be done to achieve the vision that was branded in his or her mind. Obstacles standing in the way had to be overcome, come hell or high water.

Acosta is living proof of that. Yes, we did have our "Get National!" strategy. When we set out to execute that strategy in early 1998, however, we didn't have the foggiest idea of the specific situations we might have to confront and how we would adapt—let alone all the changes our expansion would impose on our organization afterward. Yes, Acosta transformed an industry, and that transformation also transformed Acosta. When I joined our company in 1983, there were 2,500 food brokers in the U.S. Today, three national firms account for almost 90 percent of the business. That is clearly a transformational change of significant consequences.

The very uncertainty and the need to be proactive and adjust amid such change is what is best about being unreasonable! Such unreasonableness helps fight complacency and keeps an organization hungry and on its toes. Up and down the line, everyone at Acosta had to be as resourceful as possible and open to new ideas. In so doing, we were ever more mindful of opportunities and predisposed to embrace them.

"OK, we've built our national company," we started saying to each other in mid-1999. "Now, how do we make this thing work?" We figured out how, starting with our new culture. That nurtured an environment continually to strive to improve and be on the lookout for new ideas. Still, it was being unreasonable that got the ball rolling.

I can't say that we were especially conscious about this phenomenon while our sleeves were rolled up. We didn't have even one second to stand back and gaze at the so-called aerial view. It's only now that there is time for the aerial view that the long-term impact of what went on in the trenches becomes clear.

There's no question that I get a great deal of satisfaction out of telling the Acosta story. At the same time, I'd like to think that telling the story benefits Acosta's associates, especially our younger ones. It's good for them to know about their company's heritage, how the organization grew, how it transformed an industry, how close we came to plunging into the abyss, and how their peers solved assorted crises at critical times. In a way, it sends a reassuring message: *They did it, and so can you.* Moreover, implicit in our story—in an almost subconscious way—is a gentle challenge: *Here's the enterprise you now are entrusted with and responsible for; guide it carefully and resourcefully, and do your best to leave it better than you found it.*

Or, as I used to jokingly tell colleagues to put them at ease before we pitched a big client, *"Now, don't screw it up."*

My colleagues didn't screw it up, far from it.

Late in the summer of 1998, the headline of an Acosta/PMI ad appearing in trade magazines declared, "It's about getting better, not just bigger." That's exactly what's happened in the 12 years since that ad first appeared. Yes, we did keep getting bigger; Acosta actually has made more than 38 acquisitions *since* late 1999, but all those acquisitions were made in our quest to continually get better. But the number isn't what's significant. As we grew, our people truly embraced the idea of leaving Acosta better than they found it—almost instinctively, it now seems. They've made good on that ad's pledge.

Look up the word *synergy* in a dictionary, and you'll read something like this: the impact and contributions of the combined organization are greater than the combined impact or contributions that the separate parts had contributed beforehand. I can't think of a better example of synergy than today's Acosta. The whole really is bigger than the sum of its parts.

Expanding our capabilities as we improved services is exactly what Del Dallas had in mind back in 1974. And it's what I had in mind in 1997 when I started shaping our "Get National!" strategy. Neither Del nor I could pinpoint precisely *how* our capabilities would expand or what specific new benefits we might be able to offer our clients, but we were both absolutely convinced that Acosta's capabilities and benefits *would* expand, dramatically.

About the best illustration of what Acosta's synergy has fashioned remains our midsummer Grillin' & Chillin' Time displays that I described in Step 6: the combination of Kingsford charcoal, Bush's baked beans, Heinz Ketchup, Vlasic pickles, Dixie cups, and such. The displays appear prominently every summer in supermarkets all over the country, and today we all but take them for granted. Similar kinds of displays are in stores at other times of the year. But before our national platform existed, such multi-brand displays were hard to find, no matter what time of year it was. Why? Grant LaMontagne, Clorox senior vice president and chief customer officer, explains it best: "You couldn't do any of that before because there were just too many different people from different companies and agencies involved. Try to get 32 people to agree on a plan within a 24-hour time frame? It was impossible. Getting 32 people just to *understand* a plan was difficult enough. You'd be pulling your hair out."

But Acosta made it possible, and then routine—and without any tugs on anyone's hair. As we expanded into a national company, the number of products and companies we represented expanded, too—and with them, all kinds of marketing opportunities, many of them unprecedented. As we gained experience with the concept, we even found ourselves creating the initial idea, as often as not, then bringing our clients on board. But no matter where the idea originated, Acosta's position as the common representative made it far easier to plan and execute.

As Grant observes further, "Acosta unlocked the value of its entire portfolio." By working together, we strengthened the brands of all of our clients and created a kind of "critical mass" that could compete as well as marketing juggernauts like General Mills, Kraft, Procter & Gamble, and Unilever. Moreover, the supermarkets we called on were delighted to provide the space, because we helped them sell more products at the same time. We were no longer selling separate products, per se; what we were selling were targeted marketing events, and everyone benefited.

When consumers look at Grillin' and Chillin' Time, or any of our other marketing events, they have no idea that Acosta had anything to do with them. But that's okay, because our clients and customers know. They also know that there is virtually no limit to the opportunities that working together can create. In football season in New England, for instance, we might "tailgate with the Patriots," while in Pennsylvania, we might "tailgate with the Steelers" or Penn State's Nittany Lions, or with University of Florida's Gators. We're limited only by our imagination—and we're as imaginative as ever.

Indeed, to show you how contagious synergy can be, our early marketing successes prompted us to develop Acosta's MatchPoint Marketing subsidiary. A full-service creative agency, MatchPoint offers a wealth of services, including point-of-sale and coupons, interactive, outdoor advertising, event marketing, and sports marketing. In late 2008, Acosta further strengthened its creative services capabilities when it acquired Promo Depot, a Jacksonville, Florida, marketing and promotion firm that is a leader in its field. We then united Promo Depot and MatchPoint into a single organization, and its clients include not only Campbell's, Kraft, and Clorox, but also firms like Blue Cross Blue Shield, PSS World Medical, and Fidelity National.

Along with new capabilities and resources—and, yes, the greater revenues and earnings—Acosta's expansion delivered one more huge competitive advantage, old-fashioned but as valuable as ever. We operate successfully because of *economies of scale*. Raw size is really what made all the marketing ideas practical. And raw size made it economically feasible to participate in the development of increasingly sophisticated technology-based services, which we have made available to more and more clients, both large and small.

A classic example is the product bar code-based wizardry that beckoned to the grocery world at an ever-quickening pace in the 1990s, giving it incredibly valuable information; soon thereafter, other technologies were being introduced. Today we have handheld technology that gives our representatives real-time data at store level. And because we had become a large enterprise and needed literally thousands of handhelds for our representatives in the field, we could get them for an attractive price, on a per-unit basis.

Fully harnessing technology was one reason I became increasingly adamant about challenging traditional barriers like product conflicts, especially in the face of consolidations among food-manufacturing clients and the grocery chains who were our customers. Without being able to represent larger numbers of products, we couldn't afford to invest in the leading-edge technology that was being created, let alone help develop some of it. Neither could our individual clients or customers. But as a large nationwide enterprise with ties to many clients and customers large and small, we could wield all kinds of tools on their behalf that would help all of them better understand and respond to customers and shopping habits. The direct data links we established to respected research firms like ACNielsen and Information Resources, Inc., are another benefit of economies of scale.

Obviously, these technological devices and services also deliver numerous benefits to us. In our business, for instance, there's almost nothing as inefficient as an area representative driving to a customer's supermarket. Nothing else gets done! I learned that from personal experience. In my early years with Carnation, I would drive close to 50,000 miles a year in Maine, including jaunts to tiny border towns like Fort Kent.

In turn, much of the technology now in Acosta's arsenal helps us make the best possible use of a representative's time in a store and minimizes the hours spent driving to and from stores. We can document the fact that our reps spend a significantly smaller portion of a typical day driving than do those of our competitors. That has kept the cost of the services we provide our food manufacturing clients extremely low, especially when gasoline hit the $4/gallon mark, and allowed our people to spend more time where it counts: at the supermarket shelf, where the consumers make their decisions.

Today, it's also fair to say that Acosta representatives carrying handheld devices can accomplish in a single store visit what would have required several visits and many more hours not all that long ago: from placing orders electronically to gathering point-of-sale data about consumer purchases to store shelf planning and analysis, and assorted related tasks. None of that would have been possible without the critical mass Acosta has created.

The synergy our critical mass created afforded us the resources to strengthen our organization in many ways, including adding new business units and reshaping Acosta's organization itself, as opportunities and circumstances dictated. A favorite case in point was the launch of our natural foods division in 2000. It's among the ideas that Jamie Gronowski brought with him from Denver. From his vantage point in the West, Jamie was well positioned to assess the burgeoning natural foods trend in the late 1990s. "It's no passing fad, and we need to be there," he soon concluded with conviction. Citing the sector's 10-20 percent historical growth rate per year, as well as projections that natural foods would continue to grow at that clip for the next 5 to 10 years, Jamie prepared a position paper that presented a strong rationale for a concerted effort.

"Natural foods was no longer characterized by a health food shop in Boulder, Colorado, or a 50-year-old hippie reliving his or her youth," Jamie explained. If that wasn't as widely apparent in Florida, we still could see how the Whole Foods Market was fast becoming a retail chain to be reckoned with. Moreover, Jamie added, with heavyweights like General Mills, Kraft, Heinz, and Kellogg's entering the sector in earnest, it was time for Acosta to enter it, too. He cited two more reasons to dive in: First, it was an upscale market with the potential of comparatively higher commissions. Second, it signaled our company's interest and intent in representing a broader variety of products, as well as a broader variety of food producers.

It didn't take us long to say, "Go for it!" Notably, our commitment in 2000 came during the very same period when I was starting to lie awake at night worrying about cash flow and meeting payroll. It was sleeplessness well spent, for Acosta's march into natural foods has been a sound investment.

We didn't just wildly barge in. We first looked at our strengths—such as existing ties to clients like Celestial Tea, our still-new diversified channels operation, and our strong presence in the West that had come with Kelly-Clarke (which Jamie knew like the back of his hand). We also estimated we'd need to invest a good $10 million to get started; still, the prospect of generating up to $25 million in revenues in the next 12 to 18 months made it worthwhile, Jamie further projected. And we wouldn't be starting from scratch. An earlier acquisition of another Denver specialty food broker gave us a foothold in the sector, plus we knew of other firms we could acquire elsewhere around the country.

Over the next four years we made six regional acquisitions, and by 2006, Acosta was the solid leader in the field and generating revenues of $38 million, as we do today. We were representing 22 of the top 25 natural foods producers, including the number one or number two brand in virtually every specialty category.

Acosta was hardly alone in building a presence in natural foods, of course, but that only affirms its wisdom. Traditional supermarket chains have jumped into this sector, too. By mid-2009, for instance, Publix was operating three supermarkets in Florida developed as part of its Greenwise natural foods initiative. In many respects, these stores rival the Whole Foods Market concept, which keeps expanding.

The success of our natural foods division was synergistic in its own right. It gave us the experience and confidence to enter other specialty markets such as club stores like BJ's, Costco, and Sam's Club, as well as 24-hour convenience, the drug channel, dollar stores, and, more recently, what we call the military channel—selling to the commissaries and exchanges. It's a sector that Robert Hill, who succeeded me as CEO on January 1, 2009, expects to grow significantly.

Notably, we developed just about all of these new business sectors during the same years when consumers in general were shifting larger percentages of their food dollars and time to eating out. That we were able to grow as we did in the face of that shift is especially satisfying (that shift now is reversing, by the way). I like to contend that all of these initiatives exemplify how Acosta managed to grow and stay nimble and, most importantly, adapt to the changes of our customers— the supermarkets and retail chains. Before they consolidated and changed their purchasing practices, Acosta was proactive and positioned itself to respond to a new way of doing business.

We anticipated what they would do and could stay a step ahead of the market. Another internal white paper, this one a decade old and prepared by Acosta colleagues Margaret Dougherty and Greg Long, led to our creating the customer teams that flourish today, not just on behalf of Wal-Mart but also on behalf of all of the national and regional retail chains we serve. It noted how the geographical structure of most brokers hampered efficiency and would defeat one of the major benefits of nationalization. Adopting a new structure built around customer teams made us more efficient and effective. Moreover, it created a working environment that allowed new ideas, such as cooperative marketing initiatives, to flourish.

Acosta's synergy certainly wasn't flawless. Make no mistake about that. Like anyone else, we've stumbled and bet wrong—and not just on brand new ventures like Enable. In 2000, for instance, we had to shut down the international division we had had high hopes for upon launching it in October 1997. With many key clients doing business overseas, it seemed like a natural next step, almost a slam dunk. We gave the division experienced, well-connected leadership and ample resources and had what we thought was a sound strategy to create a world-wide network of distributors. But the division simply didn't fly. And by 2000, we began facing our more pressing post-merger challenges that demanded our full attention and resources. There was a residual benefit to this episode, though. Ill-fated though it was, our international division proved to be the catalyst that led to our four acquisitions in Canada. Four of the strongest regional players came together to form the first national network in Canada, and they *have* paid the dividends we envisioned.

In fiscal year 2003, dividends of any kind seemed hard to find, as an old copy of my remarks to shareholders that year acknowledge. That was another rough bump along the way. Revenues and earnings both tumbled, and we lost a few high-profile clients, too. In the aftermath of the tough times of 2000 and 2001, it was a bitter pill to have to swallow. But we did, and in 2004 our trend of annual increases in revenues and earnings resumed. In retrospect, a down year like 2003 proved to be beneficial in at least one respect. It kept us hungry and humble, taught us a few things, and helped condition us for other challenges to come.

If I've learned anything from tough times and lousy business conditions, it's to never ever think about resting on your laurels. For one thing, we learned to use our dollars ever more efficiently. Credit for that largely goes to Greg Delaney, Acosta's chief financial officer since 2002. Greg became a real master at working with our banks and building relationships. Initially, some of the challenges caught him off guard a bit, as Greg will acknowledge. In the end, though, our ability to manage our dollars helped us grow earnings at a higher rate than we were growing revenues—and what's that say about synergy?

One of Acosta's good ideas over the past ten years has been "filling in the white space." Essentially, it's the label we put on a strategy to generate more business from our existing clients, in particular our top 200 clients. There certainly is more business out there, too. It will surprise many people to learn that of Acosta's 1,200 clients, fewer than 80 are national clients; to be sure, our national accounts represent better than 75 percent of our $60 billion in annual sales. Even so, we still see an opportunity to keep growing and win more business. And that's what it's all about.

Look at it this way: Striving to win *all* of a client's business may be another unreasonable notion, but it keeps you hungry and competitive.

I've tried to keep myself hungry and competitive, too, and say, *"Don't screw it up!"* as I look in the mirror. Throughout my career, I have always wanted to improve my skills, whether I was selling, managing, or leading. There was nothing to prove to anyone, just a desire for self-improvement. As my responsibilities increased, so did my desire to get smarter. As a practical matter, I always had to keep learning, especially when it came to finance. Remember, I went off to college to be a teacher and a coach, not the leader of an enterprise with more than $60 billion in sales.

In turn, I've tried never to take myself too seriously or put myself on a pedestal. I'm just a guy from New Hampshire who "carried a bag," as we sales guys say, worked hard, and tried to take advantage of the opportunities that came along. And one of the opportunities has been to learn as much as I could about managing and leading an organization. Now that I have been able to see and assess the results, here's a selection of the cornerstone lessons that have served me—and Acosta—well:

Never be afraid to ask. It easily stands as number one on my list. You never assume what the answer might be nor predict what you'll learn simply by asking—even if the answer isn't the one you hope to hear.

I still cannot picture Acosta's being the organization and industry leader it is today had I not asked Minute Maid for financial assistance in 1998, and later Clorox. Without the combined $35 million in loans these companies provided, our expansion bid might have never gotten off the ground. We certainly would not have had the dollars to purchase Kelley-Clarke, which was a pivotal acquisition in our "Get National!" strategy.

As essential as the dollars were, getting confirmation that we would have strong influential allies supporting us as we tried to achieve the allegedly unachievable was just as important—if not more so. They were critical endorsements that told an entire industry, "This is where we're all headed."

We did have to prepare for some fallout, for there was an annoying quid pro quo that came with the Minute Maid and Clorox dollars. We had to prove that we didn't give them preferential treatment and worked just as hard for all of our other clients. As engineers say, proving a negative is virtually impossible. Despite our best efforts, news of the assistance still found its way onto the industry grapevine, where it got seriously distorted; word was that we'd given both Minute Maid and Clorox ownership stakes! Rumors were so rampant that I finally had to issue an official statement assuring the world that neither Minute Maid nor Clorox had any equity interest in our company.

Truth be told, my bold request of Minute Maid really wasn't my first one. I made a similar appeal—albeit for far less support— to Heinz in 1997, essentially to help us build a relationship with Wal-Mart. As late as 1996, we hadn't been doing any business with Wal-Mart at all. We certainly hadn't needed to do business with them, however, given the mass merchandising giant's onrushing march into the grocery business. Heinz, too, said yes, and its support helped us get our first appointment at Wal-Mart, which paid us $920,000 a year. Within 60 days, we grew that business to $2.5 million! Today it's much, much larger, of course, and we have a full team of associates in Wal-Mart's headquarters city of Bentonville, Arkansas. Notably, the leader of that team is Senior Vice President Brian Baldwin, one of the architects of Acosta's culture.

You're better off having partners who want to help you than you are with partners whose actions and attitudes could hurt you. The realization hit me during the aftermath of the H.J. Heinz appointment we received in 1997. The appointment represented $8 million worth of new business and presented an opportunity to draw a line in the sand. Representing Heinz suddenly put about $10 million of existing business in jeopardy, because in one market sector, Acosta already represented products made by a chief rival, Nestlé. As expected, Nestlé promptly cited a conflict and expected us to decline to serve Heinz. I politely declined. "You'll have to fire us, because we're not going to resign your account," I had told Nestlé's management.

It didn't come to that, as I explained in an earlier step. But at the time, I was quite willing to look Nestlé straight in the eye after asking myself this question: "Who would you rather have alongside you: Someone who wants to help you or someone who won't?" Long term, the answer was obvious: Heinz, because they were quite willing to help us and also willing to adjust their definition of conflicts. It was a key attitude shift, because I knew that Heinz's stand on that issue would help the expansion I was then envisioning.

There was irony in this dilemma over conflicts, too. A dozen or so years earlier, Acosta *had* resigned a major revenue-producing account to accept the Nestlé appointment precisely because Nestlé was eager to help us grow throughout Florida. The client we resigned had been tough to work with as well.

Fortunately, Nestlé ultimately saw the benefits of retaining us and reconsidered its position. In fact, that was another benefit of my firm stand: I helped convince Nestlé to, as Nino Cristofoli says, "Throw its conflicts policy out the window." And good riddance! I'd hate to try to total the hours I spent in the late 1980s and 1990s researching and preparing letters and memos about conflicts that now seem largely inconsequential.

Today, notably, Nestlé is Acosta's single largest client, and Heinz is among our largest clients. I have high regard for them both and am glad they are with us, helping grow our business.

The bigger the relationship, the more it becomes a partner-

ship. Representing a client in one city, or even one state, was one thing; representing that same client across the country created a much, much stronger "we need each other" kind of relationship. That enabled us to seek help when we needed it—such as the time I asked selected clients to pay us sooner than industry tradition dictated to help us cope with the aftermath of Marketing Specialists' demise in 2001. My appealing to Clorox to help us with Kelley-Clarke in late 1998 is another case in point.

Simply stated, the more we grew, and the more capabilities we acquired, the more important we became to our clients—and, to be sure, the more important our clients became to us. We each had a stake in our continued success. In turn, many client relationships steadily evolved into what are better described as partnerships. That afforded us both numerous advantages—as long as we took care not to take the partnership for granted.

The definition of leverage usually implies an attempt to gain an unfair advantage. This is not necessarily true, however; as our client relationships strengthened and business volumes increased, we gained economies of scale that enabled us to expand our capabilities. In turn, Acosta wound up with more services to offer our clients—further strengthening the relationships.

Share the wealth. As old-fashioned as it sounds, sharing the wealth still pays ample dividends. The policy Del Dallas established to allow Acosta's key managers to acquire minority ownership interests was a masterstroke that continues to serve our company. Just as becoming an owner was a powerful motivation to me in the 1980s, it remains so "for the rest of us," as executive team colleague Jack Parker quips now and then. It was a key factor that brought Jack to Acosta in 1991 (from Clorox). This policy was so important that when Berkshire Partners, LLC, first acquired its significant minority interest in 2003, we went to great lengths to protect the existing ownership interests held by Acosta's managers and executives. To Berkshire's credit, they were of the same mind-set. It added complexity to that deal, but it was well worth it.

Yes, today our company's majority owner is an outside firm. Still, a notable and significant minority percentage of Acosta stock remains in the hands of the company's executives and managers. And it remains as important an incentive as ever.

There's no magic to it at all. Ownership simply helps keep everyone's focus on performance and serving clients, because so many people have an additional stake in the outcome along with their salaries and bonuses. Throughout the tough times following the mergers, it was an especially powerful motivator for a sizable number of managers – not just a small handful of inner-circle executives. In this case, at least, there *is* strength in numbers.

Moreover, ownership helps Acosta build succeeding generations of leadership and perpetuate the business. You won't hear about exit strategies at Acosta. It's not part of our culture. Del Dallas had that in mind, too. Grooming the next generation of company leadership was always uppermost in his mind. Indeed, Del at one point advocated a new ownership team taking command about every 10 to 12 years. We still embrace that philosophy today, and it was a key reason why I stepped aside in 2009 as CEO and appointed Robert Hill to take the company into the future.

Know what you don't know. From my first day on the job with Carnation, I've always tried to take advantage of every opportunity to learn. To that end, I usually get good marks from colleagues of every rank for being a reasonably good listener and knowing when to keep my mouth shut (most of the time, anyway). It's a great way to learn. Among 10 "double-win rules" that are supposed to lead to top team performance is this one: "Listening is the most neglected skill in business today. The person who listens controls the final outcome of the discussion. Encourage others to talk, and then consciously remove any barrier to your good listening skills."

I don't know who penned that nugget of wisdom, or the nine other accompanying double-win rules. Nor can I recall where, when, or how I ran across them. But I agree with them all and have tried to embrace them—which is why all 10 double-win rules appear in Appendix A. They exemplify my long-standing habit of collecting assorted "stuff" and then stuffing it into files. As they say, "read and remember." Other anecdotes and lessons I have collected have been woven throughout these pages.

Make new friends and keep the old. Carnation's management wasn't exactly overjoyed when I resigned in late 1983 to join Acosta. Even so, I did my best to maintain the friendships I had made. By now, it should be pretty apparent how helpful those ties became after Carnation became part of Nestlé! Then again, so have all my friendships. They were essential to both planning and unrolling Acosta's "Get

National!" strategy, not to mention the tough times that followed.

Employees don't care how much you know about them as long as they know how much you care about them. This is true at least in one respect. Within reason, employees have to feel safe about their jobs and their organization to consistently deliver their best efforts over the long haul. Fear is said to be a great motivator, and within the corporate world, there are untold numbers of managers and bosses who rely on it. I'm not one of them. Certainly, there are occasions that call for discipline and rebuke, and you need to consistently set high standards. But if employees are to consistently meet and exceed high standards, they've first got to feel good about themselves and their abilities, and they have to have the latitude to succeed.

Three things will destroy any company: greed, arrogance, and complacency. Look at any enterprise that fails to endure, and you will find at least one of these characteristics ever present inside the company. Enough said.

Build with the best. To become the industry leader, we had to unite with the strongest partners we could find and be relentless about avoiding any compromises. In the final analysis, what we were acquiring were people and relationships.

"Build with the best" also applies to individuals. We had to recruit and hire the very best and brightest we could find. The flip side applies, too. As former General Electric Co. CEO Jack Welch put it, "Get the poison out early." Among my clippings of collected wisdom is an unexpected observation. The great companies that were studied became great not so much from bold vision and strategy but from getting "the right people on the bus, the wrong people off the bus and the right people in the right seats—and *then* they figured out where to drive it." Like I said during my September 1999 speech to our managers, it wasn't people who made the difference, but the *right* people.

The company's health must come first. If you don't take care of the business, the business will not take care of you. Findings of an internal survey we once commissioned, as well as assorted anecdotal comments gathered by third-party research, give Acosta's management high marks for the leadership shown throughout the tough times. Lots of factors contributed to that, but by far the most important was this: We never took our eyes off the goal. Never! No matter what happened, the company came first. That kind of focus, I have learned, is consistent among great companies and corporate leaderships studied by various researchers. Yes, incredible ambition is evident, but the ambition, and not the leaders, researchers find, "is first and foremost for the institution."

Finally, throughout my career, I have also collected assorted lists. Here's one of my favorites, because I subscribe to each and every bullet point.

Formula for Top Management Performance

- Show honest and sincere appreciation at every opportunity; make the other person feel important.
- Don't criticize, condemn, or complain.
- Make your cause bigger than your ego.
- Work for progress, not for perfection.
- Be solution-conscious, not problem-oriented.
- Invest time in the activity that brings the highest return on investment, according to the priority list of responsibilities. Effort alone doesn't count; results are the reasons for activity.
- Fulfilling responsibility is good reason to work; discipline is the method.
- Recognize and accept your own weaknesses.
- Make check lists and constantly refer to them.
- *Always* show the people in your life the humility of gratitude.

As a matter of course, however, I also showed people something else, and usually before I showed them anything else. Almost to this day, Chief Financial Officer Greg Delaney remains amazed at "what we were able to pull off," as he characterizes it. "The epitome of salesmanship" is another Delaney characterization. He describes it like this: "We'll buy your company. We're not actually going to give you all the money now, just a small down payment. Then, as we produce the profits from your business next month, next quarter, and next year, we'll give you a share of those profits. And you'll also need to assume the risk that we are going to be able to produce those profits for the period of time it takes us to pay you out."

Upon hearing Greg's observation, another friend of mine found himself recalling the proposal pitched by Wimpy, the chubby cartoon character pal of Popeye the Sailor: "I'll gladly pay you Tuesday for a hamburger today." Essentially, Acosta convinced scores of successful food brokers that we could run their businesses as well as or better than they could by making them part of Acosta, that we would pay them off with the profits our combined businesses generated, and that we would all live happily ever after.

Looking at it today, that proposition may well stand as the most unreasonable idea of all. But it worked! And it made everything else work. It's also made me appreciate the renowned observation you read at the end of Step 1. George Bernard Shaw was right. All progress comes from unreasonable people.

Food for Thought

If one advances confidently in the direction of his dreams, and endeavors to live the life which he has imagined, he will meet with a success unexpected in common hours.

— Henry David Thoreau

Appendix A

The Ten "Double-Win" Rules That Lead to Top Team Performance

1. Remember that a smile is the most powerful social tool we have at our disposal.
2. Listening is the most neglected skill in business (or home) today. The person who listens controls the final outcome of the discussion. Encourage others to talk, and then consciously remove any barriers to your good listening skills.
3. Talk in terms of the other person's interest. You will find a "uniqueness" and "specialness" in every individual you meet. Check out the other person's point of view.
4. Ask questions you already know the answer to and you will get to see the other person's perspective. Most ideas are more palatable if we "discover" them ourselves. People who truly care about others lead them down the "discovery path!"
5. "What you are speaks so loudly I can't hear what you say." Remember to model the behavior and attitude you want the other person to have.
6. Give assignments that allow you to express faith and confidence that the other person can successfully perform the task assigned.
7. Always make requests, never give orders.
8. Develop your ability to use the narrative story and the meaningful analogy—these are powerful teaching tools.
9. Always be respectful of others. Show your respect by being on time for meetings or letting others know you must be late.
10. Return phone calls and letters immediately—there is no excuse for not doing so.

Appendix B: Unreasonable Leadership Dimensions

SELF CONFIDENCE AND COURAGE	DRIVE, PASSION, & VISION
• I view myself as a leader. • I believe in myself and my ability to win big. • I believe in our team and its ability to win big. • I push myself out of my comfort zone. • I take risks and push others to do so. • I make quick and educated decisions. • I am brutally honest with myself, my team, my organization, and my clients. • I am not afraid of failure. I create and set BHAGs. • I am not afraid to challenge others and am always willing to put issues on the table. • I am not afraid to stand up for what is right and face conflict head on.	• I always want more. • I often set what might seem to others as "unattainable" goals. • I always have a strong desire to win big. • I have a strong desire to stretch and grow. • I am passionate about everything I do. • I identify intensely with the goals and mission of my organization. • I have a strong desire to create something bigger than myself. • I have a clear vision of what I want and where I want to be. • I strive to make an impact in everything I do. • I am not satisfied with moderate success or limited change. • I am able to clearly paint a picture of the goal. • I dream big. • I exhibit a strong internal will to win that permeates the team and organization. • I can create a compelling story of my vision—with clarity that others can embrace. • I seize responsibility. • I initiate "unreasonable" ideas. • I want and expect to win. • I have a strong internal drive for success that motivates my actions.

PEOPLE ORIENTATION	ACTION ORIENTATION
• I am a good listener. I care about how people feel and what they need. • I have the ability to build strong, honest relationships based on trust. • I am capable of genuinely motivating and encouraging others. • I am externally focused on my team and clients. • I enjoy helping others get what they want so they are successful as well. • I am charismatic and likable. • I spend my time influencing people, teams, and clients. • I believe in the power of team. • People work with me, not for me. • I recognize that there is no "I" in "team."	• I am capable of absorbing and practicing concepts. • I execute against goals in a consistent and structured approach. • I am action oriented. I like to get things done. • I am deliberate and intentional in my actions. • I ask for what I need. • I hold people accountable and am firm with consequences.

STRATEGY	ETHICS AND VALUES
• I see opportunity when others don't. • I paint a clear picture of where we are going so we can create it together. • I build a sense of being in this together. • I live with a sense of urgency to make a difference in the world. • I am grounded in a strong knowledge of my business. • Failure is not an option. • I empower people.	• I believe in doing the right thing. All my actions must leave me with my integrity intact. • I am honest and completely transparent. What you see is what you get. • I do not play politics. • I have a strong conviction to keep commitments. • I am principled and ethical; I will always do the right thing. • I believe in hard work. • I build teams and organizations with an underlying commitment of shared values.
PHYSICAL & EMOTIONAL WELL-BEING	**EMOTIONAL INTELLIGENCE**
• I sustain a high level of energy. • I work hard and have fun. • I have a sense of humor. • I am optimistic. • I have the will and energy to work hard.	• I am aware of my weaknesses and strengths. • I understand my emotional triggers. • I am brutally honest with myself. • I accurately perceive emotions in myself and others. • I am capable of managing and controlling my emotions. • I am aware of my self-destructive patterns and learn from them.

MY EXECUTIVE SOLUTIONS
The power of one: one leader, one team, one organization

APPENDIX C:
THE UNREASONABLE
LEADERSHIP ASSESSMENT

Created by Jane Shannon, PhD and Nina Stelfox
My Executive Solutions, Inc.

Objective

The objective of this self-assessment is to assist you in analyzing behavior patterns and increase your awareness on the core Unreasonable Leadership Competencies. This process will identify opportunities for you to maximize your strengths and develop your weaknesses.

Change is created when a series of actions create momentum and are positively reinforced. By taking the time to consider the strategies that you can begin to practice <u>now</u>, you will significantly improve your leadership effectiveness.

Remember, it's only when you move out of your comfort zone that "unreasonable" leadership occurs!

Instructions

1. Each competency is independent from the others. Per competency, rate yourself on each of the 12 areas of Unreasonable Leadership, and select the rating option that most closely and honestly reflects your current leadership effectiveness.
2. Each rating option has been assigned a value. At the end of each competency, add your response values and determine your competency level.

3. Stop and reflect, notate your ideas regarding how to improve in each area, being as specific as you can be to your particular leadership situation.

4. After you have completed your self-assessment process, create your Action Plan.

DRIVE, PASSION, AND VISION

As a Leader...

I drive results with passion and energy.
o NEVER (1)   o RARELY (2)   o FREQUENTLY (3)   o ALWAYS (4)   o UNDECIDED (0)

I have a strong desire to excel with the clear intention to produce extraordinary results.
o NEVER (1)   o RARELY (2)   o FREQUENTLY (3)   o ALWAYS (4)   o UNDECIDED (0)

I am passionate about life. I have the ability to communicate that passion with enthusiasm to others.
o NEVER (1)   o RARELY (2)   o FREQUENTLY (3)   o ALWAYS (4)   o UNDECIDED (0)

I have a strong desire to stretch and grow.
o NEVER (1)   o RARELY (2)   o FREQUENTLY (3)   o ALWAYS (4)   o UNDECIDED (0)

I passionately embrace the goals and mission of my organization. I relentlessly pursue goals, regardless of the setbacks.
o NEVER (1)   o RARELY (2)   o FREQUENTLY (3)   o ALWAYS (4)   o UNDECIDED (0)

I have a strong internal drive for success. I strive to make an impact in everything I do.
o NEVER (1)   o RARELY (2)   o FREQUENTLY (3)   o ALWAYS (4)   o UNDECIDED (0)

I initiate and embrace change. I am not satisfied with "slow, incremental" change.
o NEVER (1)   o RARELY (2)   o FREQUENTLY (3)   o ALWAYS (4)   o UNDECIDED (0)

I exhibit a strong internal will to win that permeates my interactions with the team and the organization.
o NEVER (1)   o RARELY (2)   o FREQUENTLY (3)   o ALWAYS (4)   o UNDECIDED (0)

I create a compelling story of my vision and can communicate it with clarity, and in a way that others connect with emotionally.
o NEVER (1)   o RARELY (2)   o FREQUENTLY (3)   o ALWAYS (4)   o UNDECIDED (0)

I maximize growth opportunities seeking to transform people, processes, systems, and organizations.
o NEVER (1)   o RARELY (2)   o FREQUENTLY (3)   o ALWAYS (4)   o UNDECIDED (0)

I introduce "unreasonable" ideas to challenge the status quo.
o NEVER (1)   o RARELY (2)   o FREQUENTLY (3)   o ALWAYS (4)   o UNDECIDED (0)

I expect to win. I am willing to make sacrifices and will do whatever it takes to be successful.
o NEVER (1)   o RARELY (2)   o FREQUENTLY (3)   o ALWAYS (4)   o UNDECIDED (0)

MY SCORE IS _____

DRIVE, PASSION, AND VISION

Your Rating	Your Level	Description
37–48	Level 1—High	You have the potential to transform your organization and your industry. Your passion, energy, and enthusiasm are contagious and inspiring. You create followership by your actions.
		Continue to seek opportunities to influence others at the national or global level. Dare to take the next step in your journey of unreasonable leadership by writing a book, expanding your reach, or transforming society. Offer to teach a segment of a graduate-level course; actively engage with the organization's "high potentials."
25–37	Level 2—Medium	You exhibit some passion and interest regarding your work and have ideas about what can be improved. You may struggle with clarifying your vision to others. You may not be using your own personal charisma to move others to achieve extraordinary results.
		Reevaluate how you are spending your time and energy. You have only so much energy that might scatter or defuse while you may be going through a difficult time in your life. Consider familial influences such as life-cycle changes that may diminish your power and focus at work. In these situations, you might find yourself physically and emotionally exhausted. Explore where and when the change occurred.

- Look back and determine what you were excited about when you moved into your role. Work on redefining your role. Spend your time doing more of what interests you. What is your passion?
- Find a mentor who can objectively help you assess what is occurring within the organization that may be affecting your level of passion and commitment.
- Assess the talent in your team. Determine who your "A" players are and upgrade your talent. Do you have the right people on the team to help you achieve greater results?
- Establish a series of wins. There is nothing like success to reenergize teams. Celebrate a series of these small wins to create momentum.

0–24   Level 3—Low   Organizationally, you may perceive yourself as a victim of turbulent chronic "circumstances." You have become comfortable and operate within the status quo, or you may be in transition and are uncertain as to where you fit within the organization.

You may have also become complacent or have made the decision to check out.

- Take action. Reassess whether you are in the right role or the right organization, and have the courage to make the necessary changes. Rediscover your passion, and move toward that direction.

- During transitional periods, identify and recognize your fears, and do not allow your fears to limit your success. Read *The Power of Focus* by Jack Canfield, Mark Victor Hansen, and Les Hewitt.

- Focus on reclaiming your power, and move to a place of energy and courage to face whatever is stopping you from passionately pursuing your dreams and vision.

- Life is too short. If you are not passionate about what you are doing, objectively assess what your options are and explore other opportunities. Identify a date in the future when you see yourself driven and passionate again. Use your strong analytical mind to create a strategy for yourself and your successes.

SELF-CONFIDENCE AND COURAGE

As a Leader...

I believe in myself and in my ability to "think and win big."
o NEVER (1)   o RARELY (2)   o FREQUENTLY (3)   o ALWAYS (4)   o UNDECIDED (0)

I negotiate from a position of strength.
o NEVER (1)   o RARELY (2)   o FREQUENTLY (3)   o ALWAYS (4)   o UNDECIDED (0)

I communicate with a sense of confidence. I present facts, data, analysis, and solutions in a way that demonstrates command of the content and interest of the audience and show's what's in it for them.
o NEVER (1)   o RARELY (2)   o FREQUENTLY (3)   o ALWAYS (4)   o UNDECIDED (0)

I push myself out of my comfort zone, consistently taking personal and professional risks to grow and stretch in my abilities.
o NEVER (1)   o RARELY (2)   o FREQUENTLY (3)   o ALWAYS (4)   o UNDECIDED (0)

I value people who challenge my thinking. I learn from others' points of view.
o NEVER (1)   o RARELY (2)   o FREQUENTLY (3)   o ALWAYS (4)   o UNDECIDED (0)

I am not afraid of making decisions and taking responsibility for my own mistakes instead of blaming others.
o NEVER (1)   o RARELY (2)   o FREQUENTLY (3)   o ALWAYS (4)   o UNDECIDED (0)

I use my personal power in communicating openly and honestly with others.
o NEVER (1)   o RARELY (2)   o FREQUENTLY (3)   o ALWAYS (4)   o UNDECIDED (0)

I am not afraid of failure. I create and set BHAG (big hairy audacious goals).
o NEVER (1)   o RARELY (2)   o FREQUENTLY (3)   o ALWAYS (4)   o UNDECIDED (0)

I am not afraid to challenge others and am willing to put issues on the table. Feedback is an opportunity for improvement.
o NEVER (1)   o RARELY (2)   o FREQUENTLY (3)   o ALWAYS (4)   o UNDECIDED (0)

I am able to stay objective and professional when others become emotionally reactive.
o NEVER (1)   o RARELY (2)   o FREQUENTLY (3)   o ALWAYS (4)   o UNDECIDED (0)

I face conflict openly and am not afraid to stand up for what I firmly believe is right.
o NEVER (1)   o RARELY (2)   o FREQUENTLY (3)   o ALWAYS (4)   o UNDECIDED (0)

I have a positive self-image. I know and own what I bring to my role as leader.
o NEVER (1)   o RARELY (2)   o FREQUENTLY (3)   o ALWAYS (4)   o UNDECIDED (0)

MY SCORE IS _____

SELF-CONFIDENCE AND COURAGE

Your Rating	Your Level	Description
37–48	Level 1—High	You exude a strong sense of self and inspire confidence in others. Your presence commands respect from others and is reassuring during times of crisis. You are perceived as credible and as someone who knows how to win. People listen to you; they want to be on your team and learn from you.
		Continue to use your influence to motivate and inspire high potentials. Consider writing an article in your field of study or presenting at conferences, establishing yourself as an expert in your field.
		Recognize the power and credibility that you hold in your organization. Use this power wisely to drive unreasonable results.
25–37	Level 2—Medium	You are on the right track. You are developing a stronger sense of self-confidence by becoming more grounded and developing stronger expertise in your field.
		• Remember that the most important factor in increasing your self-esteem is the power of positive thinking.
		• Visualize your future successes. Reframe failures and learning and continue to take confident actions.
		• Read *Expect to Win* by Carla Harris.
0–24	Level 3—Low	Your low self-confidence is stopping you from achieving the next level of success. Self-confidence can be developed by focusing internally and tapping into your strengths.
		• Stop comparing yourself to other people. Get in touch with your true authentic self, which is perfect in every way. Learn to appreciate who you are and what you uniquely bring to your role of leader.
		• Don't beat yourself up! Learn from your mistakes and move on. Use positive affirmations. This is an excellent way to raise your self-esteem and increase your batting average
		• Hire an executive coach who will challenge you to become the best you can be and will objectively assess and link underlying dynamics to behavioral patterns.

- Participate in leadership effectiveness workshops to help you accelerate your leadership growth.
- Read *The Power of Your Subconscious Mind* by Dr. Joseph Murphy.

ACTION ORIENTATION

As a Leader...

I am action oriented. I excel at getting things done.
o NEVER (1)   o RARELY (2)   o FREQUENTLY (3)   o ALWAYS (4)   o UNDECIDED (0)

I am intensely focused on my goals.
o NEVER (1)   o RARELY (2)   o FREQUENTLY (3)   o ALWAYS (4)   o UNDECIDED (0)

I am capable of taking action, proactively seeking out opportunities outside my comfort zone to offer solutions and strategies.
o NEVER (1)   o RARELY (2)   o FREQUENTLY (3)   o ALWAYS (4)   o UNDECIDED (0)

I create a work environment that establishes creative thinking and innovation as the norm, encouraging individuals to take risks to achieve extraordinary results.
o NEVER (1)   o RARELY (2)   o FREQUENTLY (3)   o ALWAYS (4)   o UNDECIDED (0)

I am deliberate and intentional in executing on deliverables, handling multiple challenges well and balancing heavy workloads, tight deadlines, or other pressures.
o NEVER (1)   o RARELY (2)   o FREQUENTLY (3)   o ALWAYS (4)   o UNDECIDED (0)

I ask for what I need.
o NEVER (1)   o RARELY (2)   o FREQUENTLY (3)   o ALWAYS (4)   o UNDECIDED (0)

I recover quickly from failures and setbacks and understand that learning comes from making mistakes.
o NEVER (1)   o RARELY (2)   o FREQUENTLY (3)   o ALWAYS (4)   o UNDECIDED (0)

I hold individuals and teams accountable for on time and well-executed deliverables and am firm with consequences.
o NEVER (1)   o RARELY (2)   o FREQUENTLY (3)   o ALWAYS (4)   o UNDECIDED (0)

I do not allow distractions to impede my team's focus on critical deliverables.
o NEVER (1)   o RARELY (2)   o FREQUENTLY (3)   o ALWAYS (4)   o UNDECIDED (0)

I quickly adapt to changing circumstances and proactively resolve issues with practical solutions and actions.
o NEVER (1)   o RARELY (2)   o FREQUENTLY (3)   o ALWAYS (4)   o UNDECIDED (0)

I surround myself strategically with others who are action oriented and have the ability to turn ideas and concepts into practical solutions.
o NEVER (1)   o RARELY (2)   o FREQUENTLY (3)   o ALWAYS (4)   o UNDECIDED (0)

I know and communicate my priorities. Although I do not micromanage, I consistently follow up with my team to ensure alignment on priorities and provide the necessary guidance through completion.
o NEVER (1)   o RARELY (2)   o FREQUENTLY (3)   o ALWAYS (4)   o UNDECIDED (0)

MY SCORE IS _____

ACTION ORIENTATION

Your Rating	Your Level	Description
37–48	Level 1—High	You are recognized as result-oriented. Your ability to drive results is well established within your organization. "Just do it" is your mantra, which could potentially lead to a level of disengagement with others. Celebrate your wins and recognize your team. As a precaution, be sure to schedule time for thoughtful strategy and analysis, having some white space to plan and reflect on your vision going forward. Your opportunity is to leverage your expertise and ability to get things done by choosing broader, high-profile initiatives to gain more visibility within your organization and maximize your impact.
25–37	Level 2—Medium	You have had some successes and some failures. There is something that is preventing you from executing flawlessly. You are known as someone who can get things done given the right circumstances and the right team. You might be more methodical in your approach and less prone to taking risks. You carefully weigh the pros and cons before raising your hand; you may be lacking a strong sense of urgency and tend to let circumstances or others control you and your team's outcomes. To maximize your ability to execute and achieve extraordinary results: • Assess your team. Do you have the right resources and the right level of expertise? Objectively evaluate your team's strengths and weaknesses at an individual and functional level. • Critically examine how you spend your time and identify opportunities to maximize your time and efficiency. • Step back and identify what are the fundamental issues preventing execution. Evaluate the initiatives thoroughly from end to end. Are the objectives and deliverables clear? Where are the disconnects occurring? What are the milestones? Bring the team together to establish a game plan to move forward. Link the actions to a game-changing result. Make

sure you connect the dots, communicating how the team's actions can make a difference.

- Read *Execution: The Discipline of Getting Things Done* by Larry Bossidy, Ram Charan, and Charles Burck.

0–24	Level 3—Low	

You struggle with meeting aggressive deadlines. Your team may have experienced misses in delivering on time and with quality results. You might need to reinforce your discipline, rigor, and focus, and project management skills.

To increase your efficiency:

- Begin by clearly identifying the key priorities and how they are aligned to your team's and organization's successes. Redirect your focus and time to those initiatives that bring the most value.

- Define what winning means. What are the key areas in which you must execute and be successful in your role? What specific outcomes are expected as a result of this initiative?

- Focus on a few critical projects and deep dive into your end-to-end approach. Strategize how you will most effectively get things done. Ensure that once you gain clarity on this strategy, you communicate this to your entire team.

- Initiate status reports, outline your 100-day plan, and focus on measuring your success through a disciplined approach.

- Beyond reading articles and books on execution, read *Failing Forward, Turning Mistakes into Stepping Stones for Success* by John Maxwell.

STRATEGY and BUSINESS ACUMEN

As a Leader...

I see opportunity when others don't, formulating strategies that leverage the organization's strengths to address customer and consumer trends.

o NEVER (1)   o RARELY (2)   o FREQUENTLY (3)   o ALWAYS (4)   o UNDECIDED (0)

I present a picture of where we are going so that together, as a team, we can cocreate the destination.

o NEVER (1)   o RARELY (2)   o FREQUENTLY (3)   o ALWAYS (4)   o UNDECIDED (0)

I consistently take time to step back from the operational day-to-day activities and reflect on where we are as an organization, identifying the gap between today's reality and my direction and intent for the future.

o NEVER (1)   o RARELY (2)   o FREQUENTLY (3)   o ALWAYS (4)   o UNDECIDED (0)

I maintain a competitive edge in the marketplace by understanding how we differentiate ourselves in the industry. I recognize the importance of maintaining competitive analysis data, which helps us increase our market share. I am able to adapt approaches and shift ideas when new information suggests the need to do so.

o NEVER (1)   o RARELY (2)   o FREQUENTLY (3)   o ALWAYS (4)   o UNDECIDED (0)

I focus on implementing strategies using an end-to-end approach, ensuring we have the capacity and resources to leverage growth opportunities.

o NEVER (1)   o RARELY (2)   o FREQUENTLY (3)   o ALWAYS (4)   o UNDECIDED (0)

I stay current in my field. I know and can predict industry trends and adapt easily to rapid changes in the way we execute our business.

o NEVER (1)   o RARELY (2)   o FREQUENTLY (3)   o ALWAYS (4)   o UNDECIDED (0)

I move out of my comfort zone. I seek innovation from all levels of the organization and actively create opportunities for diverse thinking.

o NEVER (1)   o RARELY (2)   o FREQUENTLY (3)   o ALWAYS (4)   o UNDECIDED (0)

I focus on building talent in my team and organization to drive change and support organizational strategies for growth.

o NEVER (1)   o RARELY (2)   o FREQUENTLY (3)   o ALWAYS (4)   o UNDECIDED (0)

I have an intuitive and applicable understanding of what drives profitability and operate with a market-focused approach. I understand the overall big picture of my business and its interrelationships, which allows me to make better business decisions. I examine facts, figures, and ideas and can intuitively gauge potential risks and successes.

o NEVER (1)   o RARELY (2)   o FREQUENTLY (3)   o ALWAYS (4)   o UNDECIDED (0)

I connect the dots for others, linking current reality to the organizational vision of the future.

o NEVER (1)   o RARELY (2)   o FREQUENTLY (3)   o ALWAYS (4)   o UNDECIDED (0)

When strategic options are being evaluated, I ask the hard questions and demand frank discussion and robust analysis prior to implementation.

o NEVER (1)   o RARELY (2)   o FREQUENTLY (3)   o ALWAYS (4)   o UNDECIDED (0)

MY SCORE IS _____

STRATEGY and BUSINESS ACUMEN

Your Rating	Your Level	Description
37–48	Level 1—High	You drive change within your industry. You take time to focus on strategy as part of your everyday practice. Rather than being seen as a once-a-quarter initiative, you are adept at making the leap between current reality and future state.
		• Continue to broaden your network of strategic partners to include industry experts. Remember to focus on building strategic relationships as you invest time with others to explore mutual opportunities.
		• Read *Billion Dollar Lessons* by Paul B. Carroll and Chunka Mui.
25–37	Level 2—Medium	You are heavily engaged in the operational aspects and have developed a high level of expertise. You may excel at identifying process improvements to gain efficiencies. You may struggle with stepping back and visualizing the bigger picture.
		• Get a mentor whose strength is strategic thinking, or hire a consulting firm who specializes in strategic planning.
		• Ensure that you are regularly gathering competitive analysis data that will help you guide your strategic decisions.
		• Don't underestimate the impact of your clients' and customers' strategic visions on your organizational success. Seek to align and proactively anticipate the next generation of thought in your industry.
		• During the analysis phase of exploring a strategic direction, ensure that a member of your team assumes the role of devil's advocate to help you thoroughly assess your analysis prior to your implementation. You objective is to weigh the pros and cons of various strategies so you can calculate and appropriately mitigate your risk.
0–24	Level 3—Low	You are successful in a functional area of the business. You may view your role as that of a subject matter expert, and you likely possess in-depth industry knowledge.
		By expanding your comfort zone and approaching your business from a broader perspective, you can increase your influence and move your organization to the next level of growth.

- Train your mind to think strategically. Block white space on your own calendar and pull your team off-site for one day each quarter to strategize and align future goals.

- Examine your ability to take risks. Start with small opportunities where the potential for failure exists but will marginally impact your budget or balance sheet.

- Focus on understanding the financial aspects of your business by analyzing data. How do you increase your profit margin? How can you accelerate growth? During the analysis phase, be transparent and objectively communicate the pros and cons of each strategy to upper management and stakeholders. Be thoroughly prepared to answer questions using supportive evidence, without becoming defensive.

- Once you have established the direction that you are going, create a compelling story so you are able to convince the organization that this is a viable strategy that must be embraced. Along the way, ensure that your key stakeholders are fully engaged.

ETHICS AND VALUES

As a Leader...

I believe in doing the right thing. I lead with integrity.
o NEVER (1)   o RARELY (2)   o FREQUENTLY (3)   o ALWAYS (4)   o UNDECIDED (0)

I am honest and direct when sharing information with others.
o NEVER (1)   o RARELY (2)   o FREQUENTLY (3)   o ALWAYS (4)   o UNDECIDED (0)

I keep my commitments.
o NEVER (1)   o RARELY (2)   o FREQUENTLY (3)   o ALWAYS (4)   o UNDECIDED (0)

I value strength in character. Actions speak louder than words.
o NEVER (1)   o RARELY (2)   o FREQUENTLY (3)   o ALWAYS (4)   o UNDECIDED (0)

I believe that hard work pays off. I have the willingness to invest my time and roll up my sleeves to learn critical aspects of my business and do what needs to get done.
o NEVER (1)   o RARELY (2)   o FREQUENTLY (3)   o ALWAYS (4)   o UNDECIDED (0)

I care deeply about the quality of all aspects of the work that I lead.
o NEVER (1)   o RARELY (2)   o FREQUENTLY (3)   o ALWAYS (4)   o UNDECIDED (0)

I build an underlying commitment of shared values.
o NEVER (1)   o RARELY (2)   o FREQUENTLY (3)   o ALWAYS (4)   o UNDECIDED (0)

I am accountable and own my failures. I take responsibility for my actions.
o NEVER (1)   o RARELY (2)   o FREQUENTLY (3)   o ALWAYS (4)   o UNDECIDED (0)

I drive results while, remaining ethically grounded.
o NEVER (1)   o RARELY (2)   o FREQUENTLY (3)   o ALWAYS (4)   o UNDECIDED (0)

By maintaining appropriate levels of confidentiality, I ensure that I do not betray trust.
o NEVER (1)   o RARELY (2)   o FREQUENTLY (3)   o ALWAYS (4)   o UNDECIDED (0)

I exercise a sense of humility and a deep sense of appreciation and gratitude for others.
o NEVER (1)   o RARELY (2)   o FREQUENTLY (3)   o ALWAYS (4)   o UNDECIDED (0)

I take personal accountability for being a responsible corporate citizen. I guard the brand of the organization that I work for.
o NEVER (1)   o RARELY (2)   o FREQUENTLY (3)   o ALWAYS (4)   o UNDECIDED (0)

MY SCORE IS _____

ETHICS AND VALUES

Your Rating	Your Level	Description
34–44	Level 1—High	You are someone whom others look up to and admire. You know your core values and have the courage to live up to them in all aspects of your life, even under pressure to compromise.
		As a leader, you expect yourself and others to actively live the values of the organization.
		• Take it upon yourself to raise the bar by setting the example and challenging unethical behaviors and practices.
		• Leverage your voice; consider ways to expand your reach. Provide opportunities to mentor those with high potential.
23–33	Level 2—Medium	You may intuitively know the right course of action but fear taking on others. You allow that fear to stop you from taking a stand.
		• Be brave enough to live your values and beliefs. Great leaders tell compelling and morally rich stories; they also live their stories.
		• Seek out individuals who exhibit a strong sense of character, and let them inspire you. Engage in dialogue with them about how they handle difficult situations.
		• Recognize where your boundaries are, and hold firm on those boundaries.
		• Consider completing a values-clarification exercise to remind yourself of your core values and put your life into perspective.
		• Identify the sabotage behaviors that are leading you off track.
0–22	Level 3—Low	You are too willing to compromise your values in exchange for success. You take too many risks without fully understanding the importance of guarding your reputation and brand.
		• Review your code of ethics and the standards by which you agreed to live your life. Step back and reconsider the principles that guide your professional and personal life.
		• Focus on organizational and team success rather than individual wins and your own ego. Ultimately, your behavior defines your credibility.

- Evaluate your communication style carefully to ensure that it provides a clear view of the situation, avoiding ambiguity.
- Be willing to fully accept responsibility for your actions.
- Put your actions into perspective by asking yourself this question: What would I want others to say about my leadership when I am gone?

EMOTIONAL INTELLIGENCE

As a Leader…

I have the ability to manage my emotions, finding ways to handle fears and anxieties, anger, and sadness appropriately. I think before responding to others.
o NEVER (1)   o RARELY (2)   o FREQUENTLY (3)   o ALWAYS (4)   o UNDECIDED (0)

I practice emotional self-control, delaying gratification and stifling impulses.
o NEVER (1)   o RARELY (2)   o FREQUENTLY (3)   o ALWAYS (4)   o UNDECIDED (0)

I am sensitive to others' feelings and concerns and to taking their perspectives, appreciating the differences in how people feel about things.
o NEVER (1)   o RARELY (2)   o FREQUENTLY (3)   o ALWAYS (4)   o UNDECIDED (0)

I am aware of my own emotions when they are occurring. I can identify and label specific feelings and can clearly communicate and discuss my emotions and express needs related to those feelings.
o NEVER (1)   o RARELY (2)   o FREQUENTLY (3)   o ALWAYS (4)   o UNDECIDED (0)

I have the ability to induce desirable responses in others by using effective diplomacy to persuade and influence.
o NEVER (1)   o RARELY (2)   o FREQUENTLY (3)   o ALWAYS (4)   o UNDECIDED (0)

While recognizing that I have opportunities for improvement, I generally like who I am.
o NEVER (1)   o RARELY (2)   o FREQUENTLY (3)   o ALWAYS (4)   o UNDECIDED (0)

When I make mistakes, I don't berate and criticize myself and my abilities.
o NEVER (1)   o RARELY (2)   o FREQUENTLY (3)   o ALWAYS (4)   o UNDECIDED (0)

I feel comfortable in emotionally charged situations.
o NEVER (1)   o RARELY (2)   o FREQUENTLY (3)   o ALWAYS (4)   o UNDECIDED (0)

I feel confident about my own skills, talents, and abilities.
o NEVER (1)   o RARELY (2)   o FREQUENTLY (3)   o ALWAYS (4)   o UNDECIDED (0)

I have an easy time meeting new people and making new friends.
o NEVER (1)   o RARELY (2)   o FREQUENTLY (3)   o ALWAYS (4)   o UNDECIDED (0)

I am able to recognize when I need help and ask for help when I need to.
o NEVER (1)   o RARELY (2)   o FREQUENTLY (3)   o ALWAYS (4)   o UNDECIDED (0)

I am able to empathize with the needs and feelings of others without judgment or criticism.
o NEVER (1)   o RARELY (2)   o FREQUENTLY (3)   o ALWAYS (4)   o UNDECIDED (0)

MY SCORE IS _____

EMOTIONAL INTELLIGENCE

Your Rating	Your Level	Description
37–48	Level 1—High	Your high score indicates that you possess one of the most important attributes to unreasonable leadership: the ability to relate to others and build strong relationships while understanding and managing your own emotions.
26–36	Level 2—Medium	Your mid-level score indicates that you are on the right track and have opportunities to continue expanding your Emotional Intelligence (EI) skills.

- Continue to seek ongoing feedback. Ask supervisors and coworkers who know you well for honest feedback on how your behavior impacts them.
- Continue developing skills in the various dimensions of EI:

  -Self-Awareness (Know your own mood and how you feel about it.)

  -Handling Emotions (Know how to handle upset feelings and stay positive under pressure.)

  -Motivation (Be able to set your own goals and work to achieve those goals.)

  -Empathy (Be able to read and understand other people's feelings.)

  -Social Skills (Be able to get along with others at all levels and build strong relationships.)

Your Rating	Your Level	Description
0–25	Level 3—Low	Your low score in Emotional Intelligence (EI) indicates that you may have difficulty building relationships and influencing others.

Develop constructive coping skills for specific moods. Learn to relax when your emotions are running high. Get up and move when you are feeling emotional.

Enhance your emotional self-awareness. Be honest with yourself. Acknowledge your negative feelings, look for their source, and come up with a way to solve the underlying problem. Ask yourself several times each day: "What am I feeling right now?" When you realize what you are feeling (such as anxiety, happiness, anger, excitement), you can make more effective decisions. For example, if you recognize that you are angry, you may choose to step back and not deal with the situation immediately, allowing yourself to deal with it in a more calm state of mind.

Begin to disclose and discuss your feelings. Don't be afraid to recognize and share your feelings in a matter-of-fact manner. If you are feeling anxious about an idea, let your team know. Anxious people tend to be critical. If you transparently communicate your emotions, your team will better understand where you are coming from. Discussing feelings improves communication and sets the tone for cooperation and trust.

Pay attention to nonverbal communication. Watch faces, listen for tone of voice, and take note of body language. Listen twice as much as you speak. Be observant. People will not always tell you when they are upset or when they are frustrated. You must learn to read their emotions to better manage situations.

Practice respect and empathy. Make conscious efforts to identify with and understand the wants, needs, and viewpoints of those around you.

Participate in a leadership development program that features self-awareness. Recognize that you can build EI skills although it will take time and effort. Individuals can achieve greater self-awareness, become empowered to set and attain goals, improve performance, and maximize their potential through focus and discipline.

PEOPLE ORIENTATION

As a Leader…

I provide feedback, and I ask clarifying questions when understanding is incomplete or when data has not yet been substantiated.
o NEVER (1)   o RARELY (2)   o FREQUENTLY (3)   o ALWAYS (4)   o UNDECIDED (0)

I persist in seeking understanding from others despite perceived obstacles.
o NEVER (1)   o RARELY (2)   o FREQUENTLY (3)   o ALWAYS (4)   o UNDECIDED (0)

I take a personal interest in others, developing relationships at all levels within the organization, including stakeholders, customers, and employees.
o NEVER (1)   o RARELY (2)   o FREQUENTLY (3)   o ALWAYS (4)   o UNDECIDED (0)

I have the ability to build strong, honest relationships based on trust and keeping my commitments.
o NEVER (1)   o RARELY (2)   o FREQUENTLY (3)   o ALWAYS (4)   o UNDECIDED (0)

I am capable of genuinely motivating and encouraging others, presenting data, information, and stories in a way that has a strong impact on others.
o NEVER (1)   o RARELY (2)   o FREQUENTLY (3)   o ALWAYS (4)   o UNDECIDED (0)

I am externally focused on my clients, making their needs and interest the primary focus of my actions.
o NEVER (1)   o RARELY (2)   o FREQUENTLY (3)   o ALWAYS (4)   o UNDECIDED (0)

I develop credibility as well as a deep level of trust with my stakeholders, customers, and employees.
o NEVER (1)   o RARELY (2)   o FREQUENTLY (3)   o ALWAYS (4)   o UNDECIDED (0)

I enjoy helping others get what they want, and I encourage their success.
o NEVER (1)   o RARELY (2)   o FREQUENTLY (3)   o ALWAYS (4)   o UNDECIDED (0)

I gain the support of my team and organization by recognizing the work efforts of others, instilling within them a deep desire to excel beyond the expected.
o NEVER (1)   o RARELY (2)   o FREQUENTLY (3)   o ALWAYS (4)   o UNDECIDED (0)

I am charismatic and likable, seeking to build relationships by being honest and direct with others.
o NEVER (1)   o RARELY (2)   o FREQUENTLY (3)   o ALWAYS (4)   o UNDECIDED (0)

11.   I influence others through my actions, words, and daily interaction with people at all levels within the organization.
o NEVER (1)   o RARELY (2)   o FREQUENTLY (3)   o ALWAYS (4)   o UNDECIDED (0)

12.   I develop, maintain, and strengthen partnerships with others inside and outside the organization.
o NEVER (1)   o RARELY (2)   o FREQUENTLY (3)   o ALWAYS (4)   o UNDECIDED (0)

MY SCORE IS _____

PEOPLE ORIENTATION

Your Rating	Your Level	Description
37–48	Level 1—High	You lead using your personal relationships and can easily connect with others. Continue to use your people skills by communicating through telling stories. Read the books *The Power of Stories* by Jim Loehr and *What Makes Successful People Tick?* by Michael J. Berland and Douglas E. Schoen.
		Continue to expand your network outside of your industry by joining nonprofit boards and increasing your visibility through community service.
25–36	Level 2—Medium	You may be more comfortable with driving projects, managing technical or logical analysis. You may be uncomfortable with leading and connecting with people.
		Start by listening and engaging with others, which will enable you to connect with people closest to you, such as your immediate team. The goal of these conversations is to learn common interests and passions. Spend time interacting either in small groups or with individuals within your organization with the intention of creating stronger relationships. Expand your comfort zone from your office or the executive suite to the ground floor.
0 –24	Level 3—Low	Your greatest opportunity is to leverage your technical and subject matter expertise (SME) to work on development of your people skills.
		Begin reading Napoleon Hill's classics *Think and Grow Rich* and *The Law of Success*, applying these lessons to your daily experiences. Step back and evaluate what you are bringing to your role as leader. Consider engaging in a 360-feedback process to help you identify the gaps that may exist and help you gain clarity on what is working and not working. Create a mentoring relationship with a seasoned executive who is a strong charismatic leader, or with an executive coach.

TEAMWORK

As a Leader...

I believe in the power of "teamwork."
o NEVER (1)   o RARELY (2)   o FREQUENTLY (3)   o ALWAYS (4)   o UNDECIDED (0)

People work with me, not for me.
o NEVER (1)   o RARELY (2)   o FREQUENTLY (3)   o ALWAYS (4)   o UNDECIDED (0)

I set high expectations for the team, and myself.
o NEVER (1)   o RARELY (2)   o FREQUENTLY (3)   o ALWAYS (4)   o UNDECIDED (0)

I show genuine interest in others by carefully listening and understanding the underlying message. I seek ways to encourage others' input.
o NEVER (1)   o RARELY (2)   o FREQUENTLY (3)   o ALWAYS (4)   o UNDECIDED (0)

I believe in the importance of synergy, which enables the combined efforts of individual contributions to far exceed the sum of their individual actions.
o NEVER (1)   o RARELY (2)   o FREQUENTLY (3)   o ALWAYS (4)   o UNDECIDED (0)

I clearly define roles and responsibilities. I hold my team and myself accountable.
o NEVER (1)   o RARELY (2)   o FREQUENTLY (3)   o ALWAYS (4)   o UNDECIDED (0)

I use my sense of humor to defuse stressful situations.
o NEVER (1)   o RARELY (2)   o FREQUENTLY (3)   o ALWAYS (4)   o UNDECIDED (0)

I deal with conflict proactively. I engage with others directly to resolve the issues at hand.
o NEVER (1)   o RARELY (2)   o FREQUENTLY (3)   o ALWAYS (4)   o UNDECIDED (0)

I give and receive feedback in an open and direct manner. I value and recognize others' contributions. I remember to say thank you.
o NEVER (1)   o RARELY (2)   o FREQUENTLY (3)   o ALWAYS (4)   o UNDECIDED (0)

I recognize the importance of solid cross-functional sharing. I create an environment that encourages the exchange of best practices and lessons learned.
o NEVER (1)   o RARELY (2)   o FREQUENTLY (3)   o ALWAYS (4)   o UNDECIDED (0)

I recognize the impact of change on my team. I recognize the importance of communication through the change process and ensure that my team connects with the organizational mission and objectives.
o NEVER (1)   o RARELY (2)   o FREQUENTLY (3)   o ALWAYS (4)   o UNDECIDED (0)

We celebrate wins as a team and learn from our mistakes.
o NEVER (1)   o RARELY (2)   o FREQUENTLY (3)   o ALWAYS (4)   o UNDECIDED (0)

MY SCORE IS _____

TEAMWORK

Your Rating	Your Level	Description
43–56	Level 1—High	You know how to build a team. You recognize the importance of teamwork as your competitive advantage. You value your people as well as your results.
		Your opportunity to move to unreasonable levels is to transform the team into a high-performance team:
		• Increase the team's visibility by actively seeking high-profile and strategic initiatives.
		Continuously challenge your individual team members to expand their skills and accelerate their professional performance.
		• Consider using leadership instruments and assessments to better understand the various leadership and communication styles among members of your team. This will increase the effectiveness of their interactions.
29–42	Level 2—Medium	You have had some success as a leader of teams. You recognize the importance of building a strong team. Your team might be in the norming or storming stage. You are getting work done, but you might not be leveraging the talent and passion within the team. You might be too focused on managing results, and your challenge is to include people as critical to the process.
		• Strengthen the people side of your leadership skills. Take the time, as a team, to step away from the work. Consider an off-site teambuilding initiative that will focus your team's efforts on increasing optimal team performance.
		• Focus your team's collective efforts on a 30-day window of time with three to four critical objectives.
		• Watch out for defensive sabotage or unhealthy competitive behaviors that negatively affect the level of teamwork.

0–28   Level 3—Low   You may tend to focus on the individual contri-
                                           butions of your team or may relying on a few key
                                           players.

- Assess your team. Do you have the right people on your team? If you have a few key players, you need to evaluate the performance strengths and gaps and take action.
- Evaluate the over-functioning–under-functioning theory. Are you over-functioning as a leader by micromanaging or rescuing your team and causing your team, as a result, to under-function?
- Build strong relationships with your team members.
- Consider a 360-feedback assessment engaging stakeholders, peers, and direct reports to help you assess what is working and what is not working. This feedback will help you identify actionable items to strengthen your team.

SELFLESS LEADERSHIP

As a Leader…

I put others' needs, desires, and goals ahead of my own. I resonate with others easily, connecting with their passion, energy, and commitment.
o NEVER (1)   o RARELY (2)   o FREQUENTLY (3)   o ALWAYS (4)   o UNDECIDED (0)

I help others feel valued, accepted, and respected.
o NEVER (1)   o RARELY (2)   o FREQUENTLY (3)   o ALWAYS (4)   o UNDECIDED (0)

I serve those I lead.
o NEVER (1)   o RARELY (2)   o FREQUENTLY (3)   o ALWAYS (4)   o UNDECIDED (0)

I am motivated by a greater good.
o NEVER (1)   o RARELY (2)   o FREQUENTLY (3)   o ALWAYS (4)   o UNDECIDED (0)

I bring out the best in others, investing in their success.
o NEVER (1)   o RARELY (2)   o FREQUENTLY (3)   o ALWAYS (4)   o UNDECIDED (0)

I give back to my community with my time, gifts, and resources.
o NEVER (1)   o RARELY (2)   o FREQUENTLY (3)   o ALWAYS (4)   o UNDECIDED (0)

I knock down roadblocks so others succeed.
o NEVER (1)   o RARELY (2)   o FREQUENTLY (3)   o ALWAYS (4)   o UNDECIDED (0)

I meet the needs of those I lead.
o NEVER (1)   o RARELY (2)   o FREQUENTLY (3)   o ALWAYS (4)   o UNDECIDED (0)

I deflect praise from myself and direct it to my team.
o NEVER (1)   o RARELY (2)   o FREQUENTLY (3)   o ALWAYS (4)   o UNDECIDED (0)

I recognize and reward talent.
o NEVER (1)   o RARELY (2)   o FREQUENTLY (3)   o ALWAYS (4)   o UNDECIDED (0)

I develop my people and provide them with the resources and tools they need.
o NEVER (1)   o RARELY (2)   o FREQUENTLY (3)   o ALWAYS (4)   o UNDECIDED (0)

MY SCORE IS _____

SELFLESS LEADERSHIP

Your Rating	Your Level	Description
43–56	Level 1—High	You define success by your ability to help others succeed. You are seen as a source of encouragement and praise. You create and build loyalty in broad segments of your organization. As you move within the organization into more challenging roles, others follow. You create an environment in which your employees want to excel and out-perform your expectations.
		Choose a cause and expand your impact.
29–42	Level 2—Medium	You might be undergoing a crisis in which your natural ability and willingness to give to others is depleted.
		• Start by giving to yourself. Allow time to energize and heal.
		• You might be caught up in the "do, do, do" of the everyday challenges and fire drills, with little energy to do things for others.
		• Select a month in which your focus is on someone else, on making someone else's life a little brighter.
		• You might not yet have developed a strong perspective of the meaning of selfless leadership.
		• Begin by reading the biographies of the leaders that have historically made a difference in the world. Study the traits that you admire and find ways to develop those traits more strongly within yourself. Become inspired to give more of yourself.
0–28	Level 3—Low	You look out for yourself first. You may be undermining others' success by focusing on your own results. You may have developed an unhealthy relationship with money that might prevent you from giving of yourself to others.
		• Explore the opportunities to invest more deeply in others.
		• Learn more from your team about what they need to be successful.
		• Volunteer one hour of your time a week to a humanitarian cause. This will help you connect with the true pleasure of giving.
		• Develop a recognition strategy for your team, which includes once-a-month recognition awards, sending note cards to individual key contributors, and praising the team.

PHYSICAL AND EMOTIONAL WELL-BEING

As a Leader...

I sustain a high level of energy.
o NEVER (1)   o RARELY (2)   o FREQUENTLY (3)   o ALWAYS (4)   o UNDECIDED (0)

I work hard and have fun.
o NEVER (1)   o RARELY (2)   o FREQUENTLY (3)   o ALWAYS (4)   o UNDECIDED (0)

I have a sense of humor.
o NEVER (1)   o RARELY (2)   o FREQUENTLY (3)   o ALWAYS (4)   o UNDECIDED (0)

I am an optimist.
o NEVER (1)   o RARELY (2)   o FREQUENTLY (3)   o ALWAYS (4)   o UNDECIDED (0)

I have the ability to trust others.
o NEVER (1)   o RARELY (2)   o FREQUENTLY (3)   o ALWAYS (4)   o UNDECIDED (0)

I manage my anxiety during transitional periods of my life.
o NEVER (1)   o RARELY (2)   o FREQUENTLY (3)   o ALWAYS (4)   o UNDECIDED (0)

I cope well with stress.
o NEVER (1)   o RARELY (2)   o FREQUENTLY (3)   o ALWAYS (4)   o UNDECIDED (0)

I have the ability to love and care for others.
o NEVER (1)   o RARELY (2)   o FREQUENTLY (3)   o ALWAYS (4)   o UNDECIDED (0)

I participate in activities I enjoy.
o NEVER (1)   o RARELY (2)   o FREQUENTLY (3)   o ALWAYS (4)   o UNDECIDED (0)

I incorporate some type of physical routine as part of my lifestyle.
o NEVER (1)   o RARELY (2)   o FREQUENTLY (3)   o ALWAYS (4)   o UNDECIDED (0)

I take time for myself to relax and clear my mind.
o NEVER (1)   o RARELY (2)   o FREQUENTLY (3)   o ALWAYS (4)   o UNDECIDED (0)

12. I have a strong sense of self.
o NEVER (1)   o RARELY (2)   o FREQUENTLY (3)   o ALWAYS (4)   o UNDECIDED (0)

MY SCORE IS _____

PHYSICAL AND EMOTIONAL WELL-BEING

Your Rating	Your Level	Description
34–44	Level 1—High	You value yourself and your well-being. You take the time to take care of yourself. You have created work-life equilibrium. People see you as an example of social, emotional, mental, spiritual, and physical balance.
		Your opportunity is to maintain that balance and keep yourself strong. Continue to add variety into your life style and explore other activities to keep you relaxed and happy.
23–33	Level 2—Medium	You recognize the impact of not caring for yourself. You have not developed a disciplined approach to support your physical and emotional well-being. You might be so focused on caring for others that you are neglecting yourself in the process. Alternatively, you may find yourself giving your all at work, while not giving yourself permission to rest and take time for yourself.
		• Establish a routine. Join a gym, sign up for yoga, take the time to take a break and walk. Incorporate some type of physical activity into your routine and commit to stay consistent with it, at least five times per week.
		• Manage your time and maximize your efficiency. Prioritize. Balance your workload to allow you to take time to take care of yourself.
		• Nourish your soul. Take the time to look inside and address underlying issues that might be affecting your emotional well-being. Sometimes all it takes is taking the time to breathe and to appreciate the beautiful things life has to offer.
0–22	Level 3—Low	You are experiencing a high level of stress, and it is negatively impacting your ability to be an effective leader.
		Start with:
		• Scheduling a complete physical examination.
		• Consider seeking professional help if you are experiencing some type of emotional loss or relationship struggle.
		• Defining your strengths and tapping into your inner resiliency.

- Seeking to discover patterns of negative emotions, identifying your triggers, and finding a release. Consider incorporating some type of physical activity to release negative energy and emotions.
- Making time for yourself; relax. Consider using a relaxation CD to learn techniques to clear your mind.
- Investing in your relationships and your support system.
- Doing something for others, particularly a physical activity that will support them.

YOUR ACTION PLAN

My three goals (The end result of what I am seeking to change!)
1.
2.
3.

Goal #1:
Projected Outcome of Change (The RESULT you are seeking):

Your Objectives (The various ACTIONS that will take to accomplish the goal):

Key Dates:

Potential Barriers to Success:

Resources and Support (Who can help you?):

Goal #2:
Projected Outcome of Change (The RESULT you are seeking):

Your Objectives (The various ACTIONS that it will take to accomplish the goal):

Key Dates:

Potential Barriers to Success:

Resources and Support (Who can help you?):

Goal #3:

Projected Outcome of Change (The RESULT you are seeking):

Your Objectives (The various ACTIONS that it will take to accomplish the goal):

Key Dates:

Potential Barriers to Success:

Resources and Support (Who can help you?):